The

Reference

Shelf

School Violence

Edited by Denise M. Bonilla

The Reference Shelf
Volume 72 • Number 1

The H.W. Wilson Company
New York • Dublin
2000

The Reference Shelf

The books in this series contain reprints of articles, excerpts from books, addresses on current issues, and studies of social trends in the United States and other countries. There are six separately bound numbers in each volume, all of which are usually published in the same calendar year. Numbers one through five are each devoted to a single subject, providing background information and discussion from various points of view and concluding with a subject index and comprehensive bibliography that lists books, pamphlets, and abstracts of additional articles on the subject. The final number of each volume is a collection of recent speeches, and it contains a cumulative speaker index. Books in the series may be purchased individually or on subscription.

Library of Congress has cataloged this serial title as follows:

School violence / edited by Denise M. Bonilla.
     p. cm. -- (The Reference shelf ; v. 72, no. 1)
    Includes bibliographical references and index.
    ISBN 0-8242-0982-6 (pbk. : alk. paper)
    1. School violence--United States. 2. School shootings--United States. I. Bonilla, Denise M. II. Series.

LB301.3 .S3764 2000   00-024137

Visit H.W. Wilson's Web site: www.hwwilson.com

Printed in the United States of America

Contents

Preface

Every day, millions of parents across the nation put the lives of their children at risk. They bundle up them up, hand them their lunch, and place them on the school bus, hoping and praying that the next time they see their children at the end of the day, they will be no more worse for wear than when they left. Placing responsibility for one's child in the hands of school officials is an act of faith that, until recent years, was usually taken for granted. The school environs have traditionally been viewed as a haven for children and teens, a small oasis of protection from the predators, the cruelty, and the violence of the outside world. That facade of safety has been shattered recently in the wake of a continuous string of mass school shootings. Children as young as 11, armed with arsenals and elaborate plans of attack, have dominated headlines, inspiring a renewed call for gun control and creating a wave of terror amongst parents and educators.

But is there validity behind this fear of an upsurge of violence in our schools? For many large, urban areas, crime and violence in the school system are not new phenomena, but rather daily scourges that communities have been battling for years. Indeed, longtime combatants in the war on teen violence have taken offense at the sudden and vast media coverage that implies school violence is only now warranting attention due to its emigration into suburban neighborhoods. While the recent incidents differ in location and scope from the everyday random stabbing or mugging, they have nevertheless served to highlight a growing concern among Americans that the public school system is, in many ways, failing to protect children from violence.

The United States first began to witness a rash of suburban shootings in the mid-1990s, after nearly a decade of steadily rising gang and crime-related violence in urban school districts. Most notable among this new epidemic, in addition to its larger mortality rate, was the apparent arbitrary and senseless nature of the crimes. A majority of previous school violence had been committed over money, jealousy, or rivalry, and in almost all cases, specific individuals were targeted. In the school shootings that began to occur after 1995, however, much of the carnage was committed randomly, with the shooters' motivation derived from a more sweeping plan of revenge seeped in anger from being outcast or shunned by classmates.

Public attention to this new wave of adolescent murders was phenomenal; newspapers blared half-page headlines and graphic photos that insinuated an approaching invasion of teen terrorism, leading some to accuse the media of sensationalism and helping to inspire copycat crimes. Still others questioned whether the panic was warranted. Granted, the crimes had been brutal and the age of the assailants shocking, but given statistical evidence that juvenile crime overall has been on a downswing, are the shootings indicative of a school violence eruption? Furthermore, with a history that goes back into the 18th century, why has adolescent violence suddenly gained such widespread attention now that it has reached its way into suburbia? Is school violence approaching epic proportions? Is this country raising a new generation of children who solve disputes and feelings of isolation by firing upon their classmates?

These types of questions have led parents, teachers, and administrators to begin searching for ways to identify and disarm potentially volatile adolescents. The response to this growing concern over school assaults has been as varied as violence itself. Most common is a desire to assign blame to a single factor, and the targets have ranged from the entertainment industry to inattentive parents. School officials, meanwhile, have looked toward preventative measures of a more concrete nature, including the placement of metal detectors inside school buildings and the implementation of zero-tolerance policies that identify troublesome youths before they commit serious crimes.

This book is intended to provide a look at these topics, as well as other current issues surrounding school violence in America. Of course, no discussion of school violence could begin with anything other than a reference to the Colorado town of Littleton and the horrific events that unfolded there in April 1999. Columbine High School has become a name synonymous with school violence, a place where two seemingly harmless teenagers unleashed a barrage of bullets, killing 12 of their classmates and one teacher before turning guns on themselves. Columbine was one of the nation's bloodiest rampages on school grounds, and as a result, most of the articles in this book include at least passing reference to the incident.

The first section looks at the various types of school violence today and the perpetrators, who range from school bullies to mass murderers. The first article provides an overall look at the various cases of school violence in the United States, including the issues of gun control and trying children as adults for their crimes. The article also places recent events within the historical context of school violence that occurred in past centuries and looks at where the problem is headed in the future. Other articles look at specific incidents of mass shootings, examine the more prevalent problem of urban school violence, and touch upon perpetrators and victims often overlooked in discussions of school violence.

The second section investigates the public discourse that has arisen in the wake of the school shootings, and the search for explanations for such violence. The articles in this section look at a wide range of issues, including the influence of popular culture, exposure to violence in the media and in video games, gun control legislation, parental responsibility, psychological disorders, biological causes, and gender factors.

In the next section, the lasting effects of mass school shootings and crime are examined. Some believe that media attention to the shootings helped inspire copycat crimes, and the first two articles look at how schools have responded to pressure to increase security and preventative measures in the wake of the fallout from high-profile incidents such as Columbine. Other articles in this section look at the impact school violence has had on gun legislation, the role of individual rights, zero-tolerance rules, and the psychological effects of strict school and juvenile law policies.

The fourth section looks at the media's role in reporting violence and the extent of the coverage that was given to incidents such as Columbine. This portion of the book explores the various issues surrounding media coverage of violent acts, including the accuracy of reports, the use of "expert" testimony, and the influence of public relations.

Finally, the last section examines violence in higher education, where crimes often go unreported or are quietly squelched by administration officials hoping to retain a reputation of safety for their school. The articles here look at crime at various campuses and the process by which a great deal of it is handled internally, within a collegiate judicial system. In this section, methods of crime reporting are analyzed, and the continuous problem of violent "hazing" by fraternities and other student groups on campus is investigated.

In closing, I would like to express my gratitude to all those at H.W. Wilson who helped make this issue of *The Reference Shelf* possible. In particular, I would like to thank Gray Young, Beth Levy, Sandra Watson, Jacquelene Latif, Sara Yoo, and Lynn Messina for their assistance with this book.

Denise M. Bonilla

February 2000

I.
Violence
in American Schools

Editor's Introduction

Throughout the past several years, news of mass school shootings in rural areas have dominated the media and seeped into the consciousness of most Americans. This first section of the book takes a look at the incidents of school violence that have rocked the country, and some of the key issues surrounding the shooters involved in those cases. In addition, this section examines some of the less-publicized episodes of violence in schools, including urban violence, female assaults, and abuse targeted at gay students.

The first article in this section, "School Violence" by Kathy Koch (*CQ Researcher*, October 9, 1998) takes an in-depth look at safety issues in America's school systems. In particular, this selection addresses the question of whether tighter gun control laws would be effective in curbing school violence, and whether juvenile criminals should be tried as adults. Koch's piece also provides a brief history of school incidents and looks at various strategies schools are using to curb violence. The article attempts to provide many viewpoints on the issues involved, and quotes a great deal of statistical analysis as well as information on current political initiatives.

As part of a series in the *Cincinnati Post*, Lisa Popyk's article "Blood in the School Yard" closely examines several specific cases of school shootings in recent years. Included in her report is information on incidents in Edinboro, PA, Paducah, KY, Pearl, MS, Moses Lake, WA, and Springfield, OR. Popyk makes particular note of media influences on the boys who committed the shootings in those incidents and looks at the impact of the violence in such movies as *Natural Born Killers* and *The Basketball Diaries*.

The third article in this section reports on the worst school violence incident in the history of this country: the Columbine High School massacre. Taken from a local newspaper, the *Denver Post*, this piece captures the essence of the shock and fear that gripped local residents during and after the ordeal. The article follows the day's events and includes reactions from local law enforcement officials as well as Columbine students and teachers. It should be noted, however, that since this was one of the earliest reports on the Columbine murders, it contains several misconceptions which were amended in later media accounts. Among these was the initial report that the teens responsible for the massacre were members of the "Trench Coat Mafia" and that they specifically targeted certain groups during their rampage.

The next two pieces explore the phenomenon of urban violence in American schools and the way in which it has been virtually ignored in recent years dues to the rise in suburban shootings. The first article, by Holly Kurtz for the *Denver Rocky Mountain News*, focuses on an anti-gang activist who has been dismayed at the inordinate amount of attention paid to isolated shooting sprees such as Columbine, compared to urban school incidents. The second article on this issue, by Jake Tapper for the online publication *Salon*, also looks at media attention to urban violence but stresses gun control as the key to reducing school violence in all sectors of the country.

The final two articles in this section look at some of the lesser-known problems schools are encountering today regarding crime and violence. "Young, Female and Turning Deadly" by Heidi Evans explores the rise of female perpetrators in schools, and how the juvenile court system treats them in comparison to male offenders. Included in the article are statistics about female violence and insights on the influence of pop culture on young girls.

Finally, in an article for the *Nation*, Doug Ireland looks at violence against gays in schools. A phenomenon only recently recognized by school officials, violence against gay students has risen in recent years due to increased visibility, as more gay men and women come out during their teen years. Ireland presents several examples of anti-gay harassment and violence, including the case of one student who was so traumatized by repeated abuse in school that he sued the school district for neglecting to protect him. This article also examines the rise of student gay/straight alliances and proposed legislation to protect gay students from violent attacks in school.

School Violence[1]

Are American Schools Safe?

By Kathy Koch
CQ Researcher, October 9, 1998

A White House conference next week will grapple with violence at public schools, including the shooting rampages last year that left 13 students and teachers dead and 47 wounded. While it was not the bloodiest year in U.S. school history, it will be remembered as the year teens turned to mass murder to solve adolescent problems. Since then, schools have adopted zero-tolerance policies on threats, established hot lines for threat tips, installed metal detectors and instituted dress codes. Many states lowered the age at which youths who murder can be tried as adults, but lawmakers refused to close gun-law loopholes that allow teens access to guns. Many parents and school officials, meanwhile, blame the deaths on society's steadily increasing glorification of violence.

THE ISSUES

When 11-year-old Logan Hamm of Seattle went to a weekend sleepover party recently, he stuffed his water pistol into his backpack along with his pajamas.

But in the school cafeteria the next Monday, when he reached into his bag for his lunch, out tumbled the gun, which he had painted black to look more realistic. Classmates alerted school authorities, who promptly expelled the middle-schooler.[1]

Seattle schools spokesman Trevor Neilson said the district's zero-tolerance weapons policy applies to toy guns as well as real ones. "In the wake of what happened in Jonesboro, Springfield and West Paducah," he said, "we take these things very, very seriously."[2]

Five times within eight months last year, troubled boys—some as young as 11—brought guns to school and fired on their classmates. Eleven students and two teachers were

---

killed, and 17 were wounded in the high-profile, small-town mass murders in Pearl, Miss., West Paducah, Ky., Jonesboro, Ark., Edinboro, Pa., and Springfield, Ore. (four other multiple murders occurred at schools last year, but they involved murder suicides by jealous boyfriends, including two by adults and a dispute between rival "party crews" at a school in California. In a separate incident at a high school in Stamps, Ark., 14-year-old Joseph Colt Todd randomly shot and wounded two students, claiming he was tired of being bullied.)

When experts gather at the White House on Oct. 15 to discuss school safety, they will be haunted by the riveting television images of schoolyards cordoned off by yellow police tape, paramedics rushing gurneys to waiting ambulances and police leading adolescent boys away in handcuffs and leg irons.

In the past, most violent school deaths occurred in urban secondary schools, involved firearms and both the victims and offenders tended to be male . . .

President Clinton called for the meeting after the massacres left a stunned nation asking how such incidents could have occurred.

"The recent series of killings in our schools has seared the heart of America about as much as anything I can remember in a long, long time," Clinton said on July 7.

At the daylong meeting, conferees will devise ways to prevent recurrences and contingency plans for the grim possibility that it might happen again. They will also grapple with the many questions prompted by the shootings. How did the boys get access to firearms? Did they give off signals indicating that they had reached the breaking point? Who is ultimately responsible for these tragedies?

In the wake of the shootings, school officials have been tightening up on security, stringently enforcing their weapons policies and trying to ensure that such horrific incidents don't happen again. Although 1997-98 was not the bloodiest year in school history more violent school deaths occurred in 1992-93 it will be remembered as the year that youngsters in America's heartland turned to mass murder to solve adolescent problems.

The most reliable statistics on school deaths come from the National School Safety Center (NSSC), which surveys press accounts of incidents each year.[3] The center counted 42 "school-associated violent deaths" in the last academic year a 68 percent jump from the previous year's total of only 25. But that was still fewer than the 55 deaths in

1992-93, the same year that juvenile crime peaked nation-wide. In the past, most violent school deaths occurred in urban secondary schools, involved firearms and both the victims and offenders tended to be male, according to the NSSC. The motives most commonly cited were interpersonal disputes. The victims last year were predominantly female.

But as many experts point out, despite the intense media attention surrounding the recent shootings, schools are the safest places for children—safer even than their own homes. "Kids are safer in schools than they are anywhere else in America," says William Modzeleski, director of the Education Department's Safe and Drug-Free Schools Program.

Shootings at schools account for less than 1 percent of the

It is difficult to ascertain whether non-homicidal school violence has increased or decreased over the years, because no one has kept comprehensive statistics in a consistent manner.

---

more than 5,000 firearms-related deaths of children under 19 in the U.S. each year. Juveniles are murdered outside of schools—and overwhelmingly by adults in or around the home—40 times more often than they are killed in school, according to a study by the Justice Policy Institute (JPI), a Washington think tank. Indeed, American children are twice as likely to be struck by lightning as they are to be shot in school, the report said.[4]

Nevertheless, nearly a million students—some as young as 10—packed guns into their backpacks along with their homework last year, according to an annual survey released June 18 by the anti-drug advocacy group PRIDE. The good news, says PRIDE, is that the number of students bringing guns to school has dropped 36 percent over the last five years.

Under federally mandated zero-tolerance policies instituted in 1994, some 6,100 students were expelled for bringing a gun to school in 1996-97, says a Department of Education report released last May 8. "Our nation's public schools are cracking down on students who bring guns to school," said U.S. Secretary of Education Richard W. Riley.[5]

But while students might be less likely to be murdered at
ool compared with the outside world, they can also be
bed, assaulted or raped at school. It is difficult to ascer-
n whether non-homicidal school violence has increased
decreased over the years, because no one has kept comprehensive statistics in a consistent manner. Existing
studies portray different snapshots of the problem.

According to the *1996 Sourcebook of Criminal Justice
Statistics*, the number of high school seniors who reported
being injured or threatened by someone with a weapon was
actually lower in 1996 than 20 years ago. For example, 3.4
percent of seniors in 1976 said they had been injured by
someone with a weapon, compared with 2.8 percent in
1996. Such assaults apparently peaked in 1991 at 3.9 per-

---

*"Gangs and the guns, drugs and
violence that go with them must be
stopped from ever reaching the schoolhouse door."*—**President Clinton**

---

cent and have been declining since.

Yet, another study released last April by the Education
and Justice departments found that the number of students physically attacked or robbed at school increased
23.5 percent between 1989 and 1995, from 3.4 percent to
4.2 percent. The increase occurred even as overall school
crime rates remained steady at about 14 percent during
the six-year period.[6]

Gang presence in schools nearly doubled during the same
period, according to the report released last April 12 by the
Bureau of Justice Statistics and the National Center for
Education Statistics. While almost none of the 10,000 students interviewed admitted taking a gun to school, 12.7
percent said they knew of another student carrying a gun
to school.

President Clinton called the trend unacceptable. "Gangs
and the guns, drugs and violence that go with them must
be stopped from ever reaching the schoolhouse door," Clinton said in a statement released with the report. He urged
Congress to approve initiatives against gangs and youth
violence that he proposed last year.

Although the NSSC's review of news reports found that
25 violent deaths occurred in schools during the 1996-97
school year, more than 1,200 public school principals sur-

veyed in a nationally representative sampling by the Education Department found that no murders occurred in their schools during that year, and only four had any suicides on campus.[7]

Ninety percent of public schools had no "serious violent crime" that year, but those that did reported 4,170 rapes, 7,150 robberies and 10,950 physical attacks or fights with weapons, according to the Education Department report. Only 4 percent of those incidents occurred in elementary schools. By far, most school crime was of a less violent nature, including 190,000 physical attacks or fights without a weapon, 116,000 thefts or larcenies and 98,000 cases of vandalism.

The report also found that most schools have a zero-tolerance policy toward weapons on campus, and 78 percent have a violence-prevention or reduction program in place. Further, violent crimes occur most often in schools with classroom discipline problems and in large schools in central cities.

Indeed, last year's high-profile shootings received overblown press coverage because of the "man-bites-dog" nature of the story: They occurred in rural schools and were perpetrated by white adolescent boys "as opposed to urban kids of color," contends JPI Director Vincent Schiraldi. As a result, public officials "from the school house to the state house to the White House" have overreacted to the shootings, he says.[8]

"We are witnessing a tragic misdirection of attention and resources . . . even though the real threat may lie elsewhere," the report said. To remedy the so-called "crisis of classroom violence," politicians have put extra police in schools, eliminated minimum ages at which children can be tried as adults and proposed expanding the death penalty to juveniles and eliminating after-school programs, the JPI report said. "If we want to reduce the overall number of childhood gun deaths we should be expanding after-school programs and restricting gun sales," Schiraldi said.

Since the shootings, many schools have adopted a no-nonsense, zero-tolerance policy on threats, similar to the attitude taken at airports if passengers make even joking references to highjacking. Teachers now report any mention of violence, even references in short stories, journal

> *"If we want to reduce the overall number of childhood gun deaths we should be expanding after-school programs and restricting gun sales."*
> —Justice Policy Institute Director Vincent Schiraldi

Zero tolerance

entries, notes passed between students and drawings of violent acts.

The new measures acknowledge the fact that in nearly all of last year's rampages, the shooters had made numerous threats or dropped hints that they were contemplating violent action. The perpetrators also had a history of violence or anti-social behavior.

"The major challenge for schools is how to react without overreacting," says Ronald D. Stephens, executive director of the California-based NSSC. He says most schools are developing comprehensive "safe school" plans, beefing up their security operations, and training their staff to recognize early warning signs of potential troublemakers. To help them do that the Education Department issued a checklist for school officials trying to sort out which threats are youthful pranks and which are coming from students likely to erupt into violence.

"Schools want to find these kids and defuse the anger before the time bomb goes off," says Barbara Wheeler, president of the National School Boards Association.

Other schools have set up hot lines for tips about threats by students so that friends worried about "ratting" on their buddies can report threats anonymously. Others have installed metal detectors, instituted uniform dress codes and hired additional school psychologists.

Yet what has profoundly shaken most parents, policy-makers, scholars, ethicists and clergy, was the detached, premeditated, cold-blooded nature of the recent incidents.

"These attacks were planned," said Gary Goldman, author of *Books and Bullets: Violence in the Public Schools.* "This wasn't a spur-of-the-moment thing. These boys had a chance to think things over. Calmly, coolly, they decided to take care of matters with pistols and rifles."[9]

"You could spend the next five years trying to figure out if big schools or single parents or a violent movie drove these kids to this," he continues. "But the only real common thread is that they saw the way to get rid of their problem was to get rid of other people. I'm not sure there is a simple way to explain a tragedy like that."[10]

As citizens and lawmakers try to make sense of recent school shootings, these are some of the questions they are asking:

fire 17 times more often than in 25 other industrialized countries—combined.

Further, between 1985 and 1994, the number of juveniles murdering with a gun quadrupled, while the number killing with all other types of weapons remained constant.[15]

Although it is illegal for anyone under 18 to possess a handgun, guns are easily accessible for juveniles in America, says Dennis Henigan, director of legal affairs for Handgun Control Inc. The primary route by which juveniles buy illegal guns is through high-volume gun sales, he says.

"In most states it's perfectly legal for a licensed dealer to sell 15 to 20 handguns to a single purchaser," he says. "Then the purchaser sells those guns in the black market." He noted the "spectacular success" of Virginia's new one-gun-a-month law which has already resulted in a 61 percent decline in guns traced back to Virginia from crimes committed in New York City. Besides Virginia, Maryland and South Carolina are the only other states that limit gun sales to 12 a year.

But John Velleco, a spokesman for the Gun Owners of America, says, "It's not access to guns that is the driving force behind juvenile violence." Because the Ten Commandments have been "ordered off the walls of our schools . . . our children are growing up in an ethical never-never land, and don't know the difference between right and wrong," he says.

If more gun laws would solve the problem, then juvenile gun-related crimes should have plummeted after the 1968 passage of the Gun Control Act, which made it illegal for juveniles to possess guns, he says. "If the gun control theory had any merit, we should have had more shootings by juveniles before 1968 and then it should have declined. But that didn't happen."

Alan Gottlieb, chairman of the 650,000-member Citizens Committee for the Right to Keep and Bear Arms, argues that "the knee-jerk reaction to impose more gun controls in the wake of these incidents fails to address the underlying problem. Gun control is a Band-Aid approach to a potentially serious hemorrhage."[16] Instead of gun control, the Congress should boost intervention and psychological counseling for anyone caught carrying a gun to school, he said.

Chief NRA lobbyist Tanya Metaksa says that additional laws are not needed because under the Gun-Free Schools Act of 1994 it is already illegal for anyone to bring a firearm to school. Pointing out that the Jonesboro shooters tried to blow-torch their way into a gun safe, she says, "No amount of laws are going to stop a juvenile or adult from illegally procuring a gun or knife or anything else."

Laws making gun owners responsible for crimes committed by a juvenile who breaks into their homes and steals their gun are akin to prosecuting a legitimate automobile owner whose car is stolen and used by criminals in a crime, she says.

The NRA opposes "one-size-fits-all" federal gun storage laws. "We think responsible gun storage comes from each gun owner looking at their environment and making an educated, informed decision," Metaksa says. That decision would be different for an elderly woman living in a high-crime area and a household where there are young children, she says.

Regarding mandatory purchase and use of trigger locks, Metzlesa says, "The recent shootings in schools have troubled and saddened us all, but it is unsound and ultimately unsafe to prescribe a single federal gun storage standard." She also stated, "When fatal firearms accidents are at an all-time low and violent crime is on the decline, it is senseless to propose ineffective laws that will only restrict the freedoms of law-abiding citizens and the fundamental right of self-defense."

One way to prevent kids from murdering at school, she says, is to "take threats more seriously. The kids involved last year gave lots of warning signs that nobody took seriously."

> *"The recent shootings in schools have troubled and saddened us all, but it is unsound and ultimately unsafe to prescribe a single federal gun storage standard."*
> —NRA lobbyist Tanya Metaksa

Should youths who commit adult crimes be tried as adults?

Shortly after the Jonesboro shootings, an elderly man sipping coffee at a Waffle House in a nearby town said, "I don't care how old they are; if they kill somebody, they ought to die. I don't care if they're 5 years old. The Bible says an eye for an eye and a tooth for a tooth. They need to change the law."[17]

He was referring to an Arkansas law under which the Jonesboro shooters, who were 11 and 13 when they were arrested, could not be tried as adults. Even though they have since been convicted, they can only be held until age 18 in a juvenile facility. The state has vowed to build a special facility to hold them until they reach 21, when they must be released.

Yet in Pearl, Miss., Luke Woodham, 17, was tried as an adult for killing his mother the same day that he opened fire on classmates. He won't be eligible for parole until he is 65.

The two cases show how state laws differ in the way they treat violent juveniles. In recent years many states have lowered the age at which violent youths can be tried as adults, and Arkansas legislators say they'll do the same.

For much of this century, the juvenile justice system subscribed to the notion that children committing crimes should be treated rather than punished. That attitude began changing in the late 1980s as crack cocaine entered the American scene, and the nature of juvenile crime changed from truancy, vandalism and joy-riding in stolen cars to assault, rape and murder.

Juveniles under 18 accounted for 13 percent of all violent crimes "cleared" by arrest in 1996, according to the FBI, and juvenile violent crime increased much faster than adult violent crime. Further, juvenile lawbreakers are getting younger and younger. Since 1965, the number of 12-year-olds arrested for violent crimes has doubled, and the number of 13- and 14-year-olds has tripled, according to the FBI.[18]

"Those statistics are a major reason why we need to revamp our antiquated juvenile justice system," wrote Linda J. Collier, a Pennsylvania juvenile court lawyer, who teaches on juvenile justice at Cabrini College in Radnor, Pa. Too many states still treat violent offenders under 16 as juveniles who belong in the juvenile system."

Since 1994, the laws in 43 states have been changed to make it easier to prosecute juveniles as adults. Proponents of the "adult-crime, adult-time" philosophy blame much of today's juvenile crime rate on an overly permissive juvenile justice system at which too many teenagers thumb their noses. The NRA says, "The young criminal's closest accomplice is a juvenile justice system that fails to mete out adult time for adult crime."[19]

School resource officer Lavarello says that when he warns kids about possible jail terms if they commit a crime, they don't believe him. "They tell me, 'That's not true because I have a friend who did that and he's not in jail,'" says Lavarello.

Under the current system, 40 percent of juveniles age 15 and older do not serve any time when they commit crimes. Rep. Mark Souder, R-Ind., said on Sept. 15, encouraging the House to pass a bill that would allow juveniles as young as 14 to be tried as adults for violent or drug crimes.

"There should be a price to pay if someone shoots somebody, if they rape somebody or if they use a gun in an armed robbery," he said. "We have spent too much time worrying about these juveniles without thinking about the people who are terrorized by these young people."

Lavarello agrees. "Kids as young as 12 know the dangers of shooting a gun," he says. They need to know that there will be consequences."

Opponents of trying youths as adults say teens do not really understand the long-range implications of their actions. Sending them to an adult prison, where they are more likely to be beaten or raped only transforms them into even harder criminals, creating more and worse crime in the long run, they argue.

"Juveniles who come from dysfunctional families need more than being locked up," said Texas Democratic Rep. Sheila Jackson-Lee, arguing against the bill. The legislation eventually passed the House, 280-126, and is awaiting conference action.

"It's just another step towards dismantling the juvenile justice system," says Charles P. Ewing, a forensic psychologist at the State University of New York at Buffalo and author of *Kids Who Kill*. "Children don't have the cognitive capacity of adults," he continues. "That's why we limit their rights to marry, drive, drink and buy cigarettes. But yet we are saying, 'Oh, but by the way, if you commit a crime, you're suddenly an adult.'

"It's a way of appearing to do something about a problem that adults created," he adds, namely a society that inundates youths with violence in music, movies, video games and television, and allows them easy access to guns. It's a social problem that we've all created."

It is more politically popular to try kids as adults and build more prisons than to fund programs known to work, like after-school recreational programs, youth development programs and crime prevention and intervention programs, he says.

Criminologist Jeffrey Fagan of the Center for Violence Research and Prevention at Columbia University's School of Public Health, agrees. "These laws are about symbolism,

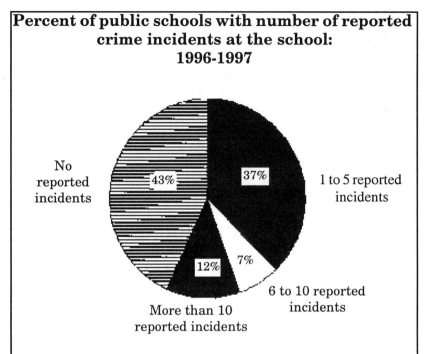

Percent of public schools with number of reported crime incidents at the school: 1996-1997

No reported incidents 43%

1 to 5 reported incidents 37%

More than 10 reported incidents 12%

6 to 10 reported incidents 7%

NOTE: The number of reported incidents of crime at the school are based on the total number of the following crimes for which the school reported that the police were contacted: murder, rape or other sexual battery, suicide, physical attack or fight with and without a weapon, robbery, theft or larceny, and vandalism. Percents may not add up to 100 because of rounding.

SOURCE: U.S. Department of Education, National Center for Education Statistics, Fast Response Survey System, "Principal/School Disciplinarian Survey on School Violence," FRSS 63, 1997.

not about substance," he says, noting that juveniles retained in adult jails have higher recidivism rates than those kept in juvenile court.

Ironically, he points out, Congress and the states are lowering the minimum ages just as juvenile crime is declining after peaking in 1994. "The laws are targeting a problem that is far less of a problem than it was five years ago," Fagan says. "So the public is being sold a bill of goods."

Some states are successfully fighting juvenile crime by taking an innovative approach that combines heavy-duty early intervention for at-risk youths, while making sure juveniles are held accountable for even minor first-offenses. Then if juveniles become violent offenders despite the early interventions, they are tried as adults.

"If the attempt to rehabilitate juvenile delinquents is unsuccessful," said Harry L. Shorstein, state attorney for Florida's 4th Judicial Circuit in Jacksonville, "then it is my firm belief that we should treat habitual and violent juvenile criminals like adults."[20]

Shorstein's innovative program, however, does not just toss juveniles into adult jails, where they are more likely to be beaten and raped. Juveniles are tried as adults but are then segregated into juvenile jail facilities, where they must attend school and meet with an adult mentor. The program has resulted in a 78 percent drop in juvenile homicide, a 53 percent reduction in rapes committed by juveniles and a 58 percent drop in juvenile auto theft.[21]

"Prevention efforts cannot succeed if those not abiding by the law do not believe there is a consequence to criminal behavior," Sh......... hearing on Sept. 1...

[handwritten note: History of Unruly students → Started in France]

> *In Colonial times, students mutinied at more than 300 schools each year, often chasing off or locking out the teacher. In 1837, nearly 400 schools in Massachusetts were vandalized.*

S... ren in 17t... dueled bra... ding to Ale... *Safe,* a stu... Reason Pub... "S... es and oth... se they wer...

St... re also common in English public schools between 1775 and 1836, forcing schoolmasters to seek help from the military, he said. In 1797 when one group of British boys was ordered to pay for damages they had done to a tradesman, they blew up their headmaster's office door, set fire to his office and withdrew to an island in a nearby lake. "British constables finally took the island by force," said Volokh.

Early American schools had their share of unruly students. In Colonial times, students mutinied at more than 300 schools each year, often chasing off or locking out the teacher. In 1837, nearly 400 schools in Massachusetts were vandalized.

Yet in modern times, standards for classroom discipline and the definition of what is acceptable student behavior have changed dramatically in America. Corporal punishment doled out by ruler-and-rod-wielding pioneer teachers is much less common today, having been replaced by judicial due process concern for students' rights and efforts to build self-esteem. Corporal punishment is still allowed in 23 states, but it has been outlawed in more than half of the individual school districts in those states.

The classroom began changing in the early 1900s with the advent of the "progressive" education movement, which eschewed authoritarian methods of discipline and encouraged teachers to recognize students as individuals. Progressive education, although criticized as too permissive, was first embraced by experimental private schools and eventually gained wide acceptance during the first 50 years of this century.[23]

Students' Rights

In the 1960s, the anti-war, anti-establishment rebellion of college students spilled over into the high schools, leading students to question authority and the status quo. Then in 1967, the Supreme Court held in *Gault v. Arizona* that juveniles in court must be given the same rights and protections as adults.[24] The decision made schools and law enforcement officials more reluctant to send kids away to training schools, especially for offenses like truancy or misbehavior, which would not be crimes if committed by an adult.

In 1975, two precedent-setting developments made it extremely difficult for teachers to kick violent or disruptive students out of class. The first was a landmark ruling in Gross v. Lopez, in which the Supreme Court said students could not be suspended without due process of law.

"Many central-city schools have tended to abandon expulsion as the ultimate enforcer of discipline," wrote Jackson Toby, director of Rutgers University's Institute for Criminological Research.[25]

Secondly, Congress passed the Education for All Handicapped Children Act, which mandated that all children be educated in the "least restrictive environment" possible. That law required that handicapped students be "mainstreamed" into regular classrooms, along with emotionally disturbed students with severe behavioral and disciplinary problems.

"Youngsters who in the past would not have gone to regular school because of their negative behavior are now attending mainstream schools," writes Connecticut school counselor Carl Bosch, in his book *Schools Under Seige, Guns, Gangs and Hidden Dangers*.[26]

At the same time, school officials became skittish about sending kids to alternative schools designed for students with severe discipline problems and those expelled for carrying weapons. The schools were criticized as "dumping grounds" for minorities.

"Schools in most big cities have given up and keep kids in school who are sufficiently troublesome that it's very difficult to maintain an educational program," wrote Toby.

Over time, lack of discipline in the classroom translates into violence in the hallways, according to several studies. "In most schools it's not the sensational acts of violence, but the smaller acts of aggression, threats, scuffles, constant back talk that take a terrible toll on the atmosphere

---

> **More than half those who carried guns to school said they had threatened to harm a teacher, and two-thirds said they had threatened to harm another student.**

---

of learning, on the morale of teachers on the attitudes of students," said Clinton, in a July 20th speech before the American Federation Of Teachers.

Guns and Gangs

In 1990 Congress created "gun-free school zones," making it a felony to bring guns within 1,000 feet of any school. Then in 1994, Congress passed the Gun-Free Schools Act, requiring mandatory one-year expulsion for any student caught with a firearm at school.

Nonetheless, of the nearly 1 million kids who carried a gun to school last year, almost half of them attended school armed on six or more occasions, according to PRIDE. More than half those who carried guns to school said they had threatened to harm a teacher, and two-thirds said they had threatened to harm another student. Of the students who carried a gun to school, 59 percent were white, 18 percent were black and 12 percent were Hispanic.[27]

"These chilling numbers suggest that for every classroom of 30 students, in every school in America, on average one student has attended school with a gun in grades six through 12," said Thomas J. Gleaton, one of the authors of the nationwide survey of 154,350 students.[28]

※ Experts say that most students who carry guns to school do so for protection.

→ is it really protection

The presence of gangs in schools contributes to the violence. In 1989 only 15.3 percent of students nationwide reported gangs in their schools, compared with 28.4 percent in 1995. Thirty-one percent of the public school students questioned had gangs in their schools, compared with 7 percent in private schools.[29]

Gangs were most prevalent in urban schools, where 40.7 percent of students in 1995 reported gangs in their schools, compared with 24.8 percent in 1989. In suburban schools the percent of students reporting gangs almost doubled, from 14 percent to 26.3 percent, during the same period. The largest growth in gangs occurred in rural schools, where the percent of students reporting gangs jumped from 7.8 percent to 19.9 percent.

Criminologists warn that statistics on gangs should be viewed skeptically. "What we used to call peer groups are now called gangs," said Jack Levin, director of the Program for the Study of Violence at Northeastern University in Boston.[30]

Declining Violence

JPI's Schiraldi says that even though the schoolhouse shootings last year occurred in rural schools, country towns and their schools are still relatively safe places. Three rural towns where school shootings occurred last year— West Paducah, Pearl and Jonesboro—had no juvenile homicide arrests in the year before these highly publicized cases, "strongly suggesting that they are idiosyncratic events rather than evidence of a trend," said a JPI press release. In Jonesboro, for example, the number of juveniles arrested for violent offenses dropped 39 percent between 1993 and 1996.

Noting that some states have reacted to the shootings by lowering the age at which juveniles who commit violent crimes can be tried as adults, Schiraldi said, "We continue to let the tail of a few isolated cases wag the dog of the juvenile justice system. Despite these tragic cases the fact remains that citizens in rural communities are still very safe from violent juvenile crime."

However, FBI statistics show that violent juvenile crime has increased in the nation's rural communities, even as juvenile crime nationwide is declining. For instance, rural juveniles were arrested for murder and manslaughter 14.9 percent more often in 1996 than in 1990, while juvenile homicide/manslaughter arrests declined 14.8 percent in the cities and a dramatic 26 percent in the suburbs during that same time period.

But only 100 murders were committed by juveniles in rural areas in 1996, compared with 1,868 in the cities, notes JPI researcher Jason Ziedenberg. "There is definitely a juvenile crime problem in this country," he says, "but it is not concentrated in rural areas. It is still most predominant in the cities."

Schools all over the country must cope with the same negative influences that society as a whole grapples with, writes Bosch. "Schools cannot shut their doors and expect a safe 'castle' where outside influences don't enter," he continues. "Violence in schools . . . is brought into classrooms because it exists in society, in the home and in entertainment."[31]

> *"Schools cannot shut their doors and expect a safe 'castle' where outside influences don't enter."*
> —**Connecticut School Counselor Carl Bosch**

Ironically, even as these bizarre school shootings were shocking the nation the overall juvenile murder rate was dropping. Federal Bureau of Investigation (FBI) 1996 statistics show that youth violence peaked in 1994 and has declined since then. Between 1994 and 1996, the number of juveniles arrested for murder declined 30 percent, and juvenile arrests for all violent crimes dropped 12 percent.

Schiraldi attributes the drop to diminished access to handguns—such as one-gun-a-month laws enacted in three states—and improving economic conditions for teenagers. For example, between 1995 and 1997, as juvenile homicide rates were falling the unemployment rate for adolescents dropped 10 percent, he points out.

Contrary to the impression that murderers are getting younger and younger, FBI statistics show that in 1965—33 years ago—25 children under the age of 13 were arrested for homicide compared with only 16 in 1996. Further, 93 percent of America's counties had either one or no juvenile homicides in 1995, up from 92 percent in 1994.[32]

Noting those encouraging statistics, JPl's Schiraldi said that while incidents like the Jonesboro shootings are "so tragic as to defy description," parents should remember that "cases like this are still very much the aberration, and not the norm."

CURRENT SITUATION

Clinton's Initiatives

Citing the Education/Justice Department report on school violence last April, Clinton called the increase in violence and gangs in schools unacceptable and urged Congress to approve anti-violence initiatives he proposed in his January budget. Those initiatives focus on "what we know works: tough, targeted deterrence and better anti-gang prevention," he said in a written statement.

Among other things, Clinton has promoted greater use of school uniforms and curfews, cracking down on truancy and zero-tolerance for guns in schools. In addition, the Department of Education has issued its "early warning" handbook for identifying violence-prone students.

In a meeting with school security officers in June, Education Secretary Riley asked what single change would help end school violence. The officers unanimously said that reducing overcrowding would help the most.

In its budget proposal for fiscal 1999, the administration asked Congress to provide $12.4 billion over seven years to help school districts hire and train 100,000 new teachers in order to reduce class size in grades one through three to an average of 18 students. Neither the House nor the Senate agreed to the request, but it was expected to be offered as an amendment before the bill is finalized.

The administration's 1999 budget also asked Congress to:

• Provide $50 million for 1,300 drug and violence prevention coordinators for 6,500 middle schools with drug and violence problems. Both the House and the Senate rejected the request.

• Dramatically increase federal funding for after-school programs, from the current $80 million level to $200 million a year. Last year the administration received 2,000 requests for after-school funds but could only fund 300. The pending House version of the Education appropriations bill

TIMELINE OF SCHOOL VIOLENCE
A sample of violent incidents at U.S. schools

February 29, 2000, Mount Morris Township, MI
After a playground dispute at Theo J. Buell Elementary School, a six-year-old boy shot and killed six-year-old classmate Kayla Rolland with a gun he had brought into school from home.

December 6, 1999, Fort Gibson, OK
A 13-year-old boy fired a 9mm semiautomatic handgun in Fort Gibson Middle School, causing a disturbance in which four students were wounded and one was severely bruised.

May 20, 1999, Conyers, GA
Fifteen-year-old T. J. Solomon, depressed after a recent breakup, shot and wounded six students at Heritage High School.

April 20, 1999, Littleton, CO
Eighteen-year-old Eric Harris and 17-year-old Dylan Klebold opened fire at Columbine High School, killing 12 students and one teacher and wounding 23 others before turning the guns on themselves.

June 15, 1998, Richmond, VA
A 14-year-old boy shot and wounded a teacher and a guidance counselor in the hallway of a high school.

May 22, 1998, Memphis, TN
Ten-year-old Travis C. Leaper pointed a loaded .25 caliber semi-automatic pistol at a classmate's head and said "pow."

May 21, 1998, Springfield, OR
Fifteen-year-old Kip Kinkel fatally shot two students and wounded 22 others in the cafeteria of Thurston High School, after killing his parents in their home.

May 21, 1998, St. Charles, MO
Three sixth-grade boys at Becky-Davis Elementary School were accused of conspiring to murder their classmates on the last day of school.

May 19, 1998, Fayetteville, TN
Eighteen-year-old honor student Jacob Davis killed a classmate in the parking lot of Lincoln County High School right before graduation because the other boy was dating his ex-girlfriend.

May 9, 1998, Memphis, TN
A five-year-old took a loaded pistol to school after he had been given a "time-out" by his teacher. According to authorities, the child had shown a fellow student a bullet and told him that he wanted to shoot his teacher and another student.

April 24, 1998, Edinboro, PA
Fourteen-year-old Andrew Wurst was charged with killing a teacher and wounding two students at a dance at James W. Parker Middle School.

March 25, 1998, Daly City, CA
A 13-year-old, supposedly angry at being sent home early from school, fired a pistol at the Principal in a crowded schoolyard of his middle school.

March 24, 1998, Jonesboro, AR
Thirteen-year-old Mitchell Johnson and his 11-year-old cousin Andrew Golden hid in the woods outside Westside Middle School and fatally shot four girls and a teacher while wounding 10 other students as they filed out of the building during a false fire alarm.

March 6, 1998, Indianapolis, IN
Teased by a female student about his ears, an eight-year-old elementary school student brought a loaded .25 caliber pistol, apparently stolen from his 19-year-old brother, to school, and subsequently pointed the handgun at a classmate.

January 15, 1998, Washington, D.C.
Sixteen-year-old Octavious Clarke shot and killed a female classmate after unsuccessfully trying to flirt with her.

December 15, 1997, Stamps, AR
Fourteen-year-old Colt Todd wounded two students who were standing in a parking lot when he fired from his hiding place in the woods.

December 1, 1997, West Paducah, KY
Fourteen-year-old Michael Carneal fired upon a group of students at Heath High School who had met in the early morning to pray together before class; three students were killed and five others were wounded.

October 15, 1997, Petersburg, FL
A thirteen-year-old student shot 13 classmates at school with a loaded .38 caliber revolver.

October 7, 1997, Moose Lake, MN
A fourteen-year-old boy was caught pointing a loaded handgun at his classmates. The boy obtained the gun from a locked cabinet in his mother's house after feeling threatened at school.

October 1, 1997, Pearl, MS
Sixteen-year-old Luke Woodham used a rifle to kill two students and wound seven others after fatally stabbing his mother in her home.

February 19, 1997, Bethel, AK
Sixteen-year-old Evan Ramsey used a shotgun to kill his high school principal and a student and wound two others.

February 2, 1996, Moses Lake, WA
Fourteen-year-old Barry Loukaitis killed two students and a teacher when he fired upon his algebra class with an assault rifle.

January 18, 1993, Grayson, KY
A 17-year-old entered East Carter High School and shot his English teacher in the head before shooting a school janitor in the abdomen.

would provide only $60 million, while the Senate would provide $75 million.

• Provide $5 billion in tax credits over five years to help school districts pay for modernizing crumbling school buildings. This tax legislation is still pending, but the Senate has included $100 million in school construction funds in its Education bill.

• Boost computer-literacy among students by providing $550 million for software and teacher training initiatives. The Senate agreed to full funding for the initiatives in its Education appropriations bill, but the House bill would fund it at lower levels.

• Provide $100 million to help support charter schools, which are public schools given "charters" allowing them flexibility in decision-making in exchange for accountability of results. The charter school movement has grown from a single school in 1992 to 1,130 today. The Senate bill contains $80 million for charter schools.

• Provide $260 million for the America Reads literacy program, which would train 30,000 reading specialists to mobilize a million volunteer reading tutors over the next five years. The program was not funded by either the Senate or the House.

"Our prisons are full of high school dropouts who cannot read. That is one reason why funding the America Reads Challenge is so important," Secretary Riley said. "Yet Congress continues to dillydally and dawdle."[33]

Aid for Worst Districts

The president also asked that $125 million of the annual $531 million in Safe and Drug-Free Schools block grants be specifically targeted at the 100 school districts with the worst drug and crime problems. Currently, the program—which is the nation's premier program for reducing school violence—distributes block grant money to school districts based on a per capita formula rather than an as-needed basis, spreading the money across all the nation's 15,000 school districts. As a result, six out of 10 school districts receive $10,000 a year or less. One district received only $53, according to the *Los Angeles Times*.[34]

"The funds are so spread out that some school districts really don't get enough money to make a difference, and that's a problem," Riley told the *Times*.[35] The administration felt that the program would be more effective if at least some of the money were specifically earmarked for school districts with the most serious violence and drug problems.

The program has been criticized recently because there is little oversight over how the money is spent. In addition, the *Times* investigation found that the money has been spent on things such as motivational speakers, tickets to Disneyland, fishing trips, resort weekends for educators and a $6,500 remote-controlled toy car. A total of $5.7 billion has been spent on the program since its inception in 1987.

"We are wasting money on programs that have been demonstrated not to work," said Debert S. Elliott, director of the University of Colorado Center for the Study and Prevention of Violence.[36]

Nevertheless, the House refused to earmark a portion of the funds for high-crime districts, preferring to continue spreading the money over all school districts on a per-student basis. But it urged the administration to develop "specific measurable standards" to show exactly how a proposed program would reduce either drug abuse or violence before receiving funding. Secretary Riley announced such guidelines in July.

The Senate bill would set aside $150 million for a new program to combat school violence through community-wide prevention programs, such as providing alternative schools for students expelled for disciplinary problems or for bringing a gun to school, mental health counseling and other services.

Clinton also asked Congress for $95 million for juvenile crime prevention programs among "at risk" populations. The money would be earmarked for community-wide programs made up of educators, police, mental health professionals and community organizations working together to prevent juvenile crime. It could be used for mentoring, after-school programs, tutoring, teaching conflict-resolution skills and reducing truancy.

The Senate version of the Justice Department appropriations bill included funds for the prevention program, but the House version did not. Instead the House created a block grant program that would coincide with programs outlined in the House's just-passed Juvenile Justice Prevention Act.

In response to last year's shootings the Senate bill also earmarked $210 million from other programs for a new Safe Schools Initiative. The funds could be used to increase community policing in and around schools, beef up crime prevention programs, weapons detection, surveillance equipment and information systems for identifying potentially violent youths. The bill is awaiting conference action.

Testing Strategies

After a comprehensive study of school violence-prevention strategies, the Reason Public Policy Institute (RPPI) found that there is no "on-size-fits-all silver bullet" approach to school violence prevention.[37]

"What works in Queens [N.Y.] is often going to be a waste of resources in Oklahoma," said Richard Seder, RPPI director of education. "Policy-makers should recognize the diversity of our schools, and rather than saddle school boards with restrictions and mandates, promote community-oriented innovation."[38]

Authors Alexander Volokh and Lisa Snell found that "The ideal violence prevention policy will likely be different for each school." Thus each school should experiment with different approaches to find out what works best in their circumstances, the authors said.[39]

Beefing up security with metal detectors, security guards or surveillance cameras has worked at some schools, the authors noted. But such strategies are expensive and can be ineffective if only random checks are made with a metal detector "wand," or if surveillance cameras are not constantly monitored.

Other schools have reduced violence by requiring school uniforms. Uniforms decrease the likelihood of fights over clothing jealousy, students carrying concealed weapons, and the wearing of gang colors. It also fosters school pride and improves the learning atmosphere.

Long Beach, Calif., for instance, saw crime decrease 36 percent the year after a dress code was adopted; fights dropped 51 percent, sex offenses 74 percent, and weapons offenses 50 percent. Many other schools have reported similar results.[40] "However, most dress codes have been at the elementary level, which isn't exactly where the violence is," the report said.

Violence is lowest in schools with effective discipline systems that mete out punishment swiftly and consistently, the researchers found. For instance, Catholic schools have been able to avoid much of the violence that exists in public schools, even among those parochial schools that cater to the difficult-to-educate, the report said. That's because public schools are "hamstrung by procedural burdens, such as hearing and notice requirements" before disciplinary action can be taken, mandated after the civil rights revolution of the 1960s.

On the other hand, private schools can require certain behavioral norms and establish certain disciplinary procedures through contract as a condition of attendance. For that reason, the authors recommend charter schools and educational choice for parents.[41]

Violence is lowest in schools with effective discipline systems that mete out punishment swiftly and consistently...

Other schools are teaching violence-prevention through conflict resolution or peer-group mediation. The Washington-based nonprofit research institute Drug Strategies "graded" dozens of such school violence-prevention programs, and only 10 out of 84 got A's. The researchers questioned violence-prevention strategies that use scare tactics, segregate aggressive students into a separate group or focus exclusively on boosting self-esteem.

Programs that work best are those that reinforce the idea that aggression and violence are not normal behavior, teach conflict-resolution skills through role-playing and involve parents, peers, media and community organizations.

"Preventing violence requires changing norms," said the report. "This is not impossible. In the past few decades, there have been dramatic changes in social norms concerning smoking, drinking and driving, and wearing seat belts."[42]

Adding School Counselors

Many school districts are also increasing the number of school counselors, psychologists and social workers, says NSSC's Stephens. In a 1997 study on student health the

National Institute of medicine recommended that there should be one school counselor—considered the first line of defense in identifying troubled youths—for every 250 students, one social worker per 800 students and a psychologist for each 1,100 students.

However, nationwide, the actual ratios are generally well below those recommended levels, and vary widely from districts to districts, says Kevin Dwyer, president-elect of the National Association of School Psychologists.

For instance, Connecticut schools have one psychologist for every 750 students, while Missouri only has one per 22,000, Dwyer says. Nationwide, the average is one for each 2,200 students, well below the recommended 1/1,000 ratio. Likewise, he says, the national average for counselors is one for every 500-750 youths, instead of the recommended 1-to-250 ratio.

Since some of the shooters last year had come back onto school grounds after being expelled for weapons offenses, some schools have begun requiring detention and psychological evaluations for anyone caught with a gun at school. Others are trying to ensure that kids caught with guns at school are not simply expelled, but are referred to alternative schools.

"I urge schools to do everything possible to make sure that expelled students are sent to alternative schools," said Secretary Riley. "A student who gets expelled for bringing a gun to school should not be allowed to just hang out on the street."

OUTLOOK

More Violence?

"There will be more killings," predicts Reisman, the Iowa-based independent criminal consultant who specializes in youth violence. Reisman, who was called in as a consultant on several of the recent shootings, said future incidents may be different. Based on the "escalation, the changes and the adaptations" that occurred from one incident to the next last year, he thinks student killers may shift to bombings on school grounds, or may try to take hostages.

Reisman has already heard about at least three telephoned threats from students this school year. "One caller said he was going to make Paducah and Jonesboro look like kindergarten," Reisman says.

Reisman has written a handbook for law enforcement officials and school and hospital administrators outlining how to devise a community-wide crisis management plan, based on the findings of a conference he organized last June, attended by about 60 emergency and school personnel involved in last year's shootings.

Reisman is not the only one who thinks school violence may increase. Within the next decade, America is expected to experience a 15 percent increase in its teen population as the last of the baby-boom generation's kids reach puberty. That could mean an unprecedented surge in youth crime as those youths reach key at-risk ages of 14-17.

Without major increases in after-school activities and child care, say others, the situation is likely to worsen as new welfare reform legislation goes into effect. The law forces single mothers to find jobs after they have been on welfare for five years. Some say that will leave more kids home alone during the dangerous 3 p.m. to 7 p.m. hours when most teenage crime occurs.

"When the school bell rings, leaving millions of young people without responsible adult supervision or constructive activities, juvenile crime suddenly triples and prime time for juvenile crime begins," said a report to Attorney General Janet Reno by James Alan Fox, dean of the College of Criminal Justice, Northeastern University.[43]

Quality after-school programs reduce crime, says Fox, not only by providing a safe haven for youngsters, but by helping them develop values and skills as a result of the positive role models and constructive activities such programs provide.

"Until the nation makes investments in after-school and other programs for children and youth we are likely to continue to pay a heavy price in crime and violence," said the report.

Dwyer agrees that more money needs to be put into after-school programs, as well as more school counselors, remedial support and conflict resolution programs. With almost full employment in America, "Our society uses all the adults to run the economy but we're not taking care of the kids," says Dwyer.

Others say it is time to make gratuitous violence politically incorrect, just as smoking drinking and driving, and not wearing seat belts have become.

"We seem to have a love affair with violence and it will take a sea change in our culture to move away from this thinking," Secretary Riley said shortly after the Springfield shooting. "As long as this society continues to glorify violence, continues to make it easy for young people to get guns and as long we continue to hide our heads in the sand or fail to reach out when a young person is truly troubled—we have to confront tragedies like Springfield and Jonesboro."

Notes

[1] "11-year-old expelled when squirt gun falls out of bag," The Associated Press, Sept. 22, 1998.

[2] Quoted on NBC's "Today" show, Sept. 23, 1998.

[3] The Department of Education has been preparing the "First Annual Report on School Safety," to be released at the White House conference.

[4] Elizabeth Donohue, Vincent Schiraldi and Jason Ziedenberg, "School House Hype: School shootings and the real risks kids face in America," Justice Policy Institute, July 29, 1998.

[5] Quoted in a press release accompanying the "Report on State Implementation of the Gun-Free Schools Act–School Year 1996-1997," U.S. Department of Education, 1998.

[6] "Students' Reports of School Crime: 1989 and 1995," National Center for Education Statistics and the Bureau of Justice Statistics, March 1998.

[7] The report, "Violence and Discipline Problems in U. S. Public Schools: 1996-97," was conducted by the National Center for Education Statistics, a division of the Department of Education.

[8] Quoted in a July 29 JPI press release.

[9] Scott Bowles, "Armed, alienated and adolescent," *USA Today*, March 31, 1998.

[10] *Ibid.*

[11] States with CAP laws are California, Connecticut, Delaware, Florida, Hawaii, Iowa, Nevada, New Jersey, North Carolina, Maryland, Massachusetts, Minnesota, Rhode Island, Texas, Virginia and Wisconsin.

[12] Peter Cummings, et. al., "State Gun-Safe Storage Laws and Child Mortality Due to Firearms," *Journal of the American Medical Association*, Oct. 1, 1997.

[13] Charlotte Faltermayer, "What is Justice for a Sixth-Grade Killer?" *Time*, April 6, 1998.

[14] National Center for Health Statistics.

[15] James A. Fox, 1996: *Trends in Juvenile Violence: A Report to the United States Attorney General on Current and Future Rates of Juvenile Offending*, U.S. Department of Justice.

[16] Quoted in a June 17 press release.

[17] Faltermayer, *op. cit.*

[18] Linda J. Collier, "Adult Crime, Adult Time," *The Washington Post*, March 29, 1998.

[19] From an NRA fact sheet on proposed CAP laws.

[20] Testimony before the Senate Judiciary Subcommittee on Youth Violence, Sept. 10, 1997.

[21] "An Evaluation of Juvenile Justice Innovations in Duval County, Fla.," was conducted by Florida State University economist David W. Rasmussen and released Aug. 21, 1996.

[22] Speech to Santa Barbara educators March 4, 1998.

[23] For background, see Sarah Glazer, "Violence in Schools," *The CQ Researcher*, Sept. 11, 1992, pp. 796-819.

[24] In *Gault v. Arizona*, the Supreme Court ruled that a youth in juvenile court is entitled to due process and representation by a lawyer. The case involved a 15-year-old who was sentenced to nearly six years in reform school for allegedly making an obscene phone call to a female neighbor, an offense for which an adult would have been sentenced to 30 days in jail.

[25] Jackson Toby, "Crime in the Schools," in James Q. Wilson, ed., *Crime and Public Policy* (1983), p. 79.

[26] Carl Bosch, *Schools Under Seige, Guns, Gangs and Hidden Dangers* (1997).

[27] According to the 1997-98 USA-PRIDE Summary Report, released June 18, 1998.

[28] Quoted in a press statement released with the report.

[29] "Report on State Implementation of the Gun-Free Schools Act– School Year 1996-1997," *op. cit.*

[30] Shannon Tangornan, "Surveys find increases in gangs, youth violence," *USA Today*, April 13, 1998.

[31] Bosch, *op. cit.*, p. 16.

[32] "Crime in the United States," Federal Bureau of Investigation, 1996.

[33] In a June speech to school safety officials gathered in Washington.

[34] Ralph Frammolino, "Failing Grade for Safe Schools Plan," *Los Angeles Times*, Sept. 8, 1998.

[35] Quoted in Frammolino, ibid.

[36] Frammolino, ibid.

[37] Alexander Volokh and Lisa Snell, "School Violence Prevention: Strategies to Keep Schools Safe," Oct. 20, 1997.

[38] Quoted in a press statement released with the report.

[39] Volokh, *ibid.*

[40] Volokh, *ibid.*

[41] For background, see Charles S. Clark, "Attack on Public Schools," *The CQ Researcher*, July 26, 1996, pp. 656-679 and Kenneth Jost, "Private Management of Public Schools," *The CQ Researcher*, March 25, 1994, pp. 282-305.

[42] "Safe Schools, Safe Students: A Guide to Violence Prevention Strategies," Drug Strategies, 1998.

[43] James Alan Fox and Sanford A. Newman, "After-School Crime or After-School Programs."

Blood in the School Yard[2]

By Lisa Popyk
Cincinnati Post, November 7, 1998

In small towns across America, the quiet, the meek, the mild-mannered are striking out with deadly, premeditated violence. A twisted view of reality tells them that killing is the best way to speak up.

The quiet youngsters next door have become today's school yard shooters—13 of them in the last five years.

The unpredictable, unforgiving and senseless force of the crimes, and the youthful faces behind them, have scarred America's image of childhood innocence.

Yet experts in psychology, psychiatry and criminology say they're surprised that there have been just 13. More, they believe, are certain to follow.

"You can't have the kind of saturation of violence that we have today without it manifesting itself somewhere," said Dewey Cornell, director of the University of Virginia Youth Violence Project.

"It's like a virus spreading through a large population of people. Not everyone gets sick. Just the most vulnerable, and then with varying degrees of illness."

The most vulnerable, he said, are today's children, particularly the lonely, disconnected, misfit child.

In each recent school yard slaying, the gunman was a young male, viewed by peers as weak and by himself as isolated, alone. He found an outlet in violence in movies, on television, on the Internet, in his own life. Often he began collecting weapons, writing about violence, torturing animals. In his confused mind, the image of him with a gun and his tormentors cowering at his feet began to loom large. He experienced a power surge beyond understanding, says John Nicoletti of Colorado, an expert in police psychology who is writing a book on school yard violence.

"Once they've drawn first blood," Nicoletti said, "you usually can't talk them down. They've reached the point of no return."

Filled with rage, the child—almost always a boy—suppresses his emotions until he explodes in a bid to take con-

---

trol of his life and be heard. Girls in such situations develop control through eating disorders and turn their rage inward; boys explode in violence, experts say.

In 1994, Greater Cincinnati awoke to the problem when a Union, Ky., teen slaughtered his upper-middle-class family one morning. Clay Shrout, who felt neglected and outcast, stood outside a convenience store drinking juice after murdering his parents and two little sisters. "You don't even know what I just did," he mumbled to passersby. He then headed to Ryle High School with his weapons cache.

For Luke Woodham, the bloody stabbing death of his mother and shooting of two students in 1997 was euphoric. He was still high on adrenaline, and smiling, when he gave police a videotaped confession 20 minutes after his arrest in Pearl, Miss. Filled with bravado and swagger, he said: "I wanted attention, someone to notice me. I guess the world's going to remember me now."

> *Clay Shrout, who felt neglected and outcast, stood outside a convenience store drinking juice after murdering his parents and two little sisters.*

And the slight, quiet Andrew Wurst was suddenly in charge, empowered by a .25 caliber Raven, when he sauntered through a panic-stricken school dance in Edinboro, Penn., in April of this year.

He waved the firearm at his friends as they fled in fear and calmly walked up behind his cowering principal. The gun aimed at her forehead, he said: "That's not going to save you."

Nicoletti and others say violent images in the media equate murder with power. And it tells lonely, isolated children that they gain control and command attention by wielding a gun. They point to movies like *Natural Born Killers,* a 1994 thinly-veiled satire featuring two brutal serial killers who become international heroes. Several of the youngsters involved in recent school yard shootings named this movie in particular as an influencing force.

In the film, lead characters Mickey and Mallory vindicate a lifetime of injustice and abuse—and find true love—by slaying more than 50 people. Murder is equated with freedom. At one point, after making his first kill, a character says, "I'm alive for the first time in my life." In the end, the killers walk free.

The controversial box-office hit is a sensational example, Cornell said, that does not stand alone.

Movies, photographs, video games and song lyrics that would have turned stomachs even five years ago, today don't raise an eyebrow.

"Maybe," Cornell said, "what we're seeing is an indication that our saturation of violence is reaching a tipping point. And early adolescents are like the miner's canaries, the first to succumb to the poisoned air.

"That doesn't mean they're not responsible, morally or legally. But we shouldn't be surprised that they're being affected by it."

At least two of the nation's recent school gunmen said

"Maybe, what we're seeing is an indication that our saturation of violence is reaching a tipping point. And early adolescents are like the miner's canaries, the first to succumb to the poisoned air."
—**Dewey Cornell, director of the University of Virginia Youth Violence Project.**

---

they were inspired by violence on television and in literature.

Fourteen-year-old Barry Loukaitis claims his shooting spree in Moses Lake, Wash., in 1996 was inspired by Pearl Jam's music video "Jeremy," the movies *Natural Born Killers* and *The Basketball Diaries,* and the book *Rage.*

All had killing as a central theme; three included a classroom mass murder.

"Jeremy" is based on the real life story of a Texas teen who in 1991 killed himself in front of his class. But the video, named Video of the Year in 1993, depicts a lonely teen who kills all his classmates after enduring taunts. Police found a copy of the video in Loukaitis' bedroom.

Loukaitis also repeatedly watched *Natural Born Killers.* He often quoted from the movie and told friends he thought it would be "fun to go on a killing spree."

Police also found in Loukaitis' bedroom a collection of Stephen King's books, including a well-worn copy of *Rage,* in which a troubled boy kills his algebra teacher and takes the class hostage.

King has since apologized for writing the book, saying he penned it during a troubling period in his life. He said he wished it never had been published.

On February 2, 1996, following weeks of discussion, Loukaitis acted out his fantasy. Dressed all in black, with boots and a long overcoat to conceal the rifle at his side—just as Leonardo DiCaprio did during a dream sequence in *The Basketball Diaries*—he sauntered into his fifth-period algebra class and opened fire.

With three people dead, a fourth critically wounded and nearly two dozen other students crying around him, Loukaitis smiled and said: "This sure beats algebra, doesn't it?"

His key target was a classmate who days earlier had called him a "fag."

> *With three people dead, a fourth critically wounded and nearly two dozen other students crying around him, Loukaitis smiled and said: "This sure beats algebra, doesn't it?"*

Less than a year later, bright, quiet Michael Carneal also said that he was inspired by *The Basketball Dairies* to murder three classmates in Paducah, Ky.

A year after seeing the movie, Carneal was still telling friends he, too, was "planning something big."

On December 12, 1997, he packed up an arsenal of stolen guns and headed to Heath High School, where the small, bespectacled freshman unpacked a .22-caliber handgun, inserted two earplugs and began shooting. Eight students fell, three were killed.

Kip Kinkel, who killed four people including his parents in Springfield, Ore., was so obsessed with excessively violent programming that his parents told friends they had to disconnect their cable TV.

"Violence is so pervasive in our culture, I don't think any child escapes it," said Charles Patrick Ewing, a clinical and forensic psychologist at the State University of New York and author of the book *Kids Who Kill*, (Lexington Books, $5.99 paperback.)

"More children think about (committing acts of violence) than don't," Ewing said. "For every one who acts on it, 99 others think about it."

Today, it's easier than ever before for children to act out those violent fantasies. Easier, experts said, because of three key factors: the consequences aren't clear, no one is listening and dangerous information is only a keyboard away.

"One of the key factors is that all children and most adolescents do not understand the finality of death," said Scott Poland, chairman of the National Emergency Disaster Team for the National Association of School Psychologists.

It's a difficult concept for any youngster, but one made even more complicated by the proliferation of quick and apparently painless death depicted on TV, in the movies and on music videos. No one suffers and no one gets punished, said Marjorie Creswell of the National School Safety Center.

Consider the following from the National Television Violence Study, which reflect three years of research:

In each of the recent school shootings, the youth involved talked about his plans before hand. Most wrote dark, morbid and death-filled papers for school assignments.

• 85 percent of all programming shown on the three premium cable channels and 44 percent of programming on broadcast networks includes violent acts;
• 73 percent of perpetrators go unpunished in these programs;
• 47 percent fail to depict the harm to victims and 58 percent show no pain.

Video games almost never show the consequences. And the running joke of the wildly-popular cable cartoon *South Park* is a child dying in a different way every week. Kip Kinkel sat down to watch it after murdering his parents in the next room.

Yet people have become so accustomed to talk of blood and gore, hate and killing, that few take a child's preoccupation with the macabre seriously, Ewing said.

"Children do things for shock value. The problem is, that we have a much greater tolerance for deviance, so it's tough to shock or alarm us," Ewing said.

"Plus, we're so into giving people their own space that the boundaries of normalcy for adolescence have become pretty broad. And honestly, that's B.S. A child talking about building bombs, abusing animals and killing people is not normal."

In each of the recent school shootings, the youth involved talked about his plans before hand. Most wrote dark, morbid and death-filled papers for school assignments. Several admitted to or bragged about abusing animals and wanting to feel the sensation of taking a life.

Making that mix even more volatile is that today's children have greater access than ever before to materials and information that can readily turn a violent fantasy into reality, Ewing said. Through the Internet they quickly can learn about bomb making, hand guns, ritualistic killings, the occult and groups ready to foster violent ideas.

"It's a whole new, secret world that they can get lost in," Nicoletti said.

Most of the school yard shooters had downloaded violence-related materials and stock piled weapons shortly before their killing sprees.

Shrout, Kinkel, Woodham and Carneal all used computers to learn about bomb building, guns and violence. Their computers served as their links to a place that their parents most likely would not have approved of, or allowed them to enter.

"Juvenile killers don't just wake up one day and become juvenile killers," Ewing said. "Homicide, like most behavior, is learned."

Colorado, World Mourn Deaths at Columbine High[3]

BY MARK OBMASCIK
DENVER POST, APRIL 22, 1999

While the world mourned the senseless killings of 14 students and one teacher at Columbine High School, survivors recalled acts of heroism as police removed bodies Wednesday from the grisly massacre site.

Thousands grieved for the dead at religious services in metro Denver, President Clinton asked for a moment of silent prayer at the White House, and the pope decried the violence from Rome. Meanwhile, investigators in Jefferson County pored over the lives of the two dead murder suspects, Eric Harris, 18, and Dylan Klebold, 17, and asked a simple but troubling question: Why? "I don't know what the motive was, other than hate," said District Attorney Dave Thomas. The Columbine crime scene was so gruesome, Thomas said, that some law enforcement officers dissolved to tears. "There were SWAT team people who were in Vietnam who were crying and weeping over what they saw," he said.

They were witnessing the worst mass school shooting in U.S. history. Though the sheriff said Tuesday that as many as 25 were dead, the confirmed number Wednesday was 15, including the two killers. Of the 22 others wounded, six have been released from hospitals. Five remain in critical condition.

At one point during the four-hour rampage, Klebold's father called the DA to offer help with his son. Law enforcement officials told the father it was too late for help.

The Klebold and Harris families both issued statements, through their attorneys, expressing grief. "Our thoughts, prayer and heartfelt apologies go out to the victims, their families, friends, and the entire community," the Klebold statement said. "Like the rest of the country, we are struggling to understand why this happened."

---

3. Copyright © 1999 *Denver Post*. Reprinted with permission. Staff writers Erin Emery, Carlos Illescas, David Olinger, J. Sebastian Sinisi, Kevin Simpson, Cindy Brovsky, Mike McPhee, Peggy Lowe, Kieran Nicholson, Angela Cortez, Patricia Callahan and Jim Kirksey contributed to this report.

Police found more than 30 pipe bombs around the school, inside boobytrapped cars and in the suspects' two suburban homes. Some bombs were palm-sized carbon-dioxide cartridges wrapped with nails and BBs to maximize killing power. Other bombs, equipped with timers, were made from propane barbecue tanks.

In the school library, where one gunman died from a gunshot wound to the back of the head and another had a hole in the side of his head, police counted four guns: a 9mm semiautomatic carbine, two sawed-off shotguns and a handgun. It's still unknown where they got the guns.

There were at least eight empty ammunition clips, which each carried at least 10 bullets, plus dozens of spent shotgun shells, investigators said.

Police investigated whether the two killers got help from friends. "This is not something they did overnight," said Sheriff John Stone. "A lot of planning went into this."

> *"This is not something they did overnight. A lot of planning went into this."*
> —Sheriff John Stone

Columbine High School will remain closed indefinitely, officials said. All other Jefferson County and Denver schools are to reopen today with heightened security.

The two teenagers, part of an outcast school group called the Trench Coat Mafia, were caught burglarizing a car in January 1998. They completed their probation in February of this year.

Rocky Hoffschneider, father of star Columbine wrestler Rocky Jr., said police told him one gunman kept a "hit list" with his son's name atop it. His son escaped unharmed. A sheriff's spokesman said he knew of no such list.

Specific targets

Witnesses said the two laughing gunmen specifically targeted prep athletes and a black youth. Several students recalled earlier tension between the gunmen and athletes.

"It was an ongoing thing. They didn't like us and we didn't like them," John House, a junior, said of the Trench Coat Mafia. Athletes often mocked the outcasts, he said, by calling them "dirt bags," and telling them, "Nice cape" or "Cute makeup."

In a before-school bowling class, the two shooters often would declare, "Heil Hitler," after scoring a strike, House said. Before the Tuesday massacre, one shooter, Harris, showed up at his 6:15 a.m. bowling class in a flannel shirt and blue jeans.

He returned to school with his friend Klebold five hours later in a black trench coat and mask, armed with an arsenal of bombs and guns.

The attack was launched during the 11:30 a.m. lunch hour when one gunman heaved a pipe bomb onto the school roof and started spraying students with gunshots, witnesses said. Two students fell dead, and the two murderers hustled into school hallways.

A sheriff's deputy stationed at the school, Neil Gardner, exchanged gunfire with one of the murderers but didn't hit him. Twenty minutes later, a SWAT team of officers from Denver, Arapahoe County and Littleton peeled into the building. Deputy Paul Smoker and Lt. Terry Manwaring fired at a gunman and missed.

At that point, because the situation was so volatile and deputies were unsure how many snipers were shooting, police said they retreated and set up a safe perimeter outside the school.

"A deputy can't help if he's dead," said department spokesman Steve Davis.

Dozens of students fled. Dozens remained trapped inside. Chaos reigned.

With pipe bombs exploding, smoke filled the hallways, and the fire alarm blared. A broken fire-sprinkler system gushed water and flooded the cafeteria. More bombs blasted, spraying students with shrapnel and collapsing ceiling tiles.

Hid under desks

Students cowered under desks. One teacher, Dave Sanders, the girls basketball coach, was shot and bleeding profusely, but still directed panicking teenagers away from the mayhem.

Teenagers ripped off their shirts and tried to save Sanders' life with makeshift tourniquets. One student, Kevin Starkey, worked to keep Sanders conscious for hours by pulling family photos from the teacher's wallet and asking about them.

The teacher died.

In the library, Crystal Woodman, 16, said a boy, Seth Houy, threw his body over hers and whispered a vow to take a bullet for her. For some reason, the gunmen spared them.

"I could feel them in there," Woodman said.

"They asked a girl if she believed in God. She said yes, and they shot her. I could hear them talking. They said they waited their whole lives for this. They were saying, 'Who's ready to die next?' Then they would whoop and holler when they shot someone."

Another student trapped in the library, Isaiah Shoels, 18, a prep wrestler, was shot and killed because he was black, survivors said.

"He had two strikes against him," said his grieving father, Mike Shoels. "He was black and he was an athlete . . . That's not a reason to die."

Outside, ambulance crews raced to the school to whisk away the injured. The gunmen fired at paramedics on the school's south end, police said.

Lakewood Sgt. George Hinkle raced to help. "There was a body of a boy in front of our armored car that I was going to rescue, but some of my guys said, 'He's dead, Sarge,' so I left the body," Hinkle said. "It was devastating. I've been a cop for 23 years and in SWAT since 1980, and this was clearly the most traumatic and devastating thing I've ever seen. I know for the next couple of weeks, I'll have nightmares."

Meanwhile, a bloody boy begged for help from a window on the school's second floor. Two Lakewood SWAT team members, Sgt. John Romaniec and Agent Donn Kraemer, saw the boy starting to pass out. They called to him, "Stay with us! Stay with us!"

The police stood on top of an armored car and caught the falling boy.

> *"I've been a cop for 23 years and in SWAT since 1980, and this was clearly the most traumatic and devastating thing I've ever seen."*
> —**Lakewood Sgt. George Hinkle**

60 in one room

Down the hall, 60 students crammed into an office next to the choir room. For 2 hours, they huddled and cried and prayed the gunmen wouldn't find them. They heard 25 shotgun blasts and 30 more shots from a handgun.

"We had a phone in there. We contacted the outside, then we said we didn't want to make any noise," said Craig Mason, 17, a junior. "We could tell they were coming closer, to the top of the stairs."

Crime in Schools

Precentage of public schools reporting one or more criminal incidents to police, 1996-1997

Elementary Schools

Rape/Sexual Battery	1%
Robbery	1%
Physical attack or fight with weapon	2%
Vandalism	31%
Theft or larceny	19%
Physical attack or fight without weapon	12%

Middle Schools

Rape/Sexual Battery	5%
Robbery	5%
Physical attack or fight with weapon	12%
Vandalism	47%
Theft or larceny	44%
Physical attack or fight without weapon	51%

High Schools

Rape/Sexual Battery	8%
Robbery	8%
Physical attack or fight with weapon	13%
Vandalism	52%
Theft or larceny	55%
Physical attack or fight without weapon	55%

Source: Indicators of School Crime and Safety, 1998, Bureau of Justice Statistics and National Center for Education Statistics

The students barricaded themselves in the office, flipped off the lights and ducked.

"You could tell he was right out side," Mason said. "After the first 20 minutes, things got quiet."

"It seemed like every kid had a pager and people's pagers started going off," said Mason. "One student called and said, 'Mom, I love you and I hope I see you, but I love you.'"

Meanwhile, Theresa Miller, a chemistry teacher, doused flames from a bomb lobbed through a window in an office next to her classroom. Her heroism was singled out by President Clinton.

"We see, in a moment of agony, what is best in our community and in our country," Clinton said on national television.

The president asked for a moment of silent prayer.

"We all must do more to recognize and look for the early warning signals that deeply troubled young people send, often before they explode into violence," Clinton said. "Surely more of them can be saved and more innocent victims and tragedies can be avoided."

From Vatican City, Pope John Paul II said he was "deeply shocked" by the rampage.

The pope sent a telegram to Denver Catholic Archbishop Charles Chaput expressing hope the American society will react "by committing itself to promoting and transmitting the moral vision and the values which alone can ensure respect for the inviolable dignity of human life."

Investigators said they need at least two more days inside the school to collect crime evidence. All bodies finally were removed by 5:30 p.m. Wednesday. The grim task was delayed in part because the killers spread live bombs around bodies. Most officers had left the scene by 7:30 p.m.

Though robots often are used to handle bombs, the machines couldn't be used in the library crime scene because the machines couldn't move around so many bodies, police said. Ten victims and both shooters died in the library.

Surrounded by scores of newspaper and television reporters from around the world, the students who returned to Columbine High School cried, hugged, reminisced and contemplated the rampage.

"I cried hysterically," said Melanie King, a 17-year-old senior who had been looking forward to her last 17 days of school. "Cried and cried and cried. Right now, I'm dry of tears."

At suburban churches and Denver's Civic Center Park, thousands of survivors and well-wishers gathered at commemorative services. Many reflected on their fate.

Justin Woods, a 15-year-old freshman, was playing soccer outside the school when shooting erupted. He saw the gunmen shoot three girls, then turn their weapons on him and his buddies.

The bullets whizzed by their heads without hitting anyone.

"I'm lucky to be here," Woods said. "I didn't eat lunch. I just wanted to play soccer. I guess soccer saved my life."

He paused and reconsidered.

"No," he said, "God saved my life."

Urban Violence Ignored, Activist Says[4]

By Holly Kurtz
Denver Rocky Mountain News, June 20, 1999

Dean Askew knows youth violence like the city streets he saves teens from each day, like the shower where he prays each morning that his son will be alive that evening.

That's why the 40-year-old anti-gang activist felt frustrated as the Columbine school shootings became a springboard for many of the discussions at Saturday's youth violence summit.

Askew, who founded Street Beat seven years ago, was saddened by the killings—but doubted such a summit would have taken place had the shootings struck an urban school, where many students were less affluent or representatives of minorities.

This tone of sympathy tinged with frustration has characterized many inner-city residents' reaction to the Columbine shootings, summit audience members said.

"We live in the cycle of violence every day," Askew said. "Nobody cared. As long as it stayed in the inner city, it was fine."

Gov. Bill Owens' press secretary Dick Wadhams disagreed. He said the summit was planned well before Columbine and that the shootings just spurred organizers to move up the date. The same event would have been held if the shootings had occurred at an inner-city school, he added.

Askew is also frustrated that people around the world have donated millions in the name of an affluent school like Columbine, while programs in his neighborhood struggle for basics. His group's budget, for example, has slipped from $130,000 to $85,000 in the past year. Askew said this sends a mixed message to inner-city kids.

"What they've told inner-city youth is that because of their socio-economic structure, you're not as important as them," he said.

---

4. Copyright © 1999 *Denver Rocky Mountain News*. Reprinted with permission.

He said he was unsure what to tell an inner-city child who asked whether President Clinton came to Columbine because the kids there "looked like him."

One student at a predominantly white high school doubted that Clinton, or the national media, would have paid as much attention had Columbine occurred in an urban high school.

"I would hope it would get as much attention," said Clif Hancock, who attends Cheyenne Mountain High School in Colorado Springs. "Naturally, it wouldn't. Unfortunately, it is more expected" in an urban school. "You have more parental involvement in schools like Cheyenne."

Elsa Banuelos disagreed. Nearly 100 percent of the 400 West High School classmates she surveyed after the Columbine killings denied the same thing could happen at their school.

In an ironic reversal of inner-city stereotypes, many urban students are shaking their heads and saying suburban killings in Littleton and other outwardly idyllic towns could never happen in their own back yards. Banuelos says the racial and cultural diversity of her school makes students less likely to taunt classmates who dress or act differently, as the Columbine shooters were allegedly teased at their more homogenous suburban school.

Antoinette Alire, a Denver School Board candidate, doubted most poor teens would have the opportunity to plan a Columbine-scale killing without being discovered. Sisters and brothers sharing their cramped bedrooms would know what they were up to, she said.

Perhaps inner-city schools can teach suburban schools a lesson about taking threats and warning signs seriously, Askew said.

"Always be on your P's and Q's," he cautioned. "Always prepare."

Littleton Every Day[5]

Guns kill a dozen kids daily, but nobody cares

BY JAKE TAPPER
SALON, APRIL 27, 1999

On the afternoon of March 29, someone pulled a gun in southeast Washington and shot Marcus Owens, a 16-year-old African-American high school student from the projects. Bang, that was it, no more Marcus: no more sweetness, no more endearing smile, no more promise. Didn't even get a mention in the *Washington Post*.

But I happened to know Marcus, through a local tutoring program, and news of his death broke my heart. Marcus was a good kid—not a criminal, not a gun-toting gang-banger who had it coming. His only crime was that he lived in a bad neighborhood, one where this kind of gun death occurs all too often.

The contrast between the silence that greeted Marcus' death and the world's reaction to the massacre in Littleton, Colo., is painful to me personally, but it makes a kind of sense. There's some racism, sure—all but one of the Littleton dead are white–but there's also our weakness for spectacle. We're riveted by mass murder; killing kids one by one doesn't get our attention the same way.

But Littleton happens every day in America. Twelve young people murdered at Columbine High School? That's the same number of kids killed by guns daily. In 1995, according to the National Center for Health Statistics, 3,280 children and teenagers were murdered with guns and 440 died in unintentional shootings. That's close to a daily dozen. Littleton is par for the course in this country. It was just a more efficient job.

But we just hear about the really big shows, the kids who had the forethought to go for the headlines. And the kids who succeeded. The week after 15-year-old Kip Kinkel opened fire with a .22 semiautomatic rifle on a crowded cafeteria in Springfield, Ore., in May 1998—killing two students and wounding 20 others—other kids had similar murderous ideas.

Check out this school-based crime log for that very same week in May: Two high school students in Camden, Del., were arrested for pointing a gun at students and teachers; a freshman in Baldwin, Mo., brought to school a .22 caliber revolver that he'd taken from home; a 10-year-old in Memphis, Tenn., pointed a loaded .25 caliber semiautomatic at the head of a classmate and said pow; a 15-year-old middle school student in Hereford, Md., brought a semiautomatic to school; and a kid in Parkersburg, W.Va., was suspended for planting a semiautomatic pistol in his teacher's backpack.

In the inner city, deaths like Marcus Owens' happen all the time. In 1992, for instance, firearm homicide became the No. 1 cause of death for black men ages 15-34. And according to the Centers for Disease Control and Prevention, the homicide rate among black men ages 15-24 rose by 66 percent from 1984 to 1997, with 95 percent of this increase due to firearm-related murders.

> *The epidemic—and it's nothing short of that—of American kids lost to guns has been estimated to be 10 times the size of the polio epidemic. Yet there are few Jonas Salks we can turn to . . .*

As Jonesboro becomes Littleton becomes fill-in-the-blank, we're going to hear myriad suggestions of how to fix the problems that once again killed American schoolchildren: metal detectors in every school; more armed guards; school uniforms; no more Nintendo; no more Internet; no more cruelty.

But nothing is going to change unless lawmakers in this country start trying to reduce the numbers of guns on the street, and the number of kids who have access to guns in their homes. How can any commentator keep a straight face when the TV pundits start blaming Marilyn Manson and Oliver Stone and killers' parents, without acknowledging that guns are part of the problem.

The epidemic—and it's nothing short of that—of American kids lost to guns has been estimated to be 10 times the size of the polio epidemic. Yet there are few Jonas Salks we can turn to; instead—to push the metaphor—we have to put up with well-funded and powerful pro-polio organizations, dedicated to the spread of the disease.

In Colorado, for instance, both the state House and Senate recently passed a law denying localities the right to pass any gun laws of their own. The law is aimed at Denver, which recently banned assault weapons; apparently NRA president Charlton Heston can't sleep at night knowing that the NRA's annual convention—to be held in Denver on Saturday—won't feature the latest in shiny new high-tech machinery that will allow future disturbed young men to kill our children quicker, faster and in greater numbers.

So prepare for more Springfields and Jonesboros and Littletons. Let the custodians clean up the blood. And I'll remember Marcus Owens, who was shot down March 29 because his life wasn't worth as much as a PAC check.

Young, Female and Turning Deadly[6]

More and More Teenage Girls Are Getting Busted in Serious Crimes

By Heidi Evans
NEW YORK DAILY NEWS, December 19, 1999

Trouble came early to Dominique Livingston. At 14, she was arrested for carrying a loaded gun to school under her shirt. Last month, she allegedly stabbed to death an 18-year-old teacher's aide at a Queens bowling alley, telling police it was over an argument they had five or six years ago. Authorities said the two exchanged heated words for 45 minutes when Livingston, 20, took a switchblade out of her pocket, pulled the girl's head back by the hair and plunged the knife into her neck.

Adrian Davis, an aspiring teacher who was out bowling with friends on a Saturday night, was pronounced dead at 3 a.m. at Jamaica Hospital.

Because murder is rare among young women, Livingston is an especially troubling example of the growing incidence of criminal violence among girls. According to the federal Office of Juvenile Justice and Delinquency Prevention, girls accounted for 27%, or 697,000, of the 2.6 million juvenile arrests in 1998.

And although their numbers are far lower than those of boys, the number of girls arrested for violent crimes in the U.S. more than doubled from 1985 to 1995—to more than 21,000 from more than 9,000.

The story is much the same in New York City, where arrests of girls for violent crime jumped 58%, to 1,766 in 1997 from 1.118 in 1987.

This alarming trend—at a time when the nation's crime rates generally are falling—has caught the attention of people in the criminal justice system.

"We used to marvel when one girl was referred to us," said Nina Jody, chief prosecutor for Manhattan Family Court, which handles juvenile crime. "Now, it's like ladies' day around here. There are many days when half the cases are girls." Just a decade ago, the girls who passed through juvenile court typically had committed minor offenses like shoplifting or purse snatching. Five years ago, girls began getting arrested for drugs. Now, Jody and other experts say, they are often picked up for crimes as violent as any that boys commit.

A Disturbing Trend

"The topography of girls and crime has changed dramatically," Jody said. "In the last two years, girls have become the main actors in assaults, robberies and even gang assaults. They are out on the street at 2 a.m., riding the subways, doing everything boys are doing."
Consider these recent cases:

• Adona A., a 15-year-old Brooklyn girl, slashed a teenager across her forehead and neck Dec. 10, while another girl held the victim down. The victim was walking in her East Flatbush neighborhood at 8:40 p.m.

• Tamika F., 15, was arrested Dec. 6 at her Manhattan high school for setting fire to a classmate's coat and test paper. Tamika was overheard telling the classmate, "If you hadn't taken my keys, this wouldn't have happened."

• Alicia A., 12, along with four other girls and two boys, ganged up on a 35-year-old flower vendor on Sept. 25 and repeatedly punched him in the face on W. 143rd St. The vendor was pushed to the ground and suffered multiple bruises on the back and side of his head.

• Maggie C., 16, of Flushing, Queens, punched a girl in the face after school on Nov. 22 near the Lincoln Center parking garage and robbed her the next day.

There are a number of factors behind the rise in violence by girls. Experts cite the easy availability of guns, poverty, the use of alcohol and drugs, and violence in the home. While these factors also affect boys, girls may have the added trauma of being victims of early childhood sexual abuse, which many advocates think can lead to violent behavior.
In 1994, for example, nearly 5 million females 12 and older nationwide were victims of violent crime, including

rape, aggravated assault, robbery and homicide. "Girls who have been physically or sexually abused are more likely than girls who have not been abused to become involved in physical fights and to believe that violence is an acceptable behavior," said Leslie Wolfe, president of the Center for Women Policy Studies in Washington.

"To continue to ignore the reality of violence on the lives of girls and young women places them and society at great risk."

Because boys commit the overwhelming number of juvenile crimes, not much attention has been paid to female offenders, either in New York or elsewhere. In fact, a study of 443 delinquency programs found that 8% focused on girls.

Different Motivation

"There has been a deafening silence about girls," said Meda Chesney-Lind, an expert on women and crime who teaches at the University of Hawaii. "The system is ill-equipped to deal with them."

What little research has been done on girls, however, shows that when girls and boys are violent, they are motivated by different forces.

Chesney-Lind says girls typically tend to fight with other girls over a challenging glance, a dispute over a boyfriend or rumors.

"With boys, violence is instrumental—they use violence to get something else they want, like money during a robbery," she said. "If girls fight with other girls or even kill, more likely it is an expression of anger or emotion."

Because boys commit the overwhelming number of juvenile crimes, not much attention has been paid to female offenders, either in New York or elsewhere.

A 1999 study by the U.S. Justice Department found that boys and girls also tend to kill different types of victims. From 1980 to 1997, 54% of male juvenile offenders killed an acquaintance, 37% killed a stranger and 9% killed a family member.

The victims of females were more likely to be family members, 39%, and far less likely to be strangers, 15%.

Moreover, males were far more likely than females to use a gun. While 73% of boys used firearms, 41% of girls used guns. Girls were more likely to use other means to kill, such as strangulation, drowning or fire.

"We do not want to believe that girls will do these things," said Dr. Deborah Prothrow-Stith of the Harvard School of

Public Health, who is in the forefront of a national movement to treat youth violence as a public health issue.

"We want to believe that girls' extra X chromosome is protective, but when you talk to middle school principals, they will tell you that girls are the more vicious, and that they often have to call an ambulance when girls fight.

"What you are seeing is the unfolding of a real tragedy—and a preventable one."

Impact of Pop Culture

Pop culture is a key reason for this, Prothrow-Stith thinks.

"We have a culture that has feminized the violent super-hero, with Pink Power Rangers and rap music, which have legitimized for girls a violent response to their problems," she said.

Indeed, there is no shortage of violent role models for girls in the hip-hop world. In one popular song, rap singer Lil' Kim, who calls herself the Queen B---h, praises sex and promiscuous behavior to the sound of a gun being cocked. Other songs openly celebrate violence, glorifying knifings, shootings and other criminal assaults.

The most dramatic increase in violent crime among girls is in the category of aggravated assault. In New York City, such arrests have risen 55% in the past decade to 930 in 1997 from 599 in 1987.

Such statistics, experts say, might be explained by today's climate, in which police feel pressured to make an arrest when domestic violence is involved, even if a child is defending herself against an abusive parent.

Last week, for example, a tearful 14-year-old was hauled into Manhattan Family Court for stabbing her intoxicated mother with a kitchen knife after the mother began beating her up. The mother called police, who reluctantly arrested the girl.

She appeared in court with circles under her eyes, exhausted from being up all night in a police station.

"There ain't no parent here for me, and I am alone with all these people I don't know," she said outside the courtroom after the judge decided to turn her over to the city's Administration for Children's Services for the weekend.

Lenient Treatment

For better or worse, girls are treated far more leniently in the juvenile justice system than boys are. Girls "get five extra bites out of the apple before anything happens to them," Jody said. "When you are sitting in front of a middle-aged judge, they are less likely to lock her up or send her away on a first arrest or conviction."

Take Livingston. She got off with 18 months' probation for bringing a loaded .22-caliber gun to Intermediate School 72 in 1994. It was her first offense, and her lawyer assured the court it would be her last.

"Dominique understands that to achieve the goals she hopes to attain, she must remain a law-abiding and productive member of society," lawyer Steven Isaacs wrote in a Family Court memorandum obtained by the Sunday News under the Freedom of Information Law. "The lessons she has learned from this experience will stay with her forever."

That is not the way it appears to have worked out.

Livingston, who confessed to police on videotape the day Davis died, has been indicted on murder charges by the Queens district attorney. If convicted, she faces up to 25 years to life in prison.

Gay Teens Fight Back[7]

A New Generation of Gay Youth Won't Tolerate Harassment in Their Schools.

By Doug Ireland
The Nation, January 31, 2000

Jared Nayfack was 11 years old and living in the heart of conservative Orange County, California, when he told his best friend from school that he was gay—"and my friend then came out to me," says Jared. When he turned 15, Jared celebrated his birthday by coming out to his parents and closest friends. By then, he was attending a Catholic high school, and on a school-sponsored overnight field trip, Jared and his schoolmates decided to spend their free evening at the movies seeing *The Rocky Horror Picture Show*. "Some of us had decided to get all costumed up to see it, and when the teacher who was with us saw us she threw a fit: She forced me to get up in front of the other twenty-one students—many of whom I didn't know—and tell them I was gay. Most of the kids supported me, but later that evening, one of them—a lot bigger than I was; he had a black belt in martial arts—came into my hotel room and beat me up. I was a bloody mess, and he could have killed me if another student hadn't heard my screams and stopped him." Instead of punishing Jared's assailant, the school's dean suspended Jared and put him on "academic and behavioral probation." "The dean told me that even though I was forced to tell the others that I was gay, I was at fault because I'd 'threatened the masculinity' of the kid who'd beat me up," Jared recalls.

In fear, Jared transferred to a public high school, the South Orange County High School of the Arts. "I thought I'd be safe and could be out when I came there—after all, it was an arts program. Boy, was I wrong. Within two weeks people were yelling 'fag' at me in the halls and in class. I was dressed a little glam, if you will—nothing really offensive, just a little makeup. But when I went to the principal to complain, she did nothing about the harassment and told me that I was 'lacking in testosterone,'" Jared

---

explains. To fight back, Jared and some gay and straight friends formed a club called PRIDE, which made a twenty-five-foot-long rainbow banner to put up in school decorated with multicolored hands and the slogan, hands for equality (the banner was banned). The club also made beaded rainbow bracelets that many students wore— "even a lot of the football players," according to Jared—but the club was forbidden by the administration "because it didn't have anything to do with the curriculum." The harassment got worse—so bad that Jared had to leave school two months before graduation. "I had to fight to *be* before I could study," Jared explains, "but I left there feeling really let down and like a failure—we hadn't gotten anywhere."

"These kids are coming out at 13, 14, 15, at the same age that straight people historically begin to experience their sexuality. But they are experiencing more violence because of that."
—**Rea Carey, executive director of the National Youth Advocacy Coalition (NYAC)**

When he enrolled as a freshman at the University of California, Santa Cruz, Jared says, "I was embraced by a huge and loving queer community. They told me, 'It's OK to be angry'—that's something I hadn't heard before." Feeling a bit burned out, for his first six months at Santa Cruz Jared avoided gay activism—until the day he attended a conference of gay youth. "There were kids pulling together—I just knew I had to help out." He attended a youth training institute run by the Gay, Lesbian and Straight Education Network (GLSEN); began working with Gay/Straight Alliances (GSAs) at two high schools near the university; edited and xerox-published an anthology of adolescent writings about AIDS; created a performance piece, as part of his self-designed major in "theatrical activism," about homophobia with a cast of seven straight boys to the hit song "Faggot" by the rock group Korn; and now speaks to gay youth groups around the country. Today Jared is only 18.

Jared's story is fairly typical of a whole new generation of lesbian and gay adolescents: brave, tough and resilient, comfortable with their sexual identity and coming out at earlier ages, inventing their own organizations—and victimized by violence and harassment in their schools. Says Rea Carey, executive director of the National Youth Advocacy Coalition (NYAC), an alliance of local and national service agencies working to empower gay youth: "Five or ten years ago, kids would go to a youth service agency and say, 'I need help because I think I'm gay.' Today, more and more they say, 'I'm gay and so what? I want friends and a place to work on the issues I care about.' Being gay is not their problem, it's their strength. These kids are coming out at 13, 14, 15, at the same age that straight people historically begin to experience their sexuality. But they are experiencing more violence because of that."

A 1997 study by the Vermont Department of Health found that gay kids were threatened or injured with a weapon at school three times more than straight kids . . .

Quantifying the number of assaults on lesbian and gay youth isn't easy. In most states, gay-run Anti-Violence Projects are woefully underfunded and understaffed (when they have any staff at all), and students are rarely aware of them, according to Jeffrey Montgomery, the director of Detroit's Triangle Foundation and the spokesman for the National Association of Anti-Violence Projects. Teachers and school administrators most often don't report such incidents. After pressure from state governments sympathetic to the Christian right, the Clinton/Gore Administration's Centers for Disease Control removed all questions regarding sexual orientation from its national Youth Risk Behavior Survey. Now the only state to include them is Massachusetts.

There, according to its most recent questioning of nearly 4,000 high school students by the Massachusetts Department of Education, kids who self-identified as gay, lesbian or bisexual were seven times more likely than other kids to have skipped school because they felt unsafe (22.2 percent versus 3.3). A 1997 study by the Vermont Department of Health found that gay kids were threatened or injured with a weapon at school three times more than straight kids (24 percent versus 8). And a five-year study released in January by Washington State's Safe Schools Coalition—

a partnership of 74 public and private agencies—documented 146 incidents in the state's schools, including eight gang rapes and 39 physical assaults (on average, a single gay kid is attacked by more than two offenders at once).

With the antigay crusades of the religious right and the verbal gay-bashings of politicians like Trent Lott legitimizing the demonization of homosexuals, it is hardly surprising that homophobia is alive and well among gay kids' classmates. In November 1998, a poll of 3,000 top high schoolers by *Who's Who Among American High School Students*—its twenty-ninth annual survey—found that 48 percent admitted they are prejudiced against gays, up 19 percent from the previous year (and these are, as *Who's Who* proclaims, "America's brightest students").

All this means that, as Jon Lasser, an Austin, Texas, school psychologist (and heterosexual parent) who has interviewed scads of gay kids for his PhD thesis, puts it, "Many have a form of post-traumatic stress syndrome that affects their schoolwork—the fear of getting hurt really shakes them up and makes it hard to concentrate."

The mushrooming growth of Gay/Straight Alliances in middle and high schools in just the past few years has been the gay kids' potent response.

The mushrooming growth of Gay/Straight Alliances in middle and high schools in just the past few years has been the gay kids' potent response. There is strength in numbers: GSAs break the immobilizing isolation of gay students and raise their visibility, creating a mechanism to pressure school authorities into tackling harassment; educate teachers as well as other students; create the kind of solidarity among straight and gay kids that fosters resistance to bigotry and violence; provide meaningful safe-sex education; and help gay adolescents to speak and fight for themselves. The GLSEN national office has identified at least 400 GSAs, but since the GSA movement has been student-initiated and many self-starting groups are still not in touch with national gay organizations, the figure is undoubtedly much higher. There are eighty-five GLSEN chapters around the country, and while GLSEN began seven years ago primarily as an organization of teachers and other school personnel, it is making an increasing effort to include students in its organizing.

Another strategy that has frightened reluctant school administrators into steps to protect gay youth has been lawsuits by the kids themselves. The first on record was brought by a 16-year-old Ashland, Wisconsin, student, Jamie Nabozny, who in 1996 won a $900,000 judgment against school authorities who failed to prevent Nabozny's torturous harassment from seventh through eleventh grades, including beatings that put him in the hospital. Currently there are nine similar suits pending, including cases in Illinois, Washington, New Jersey, Minnesota, Missouri and several in California (one brought by the first-ever group of lesbian student plaintiffs, in the San Jose area). But as David Buckel, the Lambda Legal Defense and Education Fund's staff attorney specializing in school matters, points out, "A lot of people call and say 'I can't afford to go to court,' or 'We live in a small town and I can't put my family through that,' or 'If we sue and win it'll raise our neighbors' taxes and we'll get bricks through our window.'" (And in late December, Orange County gay students filed a lawsuit against school officials, seeking to lift their ban on a GSA at El Modena High School on the grounds that the interdiction violated their First Amendment rights.)

In a civilized country, one would think, legislation to protect kids from violence and harassment in their schools should be unexceptionable. However, despite a loopy *New York Times* editorial praising the Republican Party for a kinder-and-gentler attitude toward gays, the GOP has taken the lead in opposing state-level safe-schools bills protecting gay kids. In Washington last year, for the second year in a row, openly gay State Representative Ed Murray—a progressive Seattle Democrat—led the fight for his bill that would have added lesbian and gay students to a law forbidding sexual and malicious harassment in the schools. "We had the votes to pass it this year in the House, which is split forty-nine to forty-nine—we had all forty-nine Democrats and picked up sixteen Republicans. But because of the tie in party membership, all House committees are co-chaired by Democrats and Republicans, and the GOP education committee co-chairman refused to let the bill out of committee. If it had been sent to the Senate, where Democrats have a majority, it would have passed."

The way in which the GOP continues to use same-sexers as a political football to advance its chances could be seen clearly in California, where Assemblywoman Sheila Kuehl (an open lesbian who co-starred in TV's *Dobie Gillis* series in the sixties) saw her Dignity for All Students Act beaten in the Assembly by one vote. GOP front groups "targeted only Democratic Latino legislators from swing districts in an unprecedented campaign-style effort," says Jennifer Richard, Kuehl's top aide. This included prayer vigils at their district offices, very sophisticated phone-banking that switched those called directly into Assembly members' offices to complain, mailings in Spanish to every Hispanic-surnamed household and full-page ads costing $8,000-$12,000 each in local papers. The mailings and ads featured photos of a white man embracing a Latino, a black man kissing a Latino and a Latino kid in a Boy Scout uniform, and called on voters to "stop the homosexual agenda," which "doesn't like the Boy Scout pledge to be morally

---

There is a skein of service agencies in large cities that operate effective programs for gay youth . . . But these programs are all dreadfully under-funded and in many places . . . are denied access to the schools.

---

straight." These ads were reinforced by a $30,000 radio ad blitz by the Rev. Lou Sheldon's Traditional Family Values Coalition in the targeted legislators' districts.

Despite a Youth Lobby Day that brought 700 gay students to Sacramento to support the Kuehl bill, two Latino Democrats caved in to the pressure, insuring the bill's defeat by one vote. But in a shrewd parliamentary maneuver, its supporters attached a condensed version as an amendment to an unrelated bill in the senate, which passed it—then sent it to the assembly, where it was finally approved by a six-vote margin (making California the first state to codify protections for gender-nonconforming students, who experience the most aggressive forms of harassment). Similar bills died or were defeated last year in Colorado, Delaware, Illinois and Texas (in New York, one introduced by openly gay State Senator Tom Duane is still bottled up in committee).

The difference such bills can make can be seen in Massachusetts, which has had a tough and explicit law barring discrimination against and harassment of gay students since 1993, and where its implementation benefited from strong support by then-Governor William Weld (a Republican) and his advisory council on gay and lesbian issues. Massachusetts is the only state that encourages the formation of gay student support groups as a matter of policy—which is why there are now 180 GSAs in the Bay State alone. There, the state Safe Schools program is run by GLSEN under a contract with the state's Education Department, and it organizes eight regional conferences each year for students who want to start or have just started their own GSA.

There is a skein of service agencies in large cities that operate effective programs for gay youth, including peer counseling, drop-in centers, teacher training, AIDS education and assistance for victims of violence (for listings of and links to groups for gay youth, visit *The Nation*'s website at www.thenation.com). But these programs are all dreadfully underfunded and in many places, like Texas, are denied access to the schools. Also, gay youths themselves often complain that there is a lack of support from the adult gay movement. Says Candice Clark, a 19-year-old lesbian who graduated in 1998 from a suburban Houston high school, "A lot of the older gay community here is fearful of the youth as jailbait, since so many people think that if you're gay you're a pedophile." She also notes that the failure of Congress to pass ENDA—the Employment Non-Discrimination Act for lesbians and gays—means that adults, especially teachers, can be fired if their sexual orientation is discovered.

Richard Agostinho, 22, who founded the Connecticut youth group Queer and Active after the 1998 murder of Matthew Shepard, and who serves as one of the NYAC national board's youth members, says the local adult-led groups "are not building relationships with young people—they need to go out and recruit them and engage in mentoring of sorts. There are plenty of young people who could add emotion and power to this movement. But if a 17- or 18-year-old goes to a meeting of a local group or community center in a roomful of 30- or 40-somethings, the adults frequently fail to create an atmosphere in which the youth feel comfortable contributing. It's a problem very similar to involving people of color or anyone not traditionally represented at these tables."

The urgency of putting the problems facing gay adolescents on the agenda of every local gay organization is underscored by a study released last September by GLSEN. It showed that of nearly 500 gay students surveyed, almost half said they didn't feel safe in their schools: 90 percent reported verbal harassment, 46.5 percent had experienced sexual harassment, 27.6 percent experienced physical harassment and 13.7 percent were subjected to physical assault.

But this new generation of adolescent activists won't be ignored. For, as Jared Nayfack says, "When you do this work you open up a whole area of your heart and soul, and when you stop, you feel it deeply. Activism is addictive— you don't ever want to stop unless there's nothing left to do ... and that will be a long time."

II.
Searching for
Answers

Editor's Introduction

When the dust had settled at the end of the school year in 1999, teachers, parents, students, and school officials were still trying to decipher why so many troubled teens have struck out against their classmates in recent years. The 1999 school year may not have been the most violent in U.S. history, but it was a year that will be forever etched in memory as the year of Columbine, the worst mass shooting the nation has ever witnessed. This second section of *School Violence* attempts to address some of the most plaguing questions left after young adults stand accused of assaulting their classmates. Included in this selection of articles is an exploration of such issues as media influence, violence in video games, gun control, parental-responsibility laws, anti-depressant medications, biological disorders, impersonal schools, suburban upbringing, and gender difference in schooling.

The first article, by Timothy Egan for the *New York Times*, takes a look at the mass shootings which occurred during 1998 and attempts to draw some parallel characteristics between them. Specifically, the writer focuses on three areas of similarity between the shooters: availability of guns, infatuation with violent pop culture, and missed cries for help. Although Egan does not directly blame any of these factors as a definitive cause of the violence that later erupted, he does explore how all of these elements should be deemed warning signs to parents and teachers.

Next, in an article titled "Empty Lessons" written for *Reason* magazine, writer Jessie Walker takes a cynical look at the rush for answers after the Columbine massacre. In the piece, Walker asserts, "If you didn't like some part of pop culture, Littleton was a gold mine: Anything and everything could be attacked." In the end, despite fingers being pointed at films, music, gun control, family values, public schools, and even capitalism, Walker states, the real reasons why Klebold and Harris turned into murderers will never be known.

The third selection is titled "Listen to the Children" and it looks at the role large, impersonal schools may be playing in teen angst. Author Anne C. Lewis explains how the American school system has developed over the years, so that now, an overwhelming majority of our schools are seeped in an anonymity that causes students to feel lost and disconnected. In this article, Lewis advocates a restructuring of the school system that would allow smaller classes, thereby increasing student/teacher interaction and affecting student disposition in a positive manner.

The fourth piece concerns the impacts of both anti-depressants and suburban communities on violent teens. In his article "Virtual Violence"

67

Mark Steyn argues that the "ever-swelling medicine cabinet" is partially to blame for leaving our nation's kids in a trance-like state that makes them unaware of their actions. He goes on to question whether the sprawling disconnectedness of suburban life is not also a contributing factor in making children feel alienated. In the article, Steyn additionally examines the influence of video games in the shootings while deflecting blame away from the issue of gun control.

Next, Joannie M. Schrof explores the subject of parental responsibility for teen violence in her article "Who's Guilty?" Schrof looks at recent shooting incidents and the court cases that have emerged from them, as young assailants' parents are taken to task for their children's actions. In this article, the scope and impact of parental-responsibility laws are examined, as well as lawsuits aimed at faculty and school districts.

In "Media, Littleton's Latest Suspect" by Paige Albiniak, the role of media influence on violence is explored. As one of politicians' central areas of blame, the media has taken quite a beating in recent years, with calls for less violence and stricter restraints on adolescent access to questionable programming. Here, Albiniak looks at both political and industry response to the wave of mass shootings and the connection of violent acts to movies and television shows.

The seventh article in this section, "The Shooters and the Shrinks" by Mark Boal for *Salon* magazine, investigates the validity of media reports on the detrimental nature of violent video games. Although several newspapers and magazines have mentioned school shooters' interest in graphic games, such as "Doom," Boal asserts that there is little empirical evidence to link video games with teen violence. In this article, Boal looks at studies on video games and attempts to place the importance of video games within the context of the shootings.

Next is an article that probes the possible biological reasons why young people turn violent. Anita Manning looks at studies which suggest a genetic link to violent actions, something that may help to explain otherwise good kids turning bad and committing crimes. In particular, in "Chemistry of a Killer: Is it in the Brain?" the writer explores research done on the part of the brain responsible for reason and impulse control and how abnormal functioning in that area may determine future violence.

Finally, in the last article in this section, author Sarah Glazer considers the nature of how we raise boys in our society and how it may play a part in boys turning violent later in life. All of the recent school shootings have been committed by young boys, and in "Boys' Emotional Needs," Glazer looks at the conditioning of boys versus girls in school. The article examines different emotional and learning needs among boys and girls, the role of attention deficit disorder (ADD) and how boys and girls are taught and treated differently in schools.

From Adolescent Angst To Shooting Up Schools[1]

By Timothy Egan
NEW YORK TIMES, June 14, 1998

Well before the school shootings in Oregon and the South prompted a search to the depths of the national soul, a 14-year-old honors student named Barry Loukaitis walked into his algebra class in this hard little farm town and shot his teacher in the back and two students in the chest.

Guns and violent videos were always around the boy's house. He learned how to fire weapons from his father. And he picked up a pose from the Oliver Stone movie *Natural Born Killers,* telling a friend it would be "pretty cool" to go on a killing spree just like the two lead characters in the film.

Dressed in black and armed with three of the family firearms, Barry entered Frontier Middle School in this desert town 180 miles east of Seattle on Feb. 2, 1996, and turned his guns loose on fellow ninth graders.

"This sure beats algebra, doesn't it," Barry said, according to court records, as he stood over a dying boy who was choking on his own blood. He was tackled by a teacher and hauled off to jail, where he promptly took a nap.

A sign soon appeared on a nearby school, bearing a single word: Why? Of late, that question has been asked around the nation, following a spate of multiple-victim school shootings over the last nine months that have left 15 people dead and 42 wounded. People wonder whether something aberrant and terrifying—like a lethal virus, some have called it—is in the bloodstream.

While precise answers may be elusive, the recent killing sprees share a remarkable number of common traits. The first of the rural, multiple-victim student shootings, here in Moses Lake, looks in many respects like a road map of what was to come. From this case and interviews with police officers, prosecutors, psychologists and parents of the attackers—as well as the boys' own words—several patterns emerge:

---

1. Copyright ©1998 *New York Times.* Reprinted with permission.

* Each case involved a child who felt inferior or picked on, with a grudge against some student or teacher. The attackers complained of being fat or nearsighted, short or unloved—the ordinary problems of adolescence, at first glance. But in fact, most of the assailants were suicidal, and of above-average intelligence, according to mental health experts who have examined most of the children arrested for the shootings. Their killings are now viewed by some criminologists and other experts as a way to end a tortured life with a blaze of terror.

* The killers were able to easily acquire high-powered guns, and in many cases, their parents helped the children get them, either directly or through negligence. Guns with rapid-fire capability, usually semiautomatic rifles that can spray a burst of bullets in a matter of seconds, were used in the incidents with the most victims. Single-fire, bolt-action guns or revolvers would not have caused near the damage in human life, the police say.

Their killings are now viewed by some criminologists and other experts as a way to end a tortured life with a blaze of terror.

* To varying degrees, each of the attackers seemed to have been obsessed by violent pop culture. A 14-year-old in West Paducah, Ky., was influenced by a movie in which a character's classmates are shot during a dream sequence, according to detectives. Violent rap lyrics may have influenced one of the boys in the Jonesboro, Ark., case, his mother says. In particular, a song about a stealth killing eerily matches what occurred. The killer who has confessed in Pearl, Miss., says he was a fan of violent fantasy video games and the nihilistic rock-and-roll lyrics of Marilyn Manson, as was the boy charged in the Springfield, Ore., shootings last month. The Springfield youth was so enmeshed in violent television and Internet sites that his parents recently unplugged the cable television and took away his computer, a close family friend said.

* The student killers gave ample warning signs, often in detailed writings at school, of dramatic, violent outbursts to come. The boy in Moses Lake wrote a poem about murder, saying, "I'm at my point of no return." Similar jottings were left by the boys in the South, and in Springfield. In virtually all of the cases, adults never took the threats and warning signs seriously. Or they simply overlooked them.

"When you look at the overall pattern, it's a pretty serious wake-up call," said Dr. Ronald D. Stephens, executive director of the National School Safety Center, which monitors school violence from its headquarters in Westlake Village, Calif. "We are seeing an increasing number of violent, callous, remorseless juveniles.

"What's behind it," Dr. Stephens said, "seems to be a combination of issues that range from the availability of weapons to the culture our kids immerse themselves in to the fact that many youngsters simply have no sense of the finality of death."

People argue, in the age-old debate, either that the killers are simply bad human beings or that their actions can be linked to a corrosive family environment—nature versus nurture. Certainly, the recent shootings give plenty of new material for both sides.

Parents of the young killers place blame on the surfeit of guns, the influence of junk culture and children stressed to a snapping point. But they also look at themselves, their broken marriages, their lives of stress and hurry, and wonder how all that affected their children.

"I didn't think about Barry at all," said JoAnn Phillips, the mother of Barry Loukaitis in Moses Lake, in court testimony last year in her son's case. A few weeks before the shooting, she had told her son that she planned to divorce her husband and that she herself was suicidal, but she was oblivious to how this would affect her son.

"We are responsible for our kids, but you tell me, where did I go wrong?" Gretchen Woodward said in an interview recently in which she discussed her son, Mitchell Johnson, the seventh grader accused, along with Andrew Golden, of killing 5 and wounding 10 in Jonesboro last March. "I think there's a lot more pressure on our kids today than there was when we were growing up."

THE KILLINGS

Urban Trend Takes Rural Turn

Children have long killed children in the United States. The peak was the 1992-93 school year, when nearly 50 people were killed in school-related violence, according to the School Safety Center. Most of those killings were in urban schools, and prompted a Federal law banning guns from schools, security measures like metal detectors, and efforts to control the influence of gangs. What is different now is that the shootings are largely rural, have multiple victims and, within the warped logic of homicide, seem to make no sense; many of the victims have been shot at random.

In looking at the 221 deaths at American schoolyards over the last six years, what leaps out is how the shootings changed dramatically in the last two years—not the number, but the type.

Most earlier deaths were gang-related, or they were stabbings, or they involved money or a fight over a girlfriend. (Boys are almost always the killers.) Then came the Moses Lake shooting in 1996. Barry Loukaitis, who confessed to the shootings and was found guilty as an adult in trial last fall, did have a target in mind when he walked into the afternoon algebra class—a popular boy who had teased him. He shot the boy to death.

> *When asked in a tape-recorded session with police why he shot the others, Barry [Loukaitis] said, "I don't know, I guess reflex took over."*

But then he fired away at two other students, people against whom he said he had no grudge. He shot the teacher, Leona Caires, in the back. She died with an eraser still in her hand.

When asked in a tape-recorded session with police why he shot the others, Barry said, "I don't know, I guess reflex took over."

After Moses Lake, shootings of a somewhat similar nature followed. In February 1997 in Bethel, Alaska, a boy armed with a 12-gauge shotgun that had been kept unlocked around the home killed a popular athlete, fired shots at random and then tracked and killed the principal. Like Barry, the 16-year-old Alaskan killer thought it would be "cool," prosecutors said, to shoot up the school.

"He loved what he did," said Renee Erb, who prosecuted the youth, Evan Ramsey. "This was his moment of glory."

By the end of last year, the killings seemed to come with numbing sameness. All but one of the victims apparently were chosen at random in the shootings outside a high school in Pearl, Miss.

"I wasn't aiming at anyone else," said Luke Woodham, convicted this week in the shootings, in a tape-recorded confession played at his trial in Hattiesburg, Miss. "It was like I was there, and I wasn't there."

In West Paducah, Ky., three girls were killed and five other students wounded in a shooting with no apparent motive. "It was kind of like I was in a dream," the accused attacker, 14-year-old Michael Carneal, told his principal.

In March, an 11-year-old steeped in gun culture and a 13-year-old with a troubled past opened fire, in what seemed like a military assault, at students who filed out of Westside Middle School in Jonesboro, Ark.

And finally in Springfield last month—where a boy with a love of guns is accused of mowing down as many students as possible in the crowded school cafeteria, using a semiautomatic rifle taken from his father—the victims were anyone who happened to be in the way, the police said.

People ask why this is happening now in white, rural areas, said Dr. Alan Unis, a University of Washington psychiatrist who did an examination of the Moses Lake assailant for the court. "It's happening everywhere," he said. "One of the things we're seeing in the population at large is that all the mood disorders are happening earlier and earlier. The incidence of depression and suicide has gone way up among young people."

> "One of the things we're seeing in the population at large is that all the mood disorders are happening earlier and earlier. The incidence of depression and suicide has gone way up among young people."
> —University of Washington psychiatrist Dr. Alan Unis

Suicide rates for the young have increased over the last four decades and have leveled off near their all-time highs. More than 1.5 million Americans under age 15 are seriously depressed, the National Institute of Mental Health says. The number may be twice that high, in the view of the American Academy of Child and Adolescent Psychiatry.

Most of the attackers in the recent cases had shown signs of clinical depression or other psychological problems. But schools, strapped for mental health counselors, are less likely to pick up on such behavior or to have the available help, principals at the schools where the shootings happened said.

THE GUNS

Troubled Children And Easy Access

A depressed, insecure child is one thing, and quite common. But that same boy with a gun can be a lethal threat. In all of the recent shootings, acquiring guns was easier than buying beer, or even gas. And these children armed themselves with small arsenals, as if preparing for battle.

The Moses Lake assailant used to play at home with his family guns as if they were toys, friends testified in court. In his confession, Barry Loukaitis said he took two of his father's guns from an unlocked cabinet, and a third one—a .25-caliber semiautomatic pistol—from a family car.

The gun used in the Alaska school shootings was kept unlocked at the foot of the stairs in a foster home where Evan Ramsey was living, according to police.

The shootings in West Paducah, Jonesboro and Springfield were similar in that semiautomatic weapons—capable of firing off dozens of rounds in less than a minute—were used to kill children. Weapons of less rapid-fire capability would likely have reduced the death tolls, the police said.

In Jonesboro and Springfield, the parents of the accused assailants taught their children, at an early age, how to use guns properly, which is the general advice of the National Rifle Association. The story of how Andrew Golden, accused in the Jonesboro shooting, was given a gun by Santa Claus at age 6, and was an expert marksman in the Practical Pistol Shooters Club a few years later has been widely reported.

But less well-known is how the other accused Jonesboro killer came by his knowledge of guns. Mitchell Johnson's mother, Mrs. Woodward, said in an interview that she taught her boy how to shoot a shotgun, and then he took a three-week course.

When the boys were arrested after hitting 15 human targets at Westside Middle School, police found nine guns in their possession. Most of them had been taken from the home of Andrew's grandfather, Doug Golden, a conservation officer who says he usually kept his guns unlocked in the house.

The parents of Kipland Kinkel, the boy accused of the Springfield shootings, were not gun enthusiasts, but their son was, according to interviews with family friends. The parents agonized over the boy's gun obsession, finally giving in and buying him a weapon. The father and son took courses in marksmanship and safety, and the guns were kept under lock and key.

But given Kip Kinkel's moods and temper, the parents had debated over whether to get him a single-loading bolt-action weapon or something with more rapid-fire capability. They settled on the more powerful gun, a .22-caliber semiautomatic Ruger rifle. It was a fatal mistake, said some people who are studying the recent shootings. It was that rifle that Kip used to fire off 50 rounds at Thurston High School.

"The kid had them by the throat," said Dr. Bill Reisman, who does profiling of deviant youth behavior for law-enforcement officials and recently gave a closed-door briefing to community leaders from cities where the school shootings occurred. "They were terrified of his interest in guns, but they went out and bought him guns."

A Kinkel family friend, Tom Jacobson, who played tennis every other week with the boy's father, said the parents were looking for a way to control and connect with their volatile child. The parents, Bill and Faith Kinkel, were both killed by their son, prosecutors in Oregon said.

"These were devoted parents in a tight-knit family," Mr. Jacobson said in an interview. "Bill had tried everything with Kip. I think he just ran out of ideas."

THE CULTURE

Too Influenced By Music and Film?

Just as easy to get as guns were videos or cassettes in which murder is a central theme, and often glorified. Jurors in the trial of Barry Loukaitis were shown a Pearl Jam video, "Jeremy," about a youth who fantasizes about using violence against classmates who taunt him. That video, along with *Natural Born Killers*, a movie about a pair who kill their parents and then go on nationwide shooting spree, were among Barry's favorites, his friends testified.

At least one of the boys accused in the Jonesboro attack, Mitchell Johnson, was a big fan of gangsta rap. Friends and family members say a favorite song was one by Bone Thugs-n-Harmony, called, "Crept and We Came," about killings in a massacre-like way.

The boy also played *Mortal Kombat*, a popular video game that involves graphic killing of opponents, his mother said.

"There are many cultural forces predisposing kids to violent behavior," said the Rev. Chris Perry, a youth minister for Mitchell Johnson at Central Baptist Church, who has talked to the boy three times since the shootings. "There is a profound cultural influence, like gravity, pulling kids into a world where violence is a perfectly normal way to handle our emotions."

But Mitchell also loved gospel music, the preacher said, and he sang at nursing homes. Millions of children listen to violent-themed rap music, play Mortal Kombat and witness thousands of killings on television by age 10, and do not become murderers.

"Barry Loukaitis was obviously influenced by *Natural Born Killers*," said John Knodell, who prosecuted the Moses Lake assailant. "But there are hundreds of thousands of kids who watch these things and don't blow away their schoolmates."

The psychiatrist in the Loukaitis case, Dr. Unis, also is reluctant to blame violent cultural influences. But he and other experts say there is a syndrome at work, in which a child who sees one shootout on the news may be inspired to try something similar.

"The media or violent videos do not by themselves make the event happen," said Ms. Erb, the prosecutor in Alaska. "But it shows them a way."

Millions of children listen to violent-themed rap music, play Mortal Kombat and witness thousands of killings on television by age 10, and do not become murderers.

THE SIGNS

Cries for Help Often Overlooked

The boys accused of shooting classmates are portrayed as average children. But a look inside their bedrooms or journals, or a discussion with their friends shows they left ample clues of trouble to come.

Michael Carneal was known as a slight boy who played baritone sax in the school band in West Paducah. After the killings, his principal, Bill Bond, looked at some of his writing and found a child who felt weak and powerless, with an angry desire to lash out.

A week before the shooting, Michael warned classmates that "something big was going to happen" and they should get out of the way, detectives said. At least three boys accused in other cases did the same thing.

The Alaskan assailant warned specific students the night before the killings to go up on a second-floor balcony. "These kids didn't tell anyone," said the prosecutor, Ms. Erb. "Instead, they got right up there the next day to get their view of the killings."

In his ninth-grade English class, Barry Loukaitis wrote a poem about murder that ended this way:

I look at his body on the floor,
Killing a bastard that deserves to die,
Ain't nothing like it in the world,
But he sure did bleed a lot

Kip Kinkel read a journal entry aloud in English class about killing fellow students.

Most of the attackers were also suicidal, writing notes before the killings that assumed they would die.

Luke Woodham's journal writings were particularly graphic. He left a last will and testament, leaving music cassettes to the older boy who is said by police to have influenced him. "I do this to show society, 'Push us and we will push back,'" he wrote. "I suffered all my life. No one ever truly loved me. No one ever truly cared about me."

Dr. Reisman said parents and teachers should be alarmed by such writings. Animal abuse, arson and a sudden interest in death and darkness are red flags, he said.

Often the assailants live in the shadow of successful older siblings, Dr. Reisman added. But the most common element is deep depression, he said.

"They'll all have depression, in the state in which they do these things," Dr. Reisman said. "When they're cornered, the first thing they say is, 'Kill me.' It's suicide by cop."

Empty Lessons[2]

Going to Lunch on the Ruins

BY JESSE WALKER
REASON, JULY 1999

With a tone that was simultaneously hysterical and pompous, the pundits started searching for "the lessons of Littleton." Hundreds of commentaries later, only one lesson seems clear: No event is so unique or horrific that it cannot instantly be reduced to an editorialist's cliché.

The very day of the massacre—long before we even had an accurate count of the dead—Peter Jennings was treating viewers to a clip from *The Basketball Diaries,* a fantasy sequence in which a trench coat clad Leonardo DiCaprio carries a gun to school and blows his classmates away. Littleton, Jennings announced, was sure to "reopen the debate" (had it been closed?) on the effects of media violence. He did not, however, stop showing footage of the terror, surely as intense a blast of media violence as anything in any movie.

So it began. Editorialists, activists, preachers, politicians: Everyone with a platform became an instant expert on the inner lives of Eric Harris and Dylan Klebold, the boys who killed 12 students, one teacher, and themselves at Columbine High School. Within a day of the assault, Colorado Gov. Bill Owens was declaring that the murderers didn't "have the same moral background as the rest of us." Bill Davenport, a Baptist pastor in San Clemente, confidently asserted that the killers didn't value life "because they haven't been taught about God." On CNN, criminologist Mike Rustigan declared, "Obviously, here, we are seeing non-parenting parents."

And where did these people acquire this insight into the shooters' moral upbringing? From thin air.

If you didn't like some part of pop culture, Littleton was a gold mine: Anything and everything could be attacked. Want to blame movies? MGM recalled all videos of *The Basketball Diaries*, letting the commentators turn their tut-tuts against *Heathers* and *The Matrix*. Want to blame video games? No report from Colorado was complete without the obligatory allusion to Doom. Want to blame music? Critics attacked Rammstein, KMFDM, and Marilyn Manson; the last bowed to political pressure and canceled the rest of his concert tour. (One wonders how many of the Marilyn-bashing moralists used to giggle to the folk ditty that begins, "Mine eyes have seen the glory of the burning of the school/ We have murdered every teacher, we have broken every rule . . .")

The president himself weighed in, taking a break from his own massacre in the Balkans to declare that he would meet with "some high-level folks from the entertainment industry" to ask them to tone down their products. *The Wall Street Journal* blamed the massacre on a "culture of chaos" in which one might see "surviving Columbine students willing to go on national TV to talk about the massa-

---

There were . . . calls for still more gun control, as though there were some magic number of regulations that would suddenly make a potential schoolhouse killer junk his plans.

---

cre of 15 among them, but by golly they're not going to take off those backward baseball caps to do it." Jerry Falwell suggested that the killers were gay, a cry taken up in a press release from Topeka's Westboro Baptist Church: "Two filthy fags slaughtered 13 people at Columbine High."

In the course of their crimes, Harris and Klebold broke more than a dozen gun laws already on the books. There were, nonetheless, calls for still more gun control, as though there were some magic number of regulations that would suddenly make a potential schoolhouse killer junk his plans. "By the time our children leave school at the start of the summer," announced Handgun Control, Inc. Chair Sarah Brady, "they should know that the lawmakers of this country have done something to protect them from the type of gun violence that occurred at Littleton." Further demands for gun laws issued from figures ranging from Rosie O'Donnell to . . . Marilyn Manson.

And, as always, there were attacks on the Internet. If anything was suspicious about shooter Eric Harris, surely it was that he had a *Web page*. (He kept a diary, too, but for some reason there have been no frantic denunciations of notebooks.) The BBC straightfacedly described a "probe" into "whether the killers learned how to make bombs from the Internet." On MSNBC, criminologist Casey Jordan declared that the Net was "the key" to the story: "They were in chat rooms; they had Web pages. And on the Internet, the possibility for recruiting is just unknown."

Drugs, too, took a drubbing. Reps. John Peterson (R-Pa.) and James Rogan (R-Calif.) announced that they would propose legislation allowing schools to give students random drug tests, declaring that this would make future massacres less likely. When told that no traces of any drugs had been found in the shooters' bodies, Peterson was unswayed, arguing that narcotics had been a factor in "other" incidents. The Family Research Council sent out a fax claiming that April 20, the date of the shootings, was "the national marijuana smoke-off day" and that "420" was "the police code for marijuana." (420 . . . 4/20 . . . get it?)

In fact, anyone with an agenda found that, with enough effort, he could find a way to tie his wagon to the Littleton massacre.

More often, analysts stressed that April 20 was Hitler's birthday—a sign, we were told, that the killers were neo-Nazis. (It was Marcus Aurelius' birthday too, but no one as yet has claimed the murderers were neo-Stoics.) Media reports described Harris and Klebold as inveterate racists, a charge the shooters' friends denied. No matter. Marc Fisher, in *The Washington Post*, seemed almost scrambling to find a racial angle the day after the massacre, in what might be the greatest self-undermining pair of sentences in the history of journalism: "Some witnesses said the shooters, who were white, appeared to be targeting black and Hispanic students, as well as student athletes of all races. Many whites were also among the victims."

Some pundits attacked goths; others took on trench coats; still others, the abolition of school prayer. Tipper Gore called for more therapy. George Will called for school uniforms. Camille Paglia blamed the nuclear family and the industrial revolution. Screenwriter Stephen Schiff blamed shopping malls.

In fact, anyone with an agenda found that, with enough effort, he could find a way to tie his wagon to the Littleton massacre. The Libertarian Party sent out a press release: "Public schools may be a contributing factor in the recent spate of school shootings . . ." From the privatizers to the proletarians: *The People's Tribune*, newspaper of the League of Revolutionaries for a New America, blamed the shootings on capitalism. "Our youth see what the future effort to build a sense of family among the students enrolled and to connect them to the adult world in purposeful, educationally sound ways through internships and mentoring.

In New York City, the Center for Collaborative Education is helping large high schools break up into smaller ones. More than 50 have been created in the last few years, usually by sharing the space of formerly huge schools, some of which enrolled as many as 5,000 students. These new schools are completely autonomous and so are much more accountable to the students and their families than are houses or teams set up within large high schools.

Large middle schools have begun to use "looping," allowing smaller groups of students to stay with the same set of teachers throughout their middle school years. In some areas, elementary schools are adding a grade a year through the eighth grade, a move that does away with the transition to another school and keeps family involvement intact.

Proponents of service learning argue that it should be part of the regular curriculum for all students, not just an elective or even a one-time service requirement that can be easily met. Giving students real opportunities to provide service to younger students or to help their communities solve problems and then having them reflect on their experiences is education, not an extracurricular activity, they contend.

Anecdotal evidence about the benefits of smaller schools is now reinforced by quantitative data showing that student achievement, attendance, and graduation rates are higher in such schools. According to Mary Ann Raywid, an expert on alternative schools, a recent compilation of more than 100 studies dealing with school size found that many of the studies documented superior student performance in small schools, while none found the reverse to be true.

Some of the most widely cited educational research on school success—conducted by Fred Newmann and Gary Wehlage of the Center on the Organization and Restructuring of Schools at the University of Wisconsin, Madison—concluded that smaller schools produce higher achievement. The researchers asked why this is so. One reason they found is that smaller schools allow teachers to be more flexible and to give students more individual attention. Smaller schools also make it easier for students and adults to develop close relationships. One of the major

holds for them," wrote the revolutionaries. "They know that a society based on a market economy holds them valueless."

The hubbub reached its low point on April 28, when *The Washington Post* film critic, Stephen Hunter, decided the dreadful force responsible for the deaths was . . . irony. After a labored analysis of *The Basketball Diaries*, Hunter made his point: "Jim Carroll writes a book that becomes a movie; he and everyone between him and the end user gets that it's ironic. The end user doesn't. His name is Eric Harris. The results are tragic. . . . [U]ntil the irony-addicted and the irony-impaired begin to speak the same language and make an attempt to understand each other, it seems unlikely that there will be any healing—and there may even be a lot more killing."

The Littleton murders weren't just terrible. They were mysterious. My pacifist friends have wondered why there have been so few comparisons between the violence in the Balkans and the violence in Colorado. Surely, they say, both are mass slaughter. They have a point, but they're also missing something important. When Serbs slaughter Kosovars or NATO slaughters Serbs, one can at least discern reasons for the butchery, even if those rationales are amoral and offensive. The massacre at Columbine does not yield to such explanations. It hangs in the air, a mystery that can never be completely solved.

When someone does something this awful, and this unusual, it does no good to pretend we can reduce it to any simple lesson.

And never should be solved. Human beings are ciphers, capable of terrible acts. When someone does something this awful, and this unusual, it does no good to pretend we can reduce it to any simple lesson.

In the weeks since the Littleton slaughter, we've learned that most of what the media initially told us about the Columbine killers wasn't true. They weren't Nazis. They weren't especially racist. They weren't necessarily Goths. They might not even have been members of the clique of outcasts called the Trench Coat Mafia, which, by the way, wasn't originally called the Trench Coat Mafia.

We do know that bullies routinely picked on Harris, Klebold, and others like them. We do know that such behavior goes on in most of the country's schools. But most outcasts do not take weapons to school and kill the people who tormented them. We don't know what it was inside Eric Harris and Dylan Klebold that made them into the exceptions. And we never will.

Listen to the Children[3]

By Anne C. Lewis
Phi Delta Kappan, June 1999

The airport in Burlington, Vermont, was quiet when I checked in, but the ticket agent, a young woman whose oldest child will be entering school next year, felt distraught. It was the afternoon of the Columbine High School massacre. We live in Essex Junction, said the agent, and my husband and I have talked about moving to a smaller community before our child starts school.

Everything is relative. Where I come from, Essex Junction would be considered semi-rural, a small suburb of a small city. The ticket agent's sense of wanting to escape to something even more personal, however, echoes everywhere. But most parents are helpless to do anything about the depersonalization of the schools and other community institutions that touch their lives. One can run only so far to escape population density and urbanism.

The immediate anguish of the tragedy in Littleton is over, and the long process of debate about policies to prevent a repeat in some other school will occupy us for months, if not years, to come. It seems odd that among the issues seldom mentioned is the educational structure created in the last half of this century, which has had as profound an effect on students and their families as have the mass media or changes in the patterns of family life.

Once, most of our schools were like those in Essex Junction and places even smaller. At the end of World War II, this country supported more than 200,000 school districts. Certainly, there was inefficiency in our education system, but there was also a sense of ownership. Think of the thousands of people who could serve on school boards, the opportunities for students to play on sports teams, and the role the school played as the community and family center.

Fewer than 15,000 operating school districts now exist. About one-third of the K-12 students in this country are enrolled in less than 1% of the school districts. As people have moved in from rural areas and out from cities, we have created a new type of school organization: either the suburban districts that ring our cities or the consolidated

high schools of rural counties. Long before urban chi left their neighborhoods to board buses for desegreg purposes, rural communities had to close their schools bus their children to larger consolidated schools, persu to do so by educators and county commissioners who the economies of scale and said that bigger is better.

It is as fruitless to keep trying to run back to the no gia of small-town life as it is to believe that a solutio the angst of teen life lies in re-creating the family struct of times past: the father who worked only a few min away, the mom who stayed at home, the extended fan network that was always around, and the peers who w just like everyone else. We are a different society today. are coming to terms with diversity and technology, we

> *Is the slavish esteem given high school sports as much a function of parent booster clubs as a reflection of what students really want?*

offering ever greater opportunities, but we are creati anxieties, as well.

It is not out of line, however, to reconsider how we hav organized the school life of children and to questio whether the bigness, the separation from adults, and th anonymity that can so easily overwhelm young people i large high schools is really what we want for children. W can't go back, but we needn't accept what has been createc as the only way to educate young people.

We must face some hard questions. Is the slavish esteem given high school sports as much a function of parent booster clubs as a reflection of what students really want? Can we expect a teacher who teaches 150 students each day to know more than a few of them well? Is the gradual decline in parent involvement as students move into middle schools and high schools a result of what students want (the usual excuse) or of the struggle parents must go through to make themselves noticed in more than superficial ways in places that don't really know their children?

The signals are growing stronger that a rejection of the depersonalization of schooling is under way. Charter schools re-create the smallness that seemed to be so much better for students; at the high school level, charter schools rarely enroll more than 200 students. The career academies created in large urban high schools represent a dual goals of current restructuring efforts is to create learning communities of teachers as well as students. However, Deborah Meier, founder of one of the most successful small urban high schools in the country, Central Park East Secondary School, points out that it is impossible to create a learning community of 40 to 50 teachers. They cannot even sit down together in the same room, she says.

In an occasional paper for the Small Schools Coalition in Chicago, Raywid cites much of the research supporting small schools, noting that smallness permits the sort of human connections that result in the formation of strong student/school bonds, such as those at Central Park East, which make an imprint on students and affect their attitudes and dispositions. Small school size appears to be essential to forming such an environment. We already know all these things about smaller school environments, either from educational research or from our own notions of what is right. What will it take to change our practice—to bring back that environment for students?

A week after the Littleton tragedy, I walked through Feinberg Fisher Elementary School in the South Beach section of Miami, where more than 90% of the children live in poverty. This school serves its 900 students in every way possible, dividing them into two school buildings to make an even smaller environment, providing full-service health facilities, teaching them in very small classes when necessary, providing space for both day and night classes for adults, offering day-care programs, and providing a lively parent center. Feinberg Fisher Elementary has created a modern version of a small-school community.

Anecdotal evidence about the benefits of smaller schools is now reinforced by quantitative data showing that student achievement, attendance, and graduation rates are higher in such schools.

On one wall of an open hallway were the written comments from the students about what happened in Littleton, inspired by an all-school assembly at which the principal and lead teachers served as panel members and the young students asked them questions about the tragedy. One boy advised parents: "Tell your children more often how glad you are to have kids like them." But many of the youngsters just wrote: "Don't let it happen again." We should listen to the children.

Virtual Violence[4]

What Causes American School Shootings (Not Lax Gun Laws)

By Mark Steyn
The Spectator, May 30, 1998

For the news shows, it gets a little easier each time. The "Slaughter In The Schoolyard" graphics are on permanent stand-by; the Rolodex is bulging with telegenic anger-management experts; it's just a question of finding this week's blood-spattered grove of academe on the gazetteer and dispatching the Chief Massacre Correspondent to interview surviving students, bewildered relatives and the local cops, all of whom tend to talk like the students, relatives and cops they saw on TV after the last massacre, and at least one of whom can be guaranteed to say, "We thought it couldn't happen here."

It couldn't happen in Pearl, Mississippi, site of the school year's inaugural shootout last October; nor could it happen in West Paducah, Kentucky; Fayetteville, Tennessee; Jonesboro, Arkansas; or Edinboro, Pennsylvania. This time round it was Springfield, Oregon, a town whose most famous high school alumnus hitherto had been Ken Kesey, author of *One Flew Over the Cookoo's Nest.* Ken Kesey has now been superseded by the equally alliterative Kip Kinkel, who seems to be more cuckoo than anyone in Kesey's novel. A week ago, Kip was expelled by the principal, went home, murdered his parents, returned to school the following day and opened fire on the cafeteria, killing two and injuring 22 others.

There's nothing like an American school massacre to make the rest of the world feel smug: what is it, scoff the British, with those crazy Yanks and their guns? What kind of lunatic teaches a young boy how to shoot animals when he should be inside with his computer playing *Amok!* or *Carnage!!* like a normal kid? Charlie Clydesdale, who lost his daughter at Dunblane, inclines to this view. "Isn't it time the world learned to watch what they are doing with guns?" he said after the Jonesboro bloodbath. "Have any lessons been learned since Dunblane?"

---

4. Copyright © 1998 *The Spectator.* Reprinted with permission.

Actually, yes, one or two have. For example, last fall, when that first playground whacko of the Class of '98 decided to take out the high school in Pearl, an assistant principal managed to retrieve his own gun from the car and "physically immobilise" the gunman (gunkid?) until the cops showed up. The boy had already shot two students. If not for the assistant principal, he might have shot another two, or four, or seven; he might have made it into double figures and up to Dunblane's body count. In Scotland, there was no assistant headmaster to save lives by shooting back. And now, thanks to the government's restrictions on gun ownership, there never will be.

So forget about guns. Americans have done their sums: more guns equals less crime. Vermont has more firearms per capita than any other state; it also has the second-lowest murder rate in the country (lower than the United Kingdom, too). Besides, America has always had guns and hunting. Granted that we Massacre of the Month commentators like to fit the particular situation to our own pet peeve, it still seems perverse to fixate on the constants— the guns—rather than look at what's changed. Take this kid Kinkel. When his taste for violent cartoons, the "music" of Marilyn Manson (who claims to be the Antichrist), throwing rocks at cars, torturing animals and making pipe bombs began to get out of hand, his parents took him to the doctor. The doctor put him on Prozac.

Kip may have the makings of a defense here, or at least a lawsuit. Only the other week, a ten-year-old boy, arrested after an armed stand-off with police in which he used his three-year-old niece as a human shield, entered the novel plea of "Not Guilty due to a Prozac-induced trance." Between the millions of kids on Prozac and the millions on Ritalin for Attention Deficit Disorder, America's schools are becoming one huge experiment in mood suppression. "If Huck Finn or Tom Sawyer were alive today, we'd say they had ADD or a conduct disorder," says Michael Gurian, author of *The Wonder of Boys*. "They are who they are and we need to love them for who they are. Let's not try to rewire them." But, for hassled parents and busy school administrators, rewiring is the easiest option. With half the students, you don't want to be around when the medication wears off; with the other half, you don't want to be around when it kicks in. But, as it's hard to tell which is which, you're best to steer clear entirely.

But the ever-swelling medicine cabinet is itself only a symptom of how child-rearing is increasingly contracted out. All this year's "kids who kill kids" come from what the media, in their fuzzy shorthand, call "the heartland." Springfield itself was routinely described on the news as a "small town," even, though it's, technically, a city and in combination with its larger neighbour forms what the Federal government designates as the Eugene-Springfield Metropolitan Statistical Area, with a combined population of over 300,000. To those of us in municipalities a few hundred strong, Springfield seems rather large for a small town. I suppose what the big-city reporters mean by the term is that it's a nice place, with well-kept lawns and freshly painted fences: it's not the Bronx, or South-Central LA, or Chicago's Cabrini Green housing projects, or the nation's Third World

Between the millions of kids on Prozac and the millions on Ritalin for Attention Deficit Disorder, America's schools are becoming one huge experiment in mood suppression.

capital, where the school system has collapsed and teachers feel they've come out ahead if they get through the day without being stabbed. Kip Kinkel, like his fellow boy killers, isn't the illegitimate child of a crack addict mom and jailbird dad, sleeping rough in an alley, stealing for food. So what's bugging them so much that they feel obliged to mow down their classmates?

Maybe those nice towns have something to do with it. Most of them are actually suburbs or, in the preferred oxymoron of the day, "bedroom communities": residents of Springfield drive to work in Eugene. Half a century ago, the suburbs were sold to those Americans fleeing urban decline as the natural repository of family values: all the traditional virtues of civic life, without the contemporary problems of the inner city. In fact, they've turned out to be precisely the opposite: today's bedroom communities have all the contemporary problems, without the traditional virtues. It was the physical layout of post-war suburbia which pioneered the defining problems of the age: the long-distance commute; the drifting, rootless population (20 per cent of Americans move every year); feminism, which began in part as a rebellion against the stultifying isolation of suburbia (at the time, Betty Friedan was stuck outside

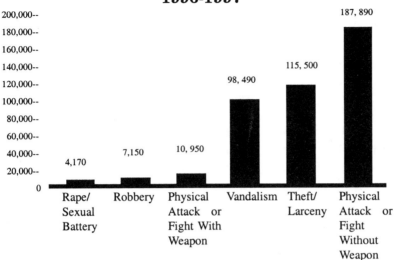

Number of Various Crimes Occurring in Public Schools
1996-1997

SOURCE: U.S. Department of Education, National Center for Education Statistics, Fast Response Survey System, "Principal/School Disciplinarian Survey on School Violence," FRSS 63, 1997.

New York in Westchester County); the working mom; the continuously flickering TV; the evening meal you pick up at the drive-thru pizza-to-go joint in the mall; the no-fault divorce; and, above all, day care. Fifty-one per cent of mothers work full-time; half of those would prefer not to. Mom's wishes notwithstanding, America's children spend their first, critical, years in what are little more than holding camps. If this year's swollen phalanx of boy killers makes anything clear, it's that there are more and more parents who don't know their children.

Grown-ups shy away from confronting the evidence about what causes violence because they don't want to be judgmental about "non-traditional" household arrangements. But, seeing Thurston High's students talking about the murder of their classmates, glassy-eyed, in dull, unexpressive monotones, you couldn't help wondering if to teenagers the very idea of something *causing* violence isn't hopelessly quaint. The so-called Information Age is actually an Entertainment Age in which violence is the most routine entertainment of all: on the accelerating descent into a "virtual childhood," violence requires nothing so humdrum as a *cause*—no motivation, no narrative drive, no character. I'd far rather an adolescent boy was out in the woods learning how to hunt deer and bear and wild turkey. But at least in 1911 a lad could come in and read *Steele of the Royal*

Mounted, in which in the frozen wastes of the far north Private Philip Steele and his villainous prey agree the terms of their duel to the death and then have a gentlemanly smoke:

"Do you mind a little sleep after we eat? I haven't slept a wink in three days and nights."

"Sleep until you're ready," urged Philip. "I don't want to fight bad eyes."

In 1936, a young chap could come inside and read *The Avenger*: "He had lost his beloved wife and small daughter in the callous machinations of a criminal ring–which loss had impelled him to dedicate his life and his great fortune to the fighting of the underworld. The tragedy had turned his coal-black hair dead white. Also the nerve shock had paralysed his facial muscles in some curious way which made the dead flesh like wax; it could not move at the command of his nerves, but when his fingers moved it, it stayed in whatever place it was prodded. Thus he became a man of a thousand faces. . . ."

Even in 1963, an adolescent could curl up with *Amazing Fantasy Introducing Spider-Man*: "'My fault—all my fault! If only I had stopped him when I could have! But I didn't—and now Uncle Ben is dead . . .' And a lean, silent figure slowly fades into the gathering darkness, aware at last that in this world with great power there must also come . . . great responsibility!"

But the codes of honour, duty, redemption, vengeance and responsibility that drove Private Steele, the Avenger and Spider-Man are all gone. Reading dime novels and pulp magazines and superhero comics were all, in their way, acts of imagination. Mowing down stick figures, blips on a screen, requires no such emotional engagement: it's a pure sensory jolt, the thrill of action divorced from human motivation. There are no causes of violence any more: you zap the aliens because that's the game; likewise, at Pearl High School, 16-year-old Luke T. Woodham "assassinated" a girl he'd once dated and another student because that was the game he and his pals had planned that day. Look at his accomplices at the Rankin County jail, or the two boys who shot up Jonesboro, or the students in Springfield—all with the same dead-eyed look of a blank computer screen. This is the way the world ends, not with a bang but an electronic whimper.

Who's Guilty?[5]

Parents are being sued and jailed for their children's sins

BY JOANNIE M. SCHROF
U.S. NEWS & WORLD REPORT, MAY 17, 1999

It is not about anger. It is not about revenge. It is not even about punishment. That is what the parents of slain Columbine High student Isaiah Shoels say of the lawsuits they may file against the parents of killers Eric Harris and Dylan Klebold. "I'm going to take my son's death and turn it into a tool," Michael Shoels told reporters. "It's time to stop."

Parents of student victims in Kentucky, Mississippi, Arkansas, and elsewhere say the same thing about court cases they have initiated. Marsha Norskog, the Chicago-area mother of a 13-year-old girl stabbed to death by a classmate, says, "This is about sending an awakening call. More must be done to save our children's lives."

Those calls resound in courtrooms throughout the country, as parents are taken to task for the sins of their children under an emerging set of rulings known as parental-responsibility laws. The rules are usually created at state or local levels after mishaps as trivial as school pranks or as monstrous as the Littleton, Colo., massacre. The result is a crazy quilt of statutes, with each court district watching the others for precedent-setting decisions.

"Parental responsibility" is actually just a new label for an old concept. In the mid-1800s, Illinois laws against contributing to the delinquency of a minor were directed mainly against bad parents, says University of Oregon family law Prof. Leslie Harris. "Every 20 years or so, people rediscover the concept of parental responsibility and pass a flurry of new laws," Harris says. "Usually they are merely a symbol of outrage and are rarely enforced." Even President Clinton's new proposal to make it a felony for parents to recklessly allow kids to use guns to commit crimes may never lead to a single conviction, say law scholars, because it would be very tough to prove.

---

5. Copyright © 1999 *U.S. News & World Report*. Reprinted with permission.

Most of the laws call for slaps on the wrist, like community service or small fines. One South Carolina judge ordered a mother and daughter, charged with truancy, to be tethered by a 2-foot rope in 1995. (Oddly enough, the pair say it was a turning point for the better in their relationship.) But as adolescent misdeeds like spray-painted lockers are overshadowed by more horrific crimes, efforts are afoot to raise the penalties for a guilty child's parents to six-figure fines and jail sentences. That is why it is wise for Eric Harris's parents to request immunity before answering police questions, says New York defense attorney Benjamin Brafman. "There are just too many potential avenues by which they can run into serious legal problems," he says.

In California, Illinois, and Oregon, parents found guilty of "failing to adequately supervise" their children can be sentenced to up to a year in jail and fined tens of thousands of dollars.

Colorado does not have many parental-responsibility laws, but even under more general statutes parents can find themselves in trouble along with their kids. In civil cases, the concept of vicarious liability dictates that parents must pay for damages caused by a child. In some states, parents are responsible for up to $300,000 in damages; in others the liability cap is as low as $3,500. Often, homeowner's insurance covers at least some of the fine under a standard liability clause, with varying deductibles.

Negligence is the more serious civil charge. In that instance, a court decides a parent (or even a teacher or counselor) should have known of the damage a child was about to inflict. Juries have found parties guilty of civil negligence and ordered them to pay up to $500,000. But parents can rarely come up with that kind of money, so plaintiffs rarely collect huge sums. Such court cases are used to make a point, not to make money, lawyers say.

Guns and minors

Criminal charges against parents are harder to prove. Parents who leave guns where a child can happen upon them can be found guilty of endangering the welfare of a minor. Those who know of a child's plans to commit a crime can be found guilty as accomplices. But more often, parents cannot be prosecuted for criminal charges unless the state has a statute specifically worded to punish parental lapses. In California, Illinois, and Oregon, parents found guilty of "failing to adequately supervise" their children can be sentenced to up to a year in jail and fined tens of thousands of dollars. In a suburb of Albuquerque, N.M., Lorraine Vallejos had to put up $10,000 to be released from jail on bond in 1997 after her son repeatedly got into trouble in gang-related incidents, including assault, robbery, and car theft. In Holiday Hills, Ill., Mark Rush spent 60 days in jail and paid $1,500 in 1996 after his son gave vodka to underage girls in his home while the father was asleep, because a county law holds parents responsible for controlling access to liquor in their homes.

Many parents express outrage at being labeled criminals because their children have misbehaved, and parental laws are often challenged as unconstitutionally vague. In Silverton, Ore., where a strict parental-responsibility law made it possible to prosecute any parent whose child had committed a crime, the American Civil Liberties Union came to the defense of Anita Beck, who was charged with failing to supervise a minor when her son was accused of shoplifting. She was subsequently acquitted, and a less severe state law replaced the Silverton statute. "At best, these laws are useless as a deterrent," says the University of Oregon's Harris. "There is not one parent alive who has not failed to adequately supervise a child at some point. That does not make us criminals."

> *"There is not one parent alive who has not failed to adequately supervise a child at some point. That does not make us criminals."*
> —University of Oregon family law professor Leslie Harris

Criminals, no, but responsible parties, yes, say child advocates who have seen parents look the other way as a child's behavior spirals out of control. "Troubled children deserve every ounce of effort their parents can muster to help them," says Chicago-Kent College of Law Prof. Richard Kling. In Dayton, Ohio, many parents whose children get into trouble with the law must attend six-week parenting classes with social workers like Jody Johnston Pawel, author of *The Parent's Toolshop.* "Most parents who come in are hostile and resentful," Pawel notes. She brags that about 90 percent of parents and children complete her course, and that as early as the second week some families say they are having better talks than before.

Parents who try to obtain help for a troubled teen usually are protected from criminal charges. Having sent Eric to a psychiatrist may well benefit the Harrises in court because it showed their good intentions. But many parents can't afford a private therapist and can't find public resources. "I can't tell you how often parents in court say that they tried desperately to get help for their child and got nowhere," says Margaret Dalton, project director of the Information Clearinghouse on Children at the University of San Diego. Parents alone do not have enough power to control a teenager, she asserts, and others agree. "It's unsettling to admit," says constitutional law scholar Marci Hamilton, "but responsibility for these youths' actions in Littleton goes far beyond their parents, in about 14 other directions. You can't sue everybody."

Yet parents whose children were killed in earlier school shootings are suing just about everyone. In Paducah, Ky.,

---

"The idea of [determining] how to punish all these people for the misdeeds of children is the wrong debate . . . We need to look at what we can do to shore up troubled kids."
—Ira Schwartz, dean of the College of Social Work at the University of Pennsylvania

---

plaintiffs have sued not only killer Michael Carneal's parents but also more than 40 students, teachers, and school officials who allegedly failed to see danger signs. They're also suing makers of violent computer games and movies. Victims in Jonesboro, Ark., are suing gun makers, and there is talk in Littleton of suing the sheriff's office for not responding more forcefully to complaints about Harris's violent behavior.

Nightly help

"The idea of [determining] how to punish all these people for the misdeeds of children is the wrong debate," says Ira Schwartz, dean of the College of Social Work at the University of Pennsylvania. "We need to look at what we can do to shore up troubled kids." One source of help, proven effective in studies from the National Institute of Mental Health, is multisystemic therapy, a program of family counseling nearly every night. But such programs are few and far between, notes University of California-Los Angeles child psychologist Gery Legagnoux, and the threat of a lawsuit is sometimes the only thing that drives people to actions they know they should take. "Everyone wants to help troubled youth," says Legagnoux. "But [that's] more likely to happen when there's a law with punishment for not doing so."

If there's a better way to prompt care for troubled teens than by taking parents to court, that's fine with Marsha Norskog, whose 13-year-old daughter, Hillary, was stabbed to death in a car by a teen who gave her a ride home from a party. The killer is now in prison for the crime, but Norskog is suing his parents for civil negligence. The process is miserable and exhausting. "But I have to use any means available to keep another child from Hillary's fate," she says. "Parents have to stop thinking these are just isolated incidents, that their own child could never do such a thing."

A valid point, says Susan Appleton, law professor at Washington University in St. Louis, but even the best parent can't always prevent a child's crime. "Some of these laws strive for an ideal that doesn't exist," she says. But in Littleton, Michael Shoels's position is firm: "It's time for a change."

Media: Littleton's Latest Suspect[6]

By PAIGE ALBINIAK
BROADCASTING & CABLE, MAY 3, 1999

As the nation anguished in its search for answers and healing in the aftermath of the Littleton, Colo., school massacre, Motion Picture Association of America President Jack Valenti summoned his broadcasting and cable counterparts to his Washington office last Thursday. The agenda: how to counter accusations that violence in the entertainment media, plain and simple, had contributed to the deadly horror at Columbine High School.

Valenti, National Association of Broadcasters President Eddie Fritts and National Cable Television Association President Decker Anstrom began forging a unified response to the policymakers, including President Clinton, who had demanded a reversal of what they called the media's irresponsible rampage toward gratuitous violence.

Clinton clearly was more restrained than many in Washington, including the powerful bipartisan coalition from Capitol Hill that flat-out called for protection from incessantly violent images on TV, movie and computer screens. But the President invited entertainment and Internet executives to join gun and explosives makers, government officials and religious leaders at a May 10 White House "strategy session" on "children, violence and responsibility."

"We must help parents to pass on their values to their children—in the face of a blizzard of popular communications that too often undermine those values," the President said in a Rose Garden address.

To be sure, when violence erupts, the nation has routinely pointed to television and its media cousins as the villains. But this time around, the deaths of 12 students and a teacher at the hands of two teen gunmen suggests that the media—and its defenders—are, in for a particularly rough time.

---

6. Copyright © 1999 *Broadcasting & Cable*. Reprinted with permission.
Bill McConnell, John M. Higgins, Richard Tedesco, Dan Trigoboff and Deborah McAdams contributed to this story.

This time around, Valenti, Anstrom and Fritts knew as much. By Thursday, each had heard the calls for summits, a Surgeon General's study, commissions—even, Heaven forbid, legislation—anything to help understand why kids are killing kids.

Anstrom, for his part, says the media has a duty to reexamine the impact of violent content. "Clearly the media and entertainment industries have some responsibility here," he said. "Parents certainly believe that."

"Violence is a predominate theme of television," said Rocky Mountain Media Watch Director Paul Klite, frequent critic of television in general and Denver television in particular. Echoing themes adopted by many pundits last week, he said: "When we see violent imagery over and over, it works the same way as a Toyota commercial. It sells that image. The explosion of copycat images across the country is evidence of the power of television to influence people."

Rep. Ed Markey (D-Mass.), author of the bill that requires TV makers to include V-chips in all new TVs, added guns to the mix: "I don't think it's possible to separate the two issues. It's a deadly cocktail of guns and media violence," he said.

The V-chip technology, mandated by federal law in 1996, will allow parents to block programs based on the now-ubiquitous TV content ratings.

Sen. Joseph Lieberman (D-Conn.), long an opponent of violent and sexual content, said: "We cannot hope to end this recurring nightmare without the help of the men and women who run the entertainment industry."

"A Sad Day"

Lieberman was joined at a Capitol Hill press conference last week by three other anti-violence crusaders: Sen. John McCain (R-Ariz.), Markey and Rep. Dan Burton (R-Ind.). The quartet called on the White House to hold a summit among entertainment industry executives, gun manufacturers, advocacy groups and policymakers to examine the effect violence in the media is having on American children. The bipartisan group of lawmakers last worked together on Markey's V-chip proposal.

At the same time, the President acknowledged a huge demand for entertainment that depicts violence. "There is a market for it. The American people buy it. They purchase it. They lap it up.

"In the end you've got to take it back to the fact that we all have responsibilities. And it starts with parents."

But it could end with censorship, warned Lieberman. "I'm telling you, the public is so fed up with the killing of innocent children and the violence generally in our society," said Lieberman, "and they're coming to a hard conclusion that the entertainment industry is contributing to those killings. . . . If they don't act to regulate themselves, there will be attempts, probably not by the four of us, but there will be attempts to impose censorship in this country, and that will be a sad day."

"When we see violent imagery over and over, it works the same way as a Toyota commercial. It sells that image."
—**Rocky Mountain Media Watch Director Paul Klite**

Lawmakers did not single out any individual TV program as particularly violent, but they think TV should share the blame. "I think TV is worse" than it used to be, said McCain. "I just think the Internet is an added layer. [And] video games are incredibly graphic and violent and there's a competition to see who can be the most graphic and violent."

Among other post-Littleton plans from Washington:

• The four policymakers last week planned to introduce a joint resolution in the Senate and the House that would require the Surgeon General to complete in 18 months a report on how violence in the media affects children.

• Senate Majority Leader Trent Lott (R-Miss.) called for a National Conference on Youth and Culture to "seek an understanding of what happened in Littleton and discuss how we can best avoid such tragedies in the future."

• Next week, Sen. Sam Brownback (R-Kansas) plans to hold a hearing to examine media violence. Scheduled to testify at the hearing are Lieberman, Valenti and Recording Industry Association President Hilary Rosen.

• At the FCC, Commissioner Gloria Tristani has been named to head a task force on implementing the V-chip. Last week, Vice-President Al Gore called on the industry to speed up implementation of the content-blocking technology.

The Net Effect

The Internet could face curbs as well. Lawmakers pummeled the evolving media for giving kids unprecedented access to violent and sexual content. The suspected lead killer, Eric Harris, was an Internet regular. He inscribed his violent thoughts on his America Online Web site.

But regulating the Intenet is not as easy as regulating TV. The Internet exists on a vast network of wires, plugged in everywhere, starting and stopping nowhere.

"We are calling for an industry effort to coordinate with parents and experts to develop software, blocking software, that makes it easier for parents to be able to control the computer, to be able to control access of this violent graphic material into the minds of their children," Markey said, later adding that the Internet is "different. You can't regulate it the same way.

"We're hoping we can do [this] within the Constitution and also pass laws that ensure that guns are not available to children," he said. "We believe that both things can be done without violating the First Amendment or the Second Amendment." (In related news, the Annenberg Foundation plans to release a survey May 4 on the Internet and parents' concerns and hopes for the new technology.)

Viewers, Influence Down?

"It's quite ironic that the [broadcast] networks are in such a bad situation that the one silver lining is that with viewership down, the politicians can't point to broadcast television as the predominant influence in people's lives anymore," noted a network executive. "We aren't dominating kids' lives, so we can't be blamed for violence in society."

"I can't help but think that television is an easy scapegoat," said Time Warner Chairman Gerald Levin, whose own son, a teacher, was shot in his apartment by a former student. "This entire exercise is a charade," said another network executive. "When they go after the guns, I'll take safe harbor a little more seriously."

The "safe harbor" refers to a bill introduced last week by Sen. Ernest "Fritz" Hollings (D-S.C.). That bill would require the FCC to provide a rule limiting all "violent" programming to hours when children are unlikely to be watching. Hollings pushed the bill in the summer of 1997, when the broadcast, cable and entertainment industries were negotiating with children's advocacy groups to come up with content-based markers to add to the age-based ratings already in use. At the time, two years ago, several lawmakers signed a letter giving the networks assurances that if they agreed to a new TV ratings system, they would be free of content-oriented legislation for the next three years. At press time, senators were unavailable to comment on whether they would adhere to the promised moratorium.

Clearly, however, Littleton puts the networks in a tough situation. They do not want new legislation and they do not think they deserve it. But if they actively fight against it, they look like the bad guys.

"Of course I'm worried about legislation," a network executive said. "It took me about two seconds after I heard about Littleton to start worrying about it." "In terms of violence on TV, I think the focus should be on cable. I don't think that this bill affects us," said another executive. Hollings' bill would apply to cable but would exempt premium and pay-per-view.

Wire on the Hook?

Cable's looser standards on sex and violence make those networks large targets.

Comedy Central each week plays for laughs the death of *South Park's* Kenny, a character who is regularly impaled, beheaded or crushed. Shootings and beatings are mixed with sexual titillation on USA Networks' action series *La Femme Nikita*. Pay networks HBO, Cinemax and The Movie Channel all routinely show violent action, as well as movies that are close to being pornographic.

Some cable network executives pointed to Hollywood, saying much of the violent content is in theatrical movies that the networks air—so the problem starts there.

"We buy the slates we buy," said HBO and Cinemax Executive Vice-President Richard Plepler.

But some of HBO's homegrown shows are fairly gritty, including Mafia shootings on *The Sopranos*, the hit of the year, and male prisoner rape scenes on *Oz*. "Hello, the subject matter is the mob," Plepler said of *The Sopranos*.

Elsewhere in Hollywood, most major broadcast networks were subdued last week when it came to discussing or implementing any possible changes post-Littleton. Several network representatives said their respective outlets were busy with the current development season (May 17-21, when all six broadcast nets will present their fall lineups to Madison Avenue) and couldn't discuss the issue.

"Does all media have some role in anesthetizing us to some of this? Maybe," said USA Networks Co-President Steve Brenner. "Every American has seen hundred of films, hundreds of news stories, hundreds of depictions, thousands of cartoons. Millions don't go out and shoot people." Brenner thinks there are "hundreds of factors affecting the way we behave in society," including violence in TV, access to guns, breakups in families, lack of respect for institutions. "How two deeply disturbed kids in a small town in Colorado acted, who knows what went into that?"

Brenner contends that his network's standards aren't much different from the broadcasters' standards. "I think I'm comfortable where we are," said Brenner. "Our standards are appropriate, I think." If USA is putting material on the air that is extreme, viewers and advertisers will pull away. "Society will force us to change," he said.

Now, a word from our sponsor

In an action plan targeting youth violence, the U.S. Conference of Mayors recommended last year that viewers boycott products that sponsor violent TV. But although the conference has stepped up its criticism of television in the wake of Littleton, no action toward a boycott appears imminent.

Gretchen Briscoe, a spokeswoman for major advertiser Procter & Gamble, said TV violence "continues to be a concern for Procter & Gamble." But she added, "We see TV violence as one element. But it's only one element. We know that that's just part of the problem." As a founding company of the Forum for Family Friendly Programming, she said the goal "is to encourage the creation" of such fare.

Other members of the forum, including General Motors and IBM, also said they've taken no direct action toward pulling away from advertising on violent programming. Jim Elder, IBM spokesman, said that IBM has been carefully avoiding ad placements in violent shows for "some time."

In a related development, J.C. Penney announced that it is pulling merchandise based on Comedy Central's *South Park* due to customer complaints.

TV on the Defense

At NBC, an executive said the network plans to step up its "The More You Know" series of public service announcements to focus on anti-violence efforts. "We're proud of that effort and we're going to accelerate it," the executive said.

Meanwhile, cable executives said they will stick by the steps they have already taken—supporting TV ratings and the V-chip, as well as teaching critical TV viewing skills to families. Cable executives also point out that cable networks, notably Home Box Office, pioneered content notices, alerting viewers if a movie depicted graphic violence or sex or had offensive language.

> *"Every American has seen hundred of films, hundreds of news stories, hundreds of depictions, thousands of cartoons. Millions don't go out and shoot people."*
> —USA Networks Co-President Steve Brenner

"NCTA believes voluntary steps are the most appropriate approach, and we oppose government regulation of television content and scheduling," said Scott Broyles, spokesman for NCTA.

Court TV has just launched an antiviolence initiative aimed at children—"Choices and Consequences"—that uses courtroom footage to show some of the consequences of violent acts. In trade ads last week, prepared before the Littleton tragedy, newspaper headlines like "Teacher Killed by 12-Year-Old Sniper," and "5 Killed at Arkansas School," asked: "Is TV teaching our kids to kill?"

The NAB last week said it plans to help local stations prepare for community crises by distributing taped educational forums to stations around the country.

"Collectively, nobody has a bigger voice to educate communities and disseminate information on early warning signs that can lead to mindless tragedies," said NAB President Eddie Fritts.

Stations also will soon get a new batch of antiviolence PSAs from The Ad Council. The spots, produced by the National Crime Prevention Council, will instruct viewers on safe storage of firearms, use of trigger locks to prevent accidental discharges and proper gun training.

"We can't overlook the obscene availability of guns," said John Calhoun, executive director of the National Crime Prevention Council. "Kids go through pain and anger. The trouble comes when they have access to guns."

The Shooters and the Shrinks[7]

After Littleton, the Media Declared That Studies Show Computer Games Lead to Violence. What Studies?

BY MARK BOAL
SALON, MAY 6, 1999

As the Littleton tragedy unfolded, David Grossman, a retired Army psychologist, emerged as the media's most quotable expert on virtual mayhem. As he hawked his book, the good soldier explained to the world that video games were "murder simulators," just like the ones used in Vietnam to mold recruits into trigger-happy killers.

His spiel, despite its flimsiness, was picked up by at least 19 media outlets. And the *New York Times* lent him its credibility in a piece headlined "All those who deny any linkage between violence in entertainment and violence in real life, think again."

The path clear, President Clinton ordered a summit with Hollywood on the culture of teen violence (oblivious to the irony as U.S. bombs pummeled Yugoslavia), while Senate Republicans announced a conference of their own. Even the digerati got a touch hysterical, with some game designers posting notices about ending digital gore for the sake of the public weal.

OK, rewind.

As of 1996, there had only been eight peer-reviewed studies testing for aggressive effects of violent video games, according to a literature review conducted in that year by *MediaScope*, a think tank that specializes in media violence. Of these, four found effects, three did not and one found effects for girls but not boys. (To put this in some perspective, I have a paper in my desk drawer on *teleportation* that cites 49 studies.)

More recent work has been done by Dr. Jeanne Funk, a psychologist at the University of Toledo, who has conducted more control-group research than anyone in the country. As both a practitioner and a parent, Funk supports labeling games for violent content; she lets her own

---

kids play, since "it's important for children to be part of the culture," but "draw[s] the line at the really violent ones."

As for Grossman, Funk tactfully points out that while "he believes in what he says," the "research is not exactly there to support it."

For starters, video games do not improve reflexes, which are innate. And while they can improve spatial recognition and coordination, the problem is "skill transfer": There's a tremendous difference between clicking a mouse in Half-Life and hefting a real eight-pound shotgun.

To put it another way, if all our GIs did was stare at monitors, Milosevic would have nothing to fear.

Putting aside the argument that computer games transform their players into soldiers, one is left with the somewhat more plausible theory that games bring out aggression among adolescents and adults. While it's been shown that 5-year-olds, after playing a karate video game, will go around chopping at each other, young children are highly impressionable by just about any stimulus. Therefore, older kids are more interesting from a scientific perspective; but they are also more problematic to study—observing them at unguarded play is nearly impossible. So most studies of adolescents and adults have them hammer on the fire button and then answer a battery of questions.

> *There's a tremendous difference between clicking a mouse in Half-Life and hefting a real eight-pound shotgun.*

Funk's most recent work in this vein will be presented in public in August at the annual meeting of the American Psychological Association. Her study hypothesized that adolescents "with a preference for violent games would be associated with more behavioral problems, particularly externalizing problems such as aggressive behavior." But the facts proved otherwise.

As it turns out, 10-year-old gamers who preferred a lot of violence scored higher on internalizing and anxious-depressed behaviors scales—meaning they were withdrawn, not aggressive. On the other hand, those with a preference for less violent games scored highest on the delinquent behavior scale. Shifting away from the aggression thesis, Funk concluded that future studies should focus on correlations between time spent playing computer games and subsequent depression.

This finding jibes with several older studies that correlate avid gaming with low self-esteem among boys. Oddly enough, girls who play a lot often didn't show the same problem. Cultural constructions of gender may account for the difference, with girls feeling good when they break out of the mold of timidity, and boys feeling lousy for being game geeks.

One 1985 study of fourth-graders showed positive effects. Quoting the abstract from the *Journal of Child Study*: "Subjects who played violent video games exhibited fewer defensive fantasies and tended to exhibit more assertive or need-persistent fantasies than did subjects who played non-violent games. For non-aggressive females, the barrier responsible for frustration was more salient in their fantasies after playing the violent video game. Results suggest that aggression in the context of a video game discharges children's aggressive impulses in a socially acceptable way, leaving the children less defensive and more assertive."

A Columbine high schooler said as much when she told the *New York Times*, "I know this sounds weird, but some violent games are a therapy for kids."

Why, then, the assertion in the *New York Times* and the *Los Angeles Times* of overwhelming evidence? The mountains of research they are referring to was done on television and film violence—and while it's presumed reasonable that video games would exhibit the same impact, a presumption is not exactly hard evidence. Though the few empirical studies on games are mixed—at best—facts alone cannot cool the media's fever.

One reason for the disconnect, argues Andrew Ross, who chairs the American studies department at NYU, is how the media handles race. Ross notes that when white suburban kids go wrong, there's enormous pressure to find a psychological cause rather than a social explanation.

White suburban kids are assumed to have an individual psychic development that can be sidetracked into dysfunctional forms of expression, if there is some sufficiently powerful external stimulus—a video game, a lurid Web site— that can knock them off course." But when it comes to inner-city black kids, "the explanations are assumed to be socially determined from the get-go." By the media's lights, "Society explains their behavior in a way that strips them of their individuality and retains only their class and race attributes"—which is why video games are never trotted out to explain homicide in inner-city schools.

In the end, says Ross, the pattern is distinctly American: "Since the early days of the republic, it has also been an elementary rule of public life for grandstanding experts and gatekeepers to hold popular culture responsible."

Chemistry of a Killer: Is It in the Brain?[8]

BY ANITA MANNING
USA TODAY, APRIL 28, 1999

What makes one out-of-control teen-ager grow up to live a normal life while another turns to murder?

A growing body of research suggests the answer may lie in a part of the brain that controls planning, reasoning and impulse control. Studies are revealing physiological differences between the brains of normal people and those of people who kill.

"There is clearly a biological predisposition to violence," says psychologist Adrian Raine of the University of Southern California. "We know there are murderers who don't have the usual signs—a history of child abuse, poverty, domestic violence, broken homes—and yet they commit violence. Research suggests the cause may lie internally, in terms of abnormal biological functioning."

Raine led studies comparing the brains of 41 murderers with those of 41 nonviolent people matched by age and gender. He found that "murderers have poorer functioning of the prefrontal cortex, the part of the brain that sits above eyes, behind the forehead. It's a part of the brain that controls regulating behaviors—the part that says 'wait a minute.'"

In another study, Raine divided the murderers into two groups: those from healthy, stable family backgrounds and those from abusive, dysfunctional homes. "It's the murderers from the good home environment who have the poorest brain functioning," he says.

That's not so surprising, Raine says. "If you are severely violent and come from a bad home environment, it's likely that bad home environment is one of the causes of your violence. On the other hand, if you're a violent offender from a good home, it's less likely the cause is from outside, and more likely that it's internal—poor brain functioning."

Exact causes of brain dysfunction are not entirely clear. Genetics plays a role, and Raine suggests that possible damage to the brain caused by early physical abuse or

---

8. Copyright © 1999 *USA Today.* Reprinted with permission.

birth complications may be a factor. Several top researchers are focusing on a brain chemical called serotonin.

"There's good evidence emerging that suggests a common biology for excessive aggression that is linked to excessiveness in other kinds of risky behavior," says behavioral neuroscientist Jim Winslow of the Yerkes Primate Research Center at Emory University in Atlanta. "The serotonin hypothesis of impulsive behavior suggests that having a defect in serotonin processing in the brain is responsible for a lot of impulsive behavior, including violence."

Serotonin is a neurotransmitter, a chemical that transmits electrical impulses in the brain from one neuron to another. While it is found in several parts of the brain, the prefrontal cortex, Winslow says, is "associated with the civilizing processes in our activities. If there's brain injury in

> ### *"There's good evidence emerging that suggests a common biology for excessive aggression that is linked to excessiveness in other kinds of risky behavior."*
> **—Emory University behavioral neuroscientist Jim Winslow**

that area, one of the outcomes often is that people are more impulsive or more violent."

While a tendency to be impulsive doesn't equal violence, he says, dysfunction in this part of the brain "does set up a susceptibility to violence, like somebody's taken the brake off things we'd normally keep in check."

Research shows that monkeys with different serotonin levels behave differently in similar situations, says J. Dee Higley of the National Institute on Alcohol Abuse and Alcoholism. In his work, Higley has observed behavior of 200-400 monkeys over a long period starting at their birth, correlating it with analysis of their spinal fluid, which indicates serotonin levels.

Monkeys whose brains are low on serotonin "are more likely to do impulsive things like jump between two tree tops," he says. "If you hang (containers of) flavored alcohol on their cages, they're more likely to drink to excess."

What causes different amounts of the brain chemical is not clear, Higley says. Monkeys raised without adult influences are more likely to have low serotonin levels, "suggesting there's something about adult monitoring and influence that is crucial to serotonin development," he says.

Not all scientists agree about the genetic links to violence, and there is no evidence that the killers in the Colorado school shooting had any brain abnormalities, says psychologist John Coie of Duke University in Durham, N.C.

"People will talk about individual differences in testosterone and serotonin as being linked to antisocial behavior, but it's a long way from saying there are differences in the brain functioning of people who are antisocial," Coie says.

Yet there is evidence of a genetic influence on serotonin function, Higley says. Research in Germany has located a gene that appears to deactivate serotonin.

"Your parents not only provide your early environment, they also provide your genes," he says. "There are probably some people who are invulnerable to the deleterious effects of environment, which could be why some people seem to survive" a difficult childhood. Conversely, he says, some people who are raised in the best homes show aggressive behavior. "They're genetically predisposed."

The environment, especially early family influences, can determine how—or if—violent impulses are controlled, Winslow says. "Most kids are pretty impulsive to begin with, so what may be retarded is the ability to learn constraints the rest of us learn."

Boys' Emotional Needs[9]

Is Growing up Tougher for Boys Than for Girls?

By Sarah Glazer
CQ Researcher, June 18, 1999

The carnage committed in April by two boys in Littleton, Colo., has forced the nation to reexamine the nature of boyhood in America. Some psychologists contend that societal pressures on boys force them to suppress their most vulnerable emotions in service to a rigid idea of manhood. They say the result is a nation of boys depressed, failing in school and occasionally exploding with murderous rage. The new concern about boys follows a decade in which adolescent girls were thought to be suffering a loss in self-esteem and academic achievement, in part because teachers gave them less attention than boys. But now it is the boys who are falling behind and more likely to be in remedial classes, to be suspended and to drop out of school.

THE ISSUES

As Americans try to fathom the recent tragedy at Columbine High School, two points of view often surface:

To some experts on adolescence, Dylan Klebold and Eric Harris were young men in whom evil triumphed despite apparently normal, loving families.

But to a growing number of professionals, the horror the pair unleashed in Littleton, Colo., reflected the difficulty inherent in growing up male in America.

"It's a national boy crisis, and the two boys in Littleton are the tip of the iceberg," says William Pollack, a clinical psychologist at Harvard Medical School. "And the iceberg is *all* boys."

Two weeks before the April 20 rampage, Pollack predicted on the "Oprah Winfrey" show that American boys were under so much pressure that an outburst of violence could occur at any time.[1] "The way we bring boys up makes it impossible for them to talk about" the kinds of humiliation Eric Harris and Dylan Klebold apparently suffered, he

---

says. "It either boils over or turns into a depressive, ongoing crisis."

The monosyllabic teenage boy wired to his computer or video game is a familiar fixture in American middle-class homes today. Indeed, the "strong, silent type" that evolved from the fictional cowboy hero who rode the range alone still occupies a position of admiration in America's individualist tradition.

But recently several child specialists have been arguing that millions of normal teenagers employing the automatic "I'm fine" response to almost any emotional difficulty "have us all fooled," writes Michael Gurian, a family therapist in Spokane, Wash.

Most boys, even apparently normal boys, are far from fine, Gurian argues in his 1998 book, *A Fine Young Man*.

"We are dealing with adolescent males experiencing post-traumatic stress," Gurian writes, referring to the "millions of our adolescent males" who have experienced the trauma of parents' divorce, failures in school or unsuccessful relationships.[2]

In America's increasingly atomized suburban culture, teenage boys are leading lonely lives, experts like Gurian say. Compared with other societies around the world, they say, America creates too little opportunity for boys to bond with older relatives in their extended family and to receive the moral development that results from connections with beloved uncles and grandfathers.

What boys do have "are peers and their TV and their computers," Gurian says. "The tragedy is when they have so little of their extended family, they put everything into the love of their peers. When their peers reject them and humiliate them, they don't have emotional and moral resources to face that."

Gurian writes that boys' difficulty in dealing with emotional traumas stems from an "inherent intellectual fragility in the male brain system."[3] Young boys start out with a disadvantage when it comes to expressing emotions, Gurian argues, in part because they tend to be less verbal than girls, and words are an important way of expressing feelings.

Other experts say it's not so much a matter of male intellectual inferiority but of society's emotional miseducation of boys. Social pressure to act manly and hide emotions, imposed early in childhood, ultimately leads to lonely men—and in some cases dangerous ones.

"I think of Dylan Klebold and Eric Harris as over-conformists—not deviants at all—to traditional notions of masculinity that say 'We don't get mad; we get even,'" says Michael Kimmel, a professor of sociology at the State University of New York at Stonybrook.

Schoolmates of Harris and Klebold have said the pair endured years of harassment from fellow students, particularly athletes. Columbine students called them "dirt hags" and often threw things at them at lunchtime, a student wounded in the assault told reporters. In their methodical carnage, the boys appeared to single out star athletes and others who had scorned them. [4]

If widespread suffering among American men seems to be a largely hidden phenomenon, some psychologists say, there's a simple explanation: Just as men typically refuse

---

... America creates too little opportunity for boys to bond with older relatives in their extended family and to receive the moral development that results from connections with beloved uncles and grandfathers.

---

to ask for directions when driving, they rarely ask for help in emotional crises. "Boys are not socialized in a way that gives them the kind of emotional repertoire that will keep them out of trouble," says child psychologist Michael Thompson. "But they make us pay."

Thompson's book, *Raising Cain: Protecting the Emotional Life of Boys*, published just days before Littleton erupted, argues that "our culture is railroading boys into lives of isolation, shame and anger." Thompson and his co-author, Harvard University psychologist Dan Kindlon, question the cost to boys of suppressing their emotional life "in service to rigid ideals of manhood." [5]

"Rejected aggressive kids are a danger to us," Thompson says. "They've been hurt, they're resentful and then they become angry and explosive. If you don't reach them, if they're not in touch with parents or any other adult, they can be quite dangerous."

The new concern about boys follows a decade in which books, studies and news articles proclaimed that adolescent girls were suffering a loss in self-esteem and academic achievement, in part because teachers gave them less

---

Results of the 1997 CDC Youth Risk Behavior Survey

In the 30 months preceding the survey:

8.3% of high school students carried a weapon (e.g., gun, knife, etc.)
5.9% of high school students carried a gun
4% of students had missed 1 or more days of school because they had felt unsafe at school or when traveling to or from school

In the 12 months preceding the survey:

7.4% of high school students were threatened or injured with a weapon on school property
14.8% of students had been in a physical fight on school property one or more times
Approximately one third (32.9%) of students nationwide had property (car, clothing, or books) stolen or deliberately damaged on school property one or more times

Overall:

Male students (12.5%) were significantly more likely than female students (3.7%) to have carried a weapon on school property
Male students (20%) were significantly more likely than female students (8.6%) to have been in a physical fight on school property

The CDC Youth Risk Behavior Survey is a school-based survey designed to produce a nationally representative sample of risk behaviors among students in grades 9-12.

---

attention than boys. But American girls have largely closed the achievement gap with boys, several experts say. Girls now compose the majority in colleges and graduate school, and they are flocking to math and science courses, historically an area of weakness for girls.

Today, it is actually boys who are suffering the most, as measured by school grades, test scores and emotional and learning disorders, say specialists who are concerned about boys. One disturbing indication is the increasing number of boys shunted off to special education classes, where they outnumber girls 3-to-1. Referrals of boys for attention deficit disorder (ADD) are surging.

In Kindlon's view, teenage boys' predominance in violence and self-destruction constitutes a public health "crisis." Boys account for some 1,600 of the almost 2,000 suicides committed by teens each year. Ninety percent of the teenage victims of homicide each year are killed by teenage boys. Male teens are also the victims in 70 percent of cases. Boys are two-and-a-half times more likely to die in car accidents than girls, much of it attributable to drunken driving, a risk-taking behavior that Kindlon closely links to emotional despair.

Some observers think the new concern about boys overstates the level of crisis. "I don't see where people are getting the idea that there's an explosion, an epidemic going on here," says Gwen J. Broude, a professor of psychology and cognitive science at Vassar College in Poughkeepsie, N.Y., and author of a recent article criticizing Pollack's and Gurian's books. [6]

"We've had eight school shootings" recently, Broude says.

"Rejected aggressive kids are a danger to us. They've been hurt, they're resentful and then they become angry and explosive." —child psychologist Michael Thompson.

"There are about 35 million boys" in the United States. "That's not a very big percentage on which to base a theory."

Despite the emotional or learning problems linked to boys today, only between 1 and 4 percent of boys are in trouble, according to Broude, and more girls than boys suffer from some of the same disorders. Far more girls than boys, for example, suffer from depression. About 80 to 90 percent of the suicide attempts among young people are made by girls, Broude points out. Girls' attempts are less successful than boys' because they're more likely to overdose on pills while boys are more likely to use guns.

Broude is also skeptical of the psychologists' suggestions that boys would be happier if they adopted an emotional style more like girls, such as examining their inner emotional despair. Psychological research identifies obsessive rumination as a classic feature of depression, she notes. "Alarmist" psychologists, she says, are "suggesting boys should learn to ruminate. They're perfectly right: If boys do that they will be just like girls—miserable."

While it's true that more girls than boys are diagnosed with depression, Gurian counters that boys' depression may be more "covert"—more likely to take the form of criminal activity, drug and alcohol use, irritability and aggressive behavior. "Like soldiers traumatized in wartime, these males act out," Gurian writes, noting that adolescent males comprise about 20 percent of the arrestees nationally.[7] Girls' unsuccessful suicide attempts may represent a cry for help, in contrast to boys' determinedly lethal methods, Kindlon suggests.

Christina Hoff Sommers, a resident scholar at the American Enterprise Institute, agrees that boys have been neglected in schools and have fallen behind girls academically after a decade of educators' efforts to render curricula and classrooms more girl-friendly.[8] But she is appalled by the contention that the Columbine violence reflects the condition of most American boys. She points to the heroic behavior of some of the male students who were caught in the shootings at Columbine High.

As symbols of American boyhood, Sommers asks, "Why not take the boy who threw his body over his sister and her friend, or the boy who, at great risk to himself, held the door open" to help other students escape the shooters? "The vast majority of boys behaved well and humanely. Look at those boys who were grieving and the boys who wrote songs," she says. "Those are our boys."

Boys are by nature a little more stoical than girls, Sommers argues. Just try to get your adolescent son to complete a homework assignment where he has to discuss his feelings about a work of fiction, she says. He'd rather memorize facts. Stoicism has been viewed as a virtue in many traditional societies, Sommers argues, and should be valued today for its traits of self-control and courage.

In the post-Littleton debate some experts have argued that the most salient feature of the tragedy was the sex of the shooters. Kimmel, for example, points out that violence and aggression are "the most intractable gender differences observed by social scientists" in males.[9] Across cultures, anthropologists have found, males are consistently the dominant sex, Kimmel notes.

Sommers agrees that boys are more aggressive than girls. "Where I part company with Kindlon and Kimmel is they tend to view masculinity as pathological," Sommers says.

While it is true that boys are less emotionally expressive than girls. Broude says, it's not necessarily a bad thing for boys' mental health. She points to research findings showing that traditionally masculine traits like independence and assertiveness are more likely to lead to good mental health than such feminine traits as emotional openness and sensitivity to others' needs.

The suggestion in the new wave of books about boys that seemingly normal boys are severely maladjusted poses the "danger of causing good parents of healthy boys to have nagging doubts about their own competence and about the well being of their sons," Broude writes. The advocates for boys, she warns, "are in danger of seducing us into interpreting sex differences, where we find them, as personal deficiencies."[10]

"There's already a lot of anger at normal, healthy boys in our society," Sommers says, "and [equating Littleton with boyhood] is going to exacerbate it."

Harvard psychologist Robert Coles says there may be limits to understanding what happened in Littleton. "[P]sychology cannot explain the enormous variations of behavior, including the fact that millions of kids listen to the same rock music, or see the same videos that Harris and Klebold did and never commit murder. The greater mystery really is that most people don't act this way."[11]

As parents, educators and child-development experts focus on boys' needs, these are some of the questions being asked:

Does the U.S. Education System Short Change Boys?

Psychologist Michael Thompson knelt beside two females who he said had misbehaved in class. In a wheedling, almost pleading tone of voice, he asked one of them, "Why did you do that to her? How do you think that made her feel?"

Thompson was role-playing to demonstrate the way elementary school teachers typically reprimand girls, and the two "girls" he addressed were actually the mothers of boys. Then he walked over to a father and towered over him to show the equivalent response to a disruptive boy student: "Cut it out young man!" he said, his voice changing to a brusque command. "I don't want to see that in my classroom!"

The parents gathered at the 92nd Street Y in New York City responded with laughs of recognition. As Thompson pointed out afterwards, "It's hard not to discipline boys differently." But the harsher response boys get in even the most caring schools tends to color their experience of school in a more negative way than girls, Thompson contends.

From an early age, many boys get the signal that "school is rigged against them," in Thompson's words. For the average boy, who learns to read about a year later than the average girl and matures more slowly socially, the message that comes across is that "school is about sitting and words." The typical boy's response: "'I'm not interested in any of that, and girls are better at it,'" Thompson said.

By school age, boys tend to be more physically active, restless and impulsive than girls. Boys' naturally higher energy level often gets them into disciplinary trouble at school, where males form the vast majority of disciplined students. "A girl can tolerate sitting and visual learning better than a boy can." Pollack says. "Some boys need five recesses a day, and when they wriggle in their chair their recess is taken away."

Boys' natural boisterousness is often misunderstood, critics say, by American schools' predominantly female teachers, who interpret normal boy behavior as discipline problems, attention disorders or learning disabilities. That may explain, at least in part, why three times as many boys as girls are enrolled in special-education classes, and why three quarters of the children taking Ritalin for ADD are boys, these psychologists suggest.[12]

While many cases of ADD are legitimate, Pollack writes, the almost 10-1 ratio of boys to girls diagnosed with the disorder raises the "possibility that many mild-to-moderate ADD cases are normal variants of boys' temperament that could be corrected by a properly trained, attentive adult." Diagnoses of ADD are often initiated by classroom teachers and school guidance counselors overwhelmed by chaotic, overcrowded classrooms. In a classroom properly designed for boys' temperament and energy levels, Pollack suggests, many of these behaviors would not even attract a teacher's attention. The typical boy with ADD may yell out impulsively, talk too much, act disorganized or be forgetful. But these behaviors are so close to those exhibited by emotionally healthy boys that it is often difficult even for trained professionals to make a diagnosis.[13]

Some research suggests that girls with learning disabilities fail to be diagnosed at the same rate as boys because girls tend to sit quietly in class even if they are having trouble learning.[14] "Boys get a lot more permission" to engage in disruptive behavior than girls, counters Heather

Johnston Nicholson, director of research for Girls Inc., which runs after-school programs for girls at 1,000 sites nationwide.

David M. Sadker, a professor of education at American University, suggests that the definition of learning disabilities is skewed toward problems that boys have—primarily reading—but neglects the problems girls have in areas such as spatial visualization which is often crucial to understanding math.

Troubling statistics showing a declining proportion of boys entering college and graduate school may be traceable to the joyless experience of school for many boys in a female-dominated environment, Kindlon suggests. "Boys tend to get a worse image of themselves because they compete with someone better than them"—namely girls. "Too many boys give up on school too early."

Diagnoses of ADD are often initiated by classroom teachers and school guidance counselors overwhelmed by chaotic, overcrowded classrooms.

The statistics confirm a dwindling interest in school on the part of boys. "Boys rather than girls are now on the short end of the gender gap in many school outcomes," concluded Providence College sociologist Cornelius Riordan.[15]

Enrollment in institutions of higher education now favors females. In 1995-1996, 55 percent of the nation's bachelor's degrees and 56 percent of the master's degrees went to girls. By comparison, in 1970, males outnumbered females receiving B.A.s 57 percent to 43 percent and M.A.s 60 percent to 40 percent.[16]

Boys seem to be lowering their expectations as well. In 1992, far more females than males among graduating high school seniors expected to attain a professional occupation by age 30. Girls usually outperform boys in reading and writing as early as the fourth grade. Girls have consistently obtained better grades and higher class ranks than boys. Eighth-grade girls were significantly more likely than boys to be in the highest quartile of self-reported grades and significantly less likely to have repeated a grade, according to a 1990 study.[17]

Boys are more likely to drop out of school, cut class, be suspended, be in trouble with the law and be placed in remedial math and English classes. Outside of school, boys appear less intellectual and studious than girls: They do less homework, work more at part-time jobs, read less for pleasure and watch more TV than girls. While in college, men spend more time than women partying, exercising, watching TV or playing video games. Consequently, says Riordan, they are less likely to graduate from college than women.[18]

In October 1998, the American Association of University Women (AAUW) reported that girls had leaped forward in math and science, two areas where they have traditionally lagged behind boys. Girls' enrollment in advanced math and science courses has increased significantly since 1990. For example, a higher proportion of females than males take algebra and geometry, and girls are more likely than their male counterparts to take both biology and chemistry.[19]

Boys are more likely to drop out of school, cut class, be suspended, be in trouble with the law and be placed in remedial math and English classes.

According to the Department of Education's National Center for Education Statistics, female high school students now take as many mathematics and science classes as males do, with the exception of physics. Growing numbers of females are also enrolling in advanced placement (AP) courses in mathematics and science.[20]

Despite these gains by girls, the AAUW report led its press release with the announcement that "a major new gender gap in technology has developed."[21]

Critics say the AAUW has seized on this issue because the argument that girls trail behind boys in school is essentially evaporating. Feminist organizations citing the low numbers of women in computer sciences and engineering are "searching for new areas of female victimization," in the words of AAUW critic Judith S. Kleinfeld, a professor of psychology at the University of Alaska, Fairbanks. Even the much-ballyhooed gap in computer-course enrollment is very small, according to Riordan: 25 percent of girls vs. 30 percent of boys.[22]

The AAUW report focused public attention on girls' tendency to sign up for courses in word processing skills associated with secretarial work. "What we were saying is girls tend to enroll in data-processing coursework for the typing of the 21st century as opposed to the more technically based or programming courses," says Maggie Ford, president of the AAUW Educational Foundation, which produced the report. "Girls are reporting they're less comfortable [than boys] with computers; they tend to come to the classroom with less prior exposure to computers at home [and] they feel less skilled."

But psychologist Kleinfeld argues that girls' choices in this area may actually reflect higher professional aspirations than boys'. "You don't need to take a computer-science course in order to work with computers any more than you need to be a car mechanic to drive a car," Kieinfeld quipped in a recent article.

"Besides, that more women prefer to be attorneys than cubicle-confined Dilberts hardly seems a social problem of great moment." [23]

"If anyone is getting shortchanged in schools, it's boys," Kleinfeld says. Boys' inferior verbal literacy should be of major national concern because reading is a skill that forms the foundation for later achievement, yet schools have paid little attention to remediating it, Kleinfeld says. Fewer boys than girls going to college could lead to the kind of social gulf African-American women already find as they search for compatible, well-educated mates, she warns.

In addition, Kleinfeld says, "We need to be very concerned about what the new studies are showing us: Boys feel that schools are hostile to them, that teachers think the girls are smarter. The newest studies are showing that girls are the new Horatio Alger. They're the ones fingered for success, and the boys are feeling alienated."

As evidence, Kleinfeld cites several recent reports. A 1998 survey sponsored by the Horatio Alger Association found one-third of high school girls said they had gotten "mostly As" on their last report card compared with less than one-fifth of the boys. The students in the study were divided into three groups. Of the successful students (those doing well in school), two-thirds were girls. At the other end of the spectrum, 70 percent of the "alienated students" were boys. [24]

Similarly, a 1997 Metropolitan Life survey of 1,306 students and teachers found "teachers nationwide view girls as higher achievers and more likely to succeed than boys." The survey also found that "girls appear to have an advantage over boys in terms of their future plans, teachers expectations, everyday experiences at school and interactions in the classroom." Of all groups, the survey found, minority boys are "the most likely to feel discouraged about the future and the least interested in getting a good education." [25]

Diane Ravitch, a senior fellow at the Brookings Institution and a former assistant secretary of Education in the Bush administration, says government-funded gender-equity programs aimed at making teachers more sensitive to girls have sent out a message of "repress the boys."

"As the mother of sons," she says. "I'm very happy they're no longer in school and too old to be affected" by what she calls a "frightening anti-male" atmosphere. "This is a very dangerous thing we've done," she says of the gender-equity programs.

Feminist organizations, which first raised alarms about the suppressed voices of girls in schools, respond with bafflement to the recent uproar of concern about boys and to the charge that anti-male sentiment has arisen in the wake of too much attention to girls. "I don't think advocating that women should be treated equally has ever implied that boys or men are suddenly painted as villains," says Patricia Ireland, president of the National Organization for Women (NOW). "I don't think the pendulum has gone anywhere near to equality for girls—much less over the line—to demonize young boys and in some way injure them in their education."

Adds the AAUW's Ford, "If there are negatives out there" from paying increased attention to girls, "we didn't see it in our work, and it's certainly not what our work is about."

> *"I don't think the pendulum has gone anywhere near to equality for girls—much less over the line—to demonize young boys and in some way injure them in their education."*
> —Patricia Ireland, president of the National Organization for Women

Vassar's Broude says she's not at all convinced that schools have become such an uncomfortable place for boys. In fact for many boys, it's a welcoming place, she maintains. Although teachers do believe that girls are better behaved in the early grades, research indicates that in the later grades the pattern reverses, and teachers see masculine characteristics as indicative of intelligence, independence and success in school, according to Broude.

In addition, sometimes drops in self-esteem result when children get the opportunity to compare themselves to their peers in school and revise their inflated ideas of themselves, Broude maintains.

Questionnaires and interviews cited by Broude find that both boys and girls have high self-esteem in kindergarten, when they first enter school, that self-esteem falls for both sexes throughout the first few years of school and then recovers. Another dip in self-esteem occurs in seventh and eighth grade, when teenagers become especially sensitive to how they measure up against their age group. But Broude sees these hits to self-esteem as part of normal growing pains.

In her critique of Gurian and Pollack, Broude says the contention that boys are emotionally fragile can have dangerous consequences for childrearing. That premise of fragility, she argues, underestimates the importance of fortifying children with resilience against hardship—and thus deprives them of the skills they need to weather adulthood. Besides, she notes, modern suburban American children enjoy one of the most comfortable lives imaginable in history. "If we buy into the fantasy that boys are china dolls," she warns, "we are in danger of making them just that."

Do Boys and Girls Learn in Different Ways?

The public's current fascination with gender differences often blurs how small the differences are between girls and boys. In the most comprehensive study done to date, the Educational Testing Service (ETS) looked at data from more than 400 tests to determine gender differences. Contrary to public opinion, ETS concluded that by 12th grade gender differences accounted for no more than 1 percent of all variation in scores on most tests. That's partly because boys' and girls' different areas of superiority tend to cancel one another out. At the same time, some intriguing differences in the intellectual strengths of boys and girls persist when the average boy is compared with the average girl. [26]

In the fourth grade, the ETS research showed, there are only small differences in scores between boys and girls, which become more pronounced as students move up through the grades. Girls' small advantage in writing and language skills gets larger between the fourth and eighth grades. Boys tend to gain on girls in math, science and geopolitical subjects between the eighth and 12th grades.

The classic work on sex differences, *The Psychology of Sex Differences,* concluded that four main sex differences are fairly well-established: Girls have greater verbal ability than boys; boys excel in visual spatial ability, boys excel in mathematics and males are more aggressive. [27]

The ETS study confirmed some of these differences. Among 12th-graders, girls tend to perform better on verbal and writing subjects while males perform better in mechanical and electronic areas. For example, on open-ended questions (as opposed to multiple choice) from advanced placement tests, females tended to do better if the response was written. Males tended to do better if the response was to produce a figure, such as a graph, or part of a figure to explain or interpret information. [28]

Yet girls appear to be overcoming their historical weakness in math better than boys have in language. While

---

Those who argue that schools are failing boys point out that while high-achieving boys tend to attract the most attention, more boys than girls are clumped at the bottom of the academic ladder.

---

girls have reduced the familiar math and science gap in test scores to a quarter of what it was 30 years ago, boys have not closed the sizable gap in writing skills since 1960, according to ETS.

Those who argue that schools are failing boys point out that while high-achieving boys tend to attract the most attention, more boys than girls are clumped at the bottom of the academic ladder. This seeming paradox is explained by the fact that males tend to be more variable in performance than females, whether comparing cognitive, physical or behavioral traits. For example, the ETS study found that among 12th-graders, there are about five males for every four females below the 10th percentile and above the 90th percentile—more boys at the bottom and more at the top. [29]

But critics say the ETS study gives short shrift to an important area where girls still lag behind boys: the "high-stakes" tests like the Scholastic Assessment Test (SAT), required for college entrance, and the Graduate Record Exam (GRE), needed for entrance to graduate school. In 1998, female college-bound seniors scored an average of 496 on the math section of the SAT, 35 points behind the average male score of 531. Surprisingly, even on the verbal SAT, girls scored lower than boys, though by a much smaller margin. Girls averaged 502 compared with boys' 509. [30]

"My question to ETS is why are the girls doing so much worse on the tests that affect their lives?" asks Sadker of American University. Sadker and his late wife Myra authored several influential studies concluding that teachers give more attention in the classroom to boys than to girls. In a widely cited finding, they reported that elementary and middle-school boys called out answers more often than girls. When boys called out, teachers typically listened to the comment, according to the Sadkers. But when girls called out, they were usually corrected with comments like, "Please raise your hand if you want to speak."[31]

Sadker believes that the more intense spotlight experienced by boys in the classroom serves as a training ground for the high-stakes tests. "I think when you get more attention in the classroom, you have more confidence going into a test," he says. "Boys' performance on those tests is more aggressive, more risk-taking, more confident. One hypothesis I have is that boys perform better in stress situations," Sadker says. "They've been put on the spot to come up with the answer."

By contrast, girls treat multiple-choice tests more like social or classroom situations where they don't want to offend someone by claiming to know something that they don't, according to Sadker. He cites a study of a fourth-grade science test where the researchers added "I don't know" as one of the multiple-choice answers. Girls were four to five times more likely than boys to answer "I don't know"—an answer for which they got no credit.

Brookings' Ravitch suggests the boys' superior performance on the SAT may lie in the fact that a broader range of female than male students take the test. For example, among African-Americans, girls taking the test outnumber boys 2-to-1, Ravitch notes. The predominance of girls in every ethnic group except for Asian-Americans suggests they represent a wider range of talents, including those at the low end of the ability scale, than the college-bound boys, who represent a self-selected group of excelling students.

But Sadker argues that in some sense women, who do better than men, "aren't believing the grades." They are believing the SATs. He sees a straight line from the classroom atmosphere, where boys aggressively shout out answers, and the workplace, where women earn less money than men with the same level of education.

"Part of what goes on in the classroom is a laboratory for life," Sadker maintains. "Women who sometimes do extraordinarily well on report card grades in school report to me 20 or 30 years later they don't understand what happened. They see guys get promoted, make higher salaries."

His explanation is that in the classroom the boys have learned how to have a "public voice." They've learned how to claim credit for their ideas in public meetings and how to demand a raise from the boss. By contrast, Sadker says, "The women haven't learned that unlike school, there isn't a quiz on Friday; you don't get smiles and pats on the back for being quiet in class."

Women's lack of assertiveness in the workplace, Sadker suggests, may explain in large part why women still earn significantly less than men with the same education. According to government statistics, a full-time working woman with a B.A. earns $13,237 less than a man with an equivalent education. A woman with an M.A. still earns $16,741 less than a male with the same degree.[32]

Ravitch dismisses Sadker's hypothesis that there's a link between classroom neglect of females and women's lower earnings. "I wouldn't trust any research he produces because I've never seen the replication of his research and its relevance to achievement," she says. "I think the kind of [teachers] calling-on [boys] he talks about is reprimand. And reprimand does not produce higher achievement." As for women's lower wages in the workplace, Ravitch says, some of the differential may result from choices women make to interrupt careers to have children and take lower-paying jobs.

In the last analysis, researchers on both sides of the debate agree that girls and boys are much more alike than they are different. Statistically, differences between genders on tests, for example, are dwarfed by the large amount of overlap in the male and female distribution along the achievement scale, ETS notes.

The leap forward of girls in math and science in recent years is one indication that differences formerly viewed as sex-linked are not as genetically predetermined as was once widely believed. "What we're seeing is girls' performance changing faster than the gene can travel," says Sadker.

"There's not a girls' style of learning; there's not a boys' style of learning. Boys and girls mostly learn the same way and mostly respond the same way," Ravitch maintains. "In any generalization, there's enormous overlap; there will be boys who are fine readers and writers and girls who are good in math and science."

Notes:

[1] Pollack appeared on "Oprah" to promote his book, *Real Boys; Rescuing Our Sons from the Myths of Boyhood* (1998). For background, see Kathy Koch, "School Violence," *The CQ Researcher*, Oct. 9, 1998, pp. 888-911.

[2] Michael Gurian, *A Fine Young Man* (1998), p. 24.

[3] *Ibid.*, p. 17. For background, see Charles S. Clark, "Sex, Violence and the Media," *The CQ Researcher*, Nov. 17, 1995, pp. 1017-1040.

[4] Michael D. Shear and Jacqueline L. Salmon, "An Education in Taunting," *The Washington Post*, May 2, 1999, pp. C1, C9.

[5] Dan Kindlon and Michael Thompson, *Raising Cain: Protecting the Emotional Life of Boys* (1999).

[6] Gwen J. Broude, "Boys will be boys," *The Public Interest*, Summer 1999.

[7] Gurian, *op cit.*, pp. 24, 25.

[8] Sommers' new book, *The War Against Boys*, is due to be published this year.

[9] Michael Kimmel, "Shooting Sheds Light on Problems Boys Face," letter to the editor, *The New York Times*, May 5, 1999, p. A32.

[10] Broude, *op. cit.*, p. 16.

[11] Quoted in Jay Tolson, "The Vocabulary of Evil," *U.S. News & World Report*, May 10, 1999, p. 72.

[12] Pollack, *op. cit.*, p. 254.

[13] *Ibid.*, p. 255.

[14] American Association of University Women (AAUW) Educational Foundation, *How Schools Shortchange Girls–the AAUW Report 1992* (1995), pp. 29-31.

[15] Cornelius Riordan, "Student Outcomes in Public Secondary Schools: Gender Gap Comparisons from 1972 to 1992," unpublished paper presented at annual meeting of the American Sociological Association, Aug. 21, 1998.

[16] National Center for Education Statistics, Department of Education, "Earned Degrees Conferred: Projections of Education Statistics to 2008," May 1998.

[17] Riordan, *op. cit.*, pp. 1-3.

[18] *Ibid*, pp. 3-4, 12.

[19] AAUW Educational Foundation, "Gender Gaps: Where Schools Still Fail Our Children," 1998.

[20] Judith Kleinfeld, "Student Performance: Males vs. Females," *The Public Interest*, Winter 1999, p. 10.

[21] AAUW Education Foundation news release, "Technology Gender Gap Develops while Gaps in Math and Science Narrow, AAUW Foundation Report Shows," Oct. 14, 1998. Also see, "Gender Gaps: Where Schools Still Fail Our Children," *op. cit.*, pp. 10, 13, 14, 103.

[22] Riordan, *op. cit.*, p. 4.

[28] Kleinfeld, *op. cit.*, p. 13.

[24] The "State of Our Nation's Youth" survey covered 1,195 randomly selected high school students. The Horatio Alger Association is a non-profit educational organization in Alexandria, Va., that gives out more than $1 million yearly in college scholarships.

[25] Kleinfeld, *op. cit.*, pp. 6, 18-19.

[26] Nancy S. Cole, "The ETS Gender Study: How Females and Males Perform in Educational Settings," 1997.

[27] E.E. Maccoby and C.N. Jacklin, *The Psychology of Sex Differences* (1974).

[28] Cole, *op. cit.*, p. 23.

[29] *Ibid*, p. 18.

[30] Educational Testing Service, "Profile of College-Bound Seniors," 1998.

[31] Quoted in AAUW Educational Foundation, pp. 118-119 (1995 paperback edition).

[32] U.S. Department of Education, "Outcomes of Education, Median Annual Income of Year-Round Full-Time Workers 25 Years Old and Over, by level of Education Completed and Sex: 1989 to 1997," 1998.

III.
The Aftermath

Editor's Introduction

W henever there is an incident of mass violence, the effects inevitably ripple through society in both subtle and overt ways. Security is tightened, legislation is passed, "suspicious" individuals are identified, policies are re-formulated—anything to prevent future occurrences of violence and to let people sleep easier at night knowing that the kinks in the system are being worked out. Nowhere is this more clearly evident than when violence enters our school systems. The third section of this book examines the aftermath of the school shootings that plagued this country from 1998 to 1999. Included in this portion of the book is a look at copycat crimes, new school security measures, new gun control legislation, student civil rights issues, trying youths as adults, and zero-tolerance policies.

The first selection, written for the *Washington Post*, examines some of the more disturbing copycat crimes that began to emerge around the country after the Columbine shooting. Author Kenneth J. Cooper looks at the extent of these incidents and the possible reasons why they are being carried out.

Next, Kevin Sack writes of the host of new school safety measures being implemented in the wake of the increase of school violence in recent years. In this *New York Times* article, Sack also discusses legislation aimed at curbing teen exposure to Internet violence and the impact of all of these policies on student rights.

The third article, "The Loud Echo of Littleton's Gunfire" by Angie Cannon, explores the gun control debate that has been fueled by these recent school shooting incidents. This hotly debated issue is being considered by all sides of the political battlefield, and Cannon discusses some of the more pressing legislation, both gun and media-related, that is currently being lobbied about in Congress.

In the fourth article, by Kenneth J. Cooper and Dale Russakoff for the *Washington Post*, the central topic is that of student rights violated in the aftermath of Columbine. The authors look at various cases in which simple statements or innuendo were treated with urgent punishments by school officials in an effort to prevent another school shooting. The result of this intense crack-down on students, according to the authors, is that civil liberties lawyers are being approached by concerned parents who say their children's civil rights were violated.

The subject of trying youths as adults for crimes is presented in the next article, written by Annette Fuentes for *The Nation*. Fuentes probes the question of whether juvenile crime has actually increased over the past few years, and whether offenses deserve punishment equal to that of adult crimes. The article further questions whether young adults are being unfairly targeted in our society and are being set up to fail the process of our criminal system.

The next piece delves into an issue that is the backbone of most school policy debates today: zero tolerance. The authors of "Zap Zero Tolerance," Russ Skiba and Reece Peterson, take the controversial stance that zero-tolerance policies are ineffective and largely untested. Furthermore, they assert that the entire reason why such policies were implemented—in response to a perceived increase in crime and violence in school—is unfounded. Skiba and Peterson also take exception to such strict policies, for fear that they infringe upon students' rights and create an atmosphere of authoritarianism in schools.

Finally, in an article for *Psychology Today*, Michael Easterbrook examines the increase in school security measures and the impact such actions may have on students. The author discusses the emerging belief that such stringent safety procedures may be affecting the students' education and looks into the accusation that these measures may even contribute to crimes and violence in schools.

This Time, Copycat Wave Is Broader; Schools Scramble to Respond to Violent Threats Since Littleton[1]

By Kenneth J. Cooper
Washington Post, May 1, 1999

In the eight school days since the deadly rampage at Columbine High School, panic has swept schools in nearly every state as administrators and teachers scramble to deal with hundreds of copycat incidents—most often bomb threats or scares, but in a few cases acts of violence.

The incidents have ranged from a boy tossing chemical bombs outside a Michigan high school and four Texas boys plotting a bomb attack on their middle school to an Alaska boy who brought a stolen .44-caliber Magnum pistol to his middle school. A New Hampshire high school received an untraceable threat just hours before Tipper Gore arrived for a discussion about the Columbine High shooting, which left 15 dead.

Other schools have reported cases of young girls making violent threats, including an 11-year-old in New Jersey who sent e-mails suggesting that her fifth-grade classmates would become targets of gunfire.

Educators around the country agree that the copycat phenomenon has been broader and scarier this time than in the aftermath of past school shootings, provoking intense fears among both students and parents and prompting school officials to intensify security measures. While there have been bomb threats after previous school shootings, this time they appear to be far more prevalent.

"It's a kind of hysteria. It has a mind of its own, a face of its own. It has taken on its own personality. I've never experienced it as a professional" for 40 years, said Dale Glynn, principal of Everett High School in Lansing, Mich., where on Monday a student hurled simple, not terribly powerful bombs on the 52-acre campus.

---

1. Copyright © 1999 *Washington Post*. Reprinted with permission.
Staff writers Victoria Benning, Christina A. Samuels and Craig Whitlock contributed to this report.

Since two teenage boys carried out the April 20 shooting and bombing in Littleton, Colo., there have been reports of mimicking behavior at schools in every state except Vermont. Pennsylvania, a state with rare centralized records, reported 60 threats of school violence.

Washington area schools have been plagued by bomb threats and rumors of student "hit lists" since the Colorado shooting. The trend continued yesterday, with bomb searches at schools in Arlington and Fairfax counties and the arrests of two Prince George's County students on charges of making threats.

Prince George's police said a 15-year-old at Oxon Hill High School repeatedly told his teacher that he would blow up the school if he continued to get bad grades in algebra. They also arrested an 11-year-old boy at Waldon Woods Elementary School after his classmates told a teacher that he had been spreading rumors about bombs.

For the second day in a row, some Prince William County schools had unusually high numbers of absent students. At Gar-Field High School in Woodbridge, 1,385 of the school's 2,600 students stayed home yesterday because of vague rumors that violence would occur, said Superintendent Edward L. Kelly.

At Meyers Junior-Senior High School in Wilkes-Barre, Pa., an unsubstantiated warning of a possible bombing made during an Internet chat of local students was enough to force cancellation of classes Monday afternoon.

Since two teenage boys carried out the April 20 shooting and bombing in Littleton, Colo., there have been reports of mimicking behavior at schools in every state except Vermont.

"I've got 37 years in, and I've seen nothing like this before," said Principal Michael Gorham.

School psychology experts attributed the stronger emotional reaction to the fact that Eric Harris, 18, and Dylan Klebold, 17, had planted hidden bombs—potentially more deadly than guns—before they shot and killed 13 people and then themselves at Columbine High.

"I think it's the bomb element," said Maurice Elias, a Rutgers University psychologist who specializes in children, schools and families.

What has motivated school children to imitate the violent behavior behind one of the worst school shootings ever?

Least worrisome to some parents and school officials is the springtime impulse to pull pranks: Calling in a bomb threat, like secretly pulling the school fire alarm, gives students a break from classes while bomb-sniffing dogs are sent into empty buildings.

Experts say that other possible motivations reflect the unmet needs of teenagers for attention and a sense of belonging to peer groups, in some cases signaling deeper personal troubles.

"A lot of our kids are looking for an identity," said Gorham. "To see their picture in the newspaper or on TV, they think it's an ego massage, and they'll be more accepted by their peer group."

Elias said such behavior could be "a signal of how disconnected and disaffected kids feel from schools."

"I think kids are angry at schools . . . because they feel schools have no place for them and no concern for them," he said. "The only ones who are valued are very smart or very athletic. If you're not at the top of the game, you don't matter."

> *"I think kids are angry at schools . . . because they feel schools have no place for them and no concern for them."*
> —**Maurice Elias, Rutgers University psychologist**

Many schools had already upgraded their security and instituted measures to identify and help troubled students after a rash of school shootings during the past three years. Now these schools are responding to the surge of Columbine copycat incidents with stern disciplinary actions, dozens of arrests and more changes in school security.

Students in North Carolina and New Jersey were suspended, for instance, for wearing black trench coats similar to the ones that were the trademark of the Gothic clique that embraced Harris and Klebold. Others have been arrested for making threats verbally or in graffiti, sometimes using words deemed "terroristic" only because they alluded to Columbine High.

While some civil libertarians have worried that the crackdown may be too invasive or violate the free speech rights of students, most school and law enforcement officials have generally taken a tough line in a climate of public anxiety.

But Paul Houston, executive director of the American Association of School Administrators, cautioned against going too far in tightening security and creating an atmosphere only marginally safer but "completely sterile."

"The problem is that in an open society, no matter how much security you provide, those who are bent on destruction—particularly where it involves self-destruction—cannot be stopped," Houston said in a commentary on Columbine High.

While parents in some places have called for the installation of metal detectors at schools, administrators have more often reduced the number of unlocked school doors or adopted new policies requiring visitors to show identification or get passes. Police have also stepped up routine patrols around some schools.

In responding to bomb threats, schools have opened late, dismissed classes early, evacuated students during police searches or closed for the day, as Fairfax High School did on Thursday.

"There's no way that I would want them to take a risk with my child's safety," said Margaret Ochs, whose daughter attends Fairfax. "I think it was handled the way it needed to be handled."

School Officials Are Seeking New Safety Measures[2]

Schools Look Hard At Lockers, Shirts, Bags and Manners

BY KEVIN SACK
NEW YORK TIMES, MAY 24, 1999

The members of the Coweta County Board of Education are not naive enough to think that they vanquished school violence two weeks ago when they voted to prohibit students from carrying book bags unless the bags were transparent or made of mesh.

But at least it is something, they say. And after last month's deadly attack in Littleton, Colo., and now Thursday's shootings in Conyers, Ga., school officials and political leaders here and around the country feel an urgency to do something, to do anything, really, that will ease the anxieties of students and parents.

In such a frantic atmosphere, the pressure to act is increasingly winning out over concerns about privacy and constitutionality.

"We've got to let the kids know who's in charge of the schools," said Michael E. Sumner, a Newnan lawyer who is chairman of the school board in Coweta County, about 45 miles southwest of Atlanta. "And if that means we're infringing on somebody's individual freedom of expression, then so be it.

"There's been some criticism that, well, where does it end? And my point would be that I don't know where it ends but it's sure going to begin with book bags. Just because we can't do everything to make our schools absolutely safe doesn't mean we shouldn't take the first step."

Mr. Sumner's attitude is far from unique. Since the shootings at Columbine High School in Littleton, school boards, county commissions and state legislatures across the country have proposed and enacted a broad series of measures intended to attack the youth violence problem at the margins. In each case, the proponents acknowledge that their actions are not cure-alls and that a more enduring solution

---

will require sweeping reassessments of today's youth culture and its countless corrupting influences.

But with six shooting rampages at American schools in the last 20 months, few parents and school administrators have the patience to wait. And so they are darning a patchwork strategy and praying that incremental changes will ward off the next tragedy.

In an effort to eliminate hiding places for weapons, proposals to require mesh book bags have become commonplace. For the same reason, some school districts are discussing the removal of student lockers. Here in Coweta County, the school board is already thinking about amending its new policy on book bags by banning them altogether and buying each student two sets of books, one for home and one for school.

Many schools, even in the most pastoral settings, are installing locks and buzzers on doors, positioning surveillance cameras in hallways and placing two-way intercoms in classrooms.

Some school districts also are considering dress codes that would require students to tuck in shirts, so that weapons could not be hidden in waistbands. And public school districts are discussing mandatory uniforms for students, at least partly because officials think uniforms deter gang activity and help administrators determine who belongs on their campuses.

Many schools, even in the most pastoral settings, are installing locks and buzzers on doors, positioning surveillance cameras in hallways and placing two-way intercoms in classrooms. Budgets are being reconfigured to find money for metal detectors.

At meetings with faculty members, parents and students on this morning, the day after six students were shot at Heritage High School in Conyers, Donald A. Peccia, superintendent of the district that includes Heritage, discussed banning opaque book bags, removing lockers, installing metal detectors and imposing a strict dress code.

In Lexington, Ky., the Fayette County school board freed up $125,000 after the Littleton shootings to buy a surveillance camera and door buzzers for each of its 54 schools. John E. Toye, the district's director of law enforcement, said the security plans had been discussed before the April 20 attack, but money was appropriated only afterward. "It got everybody's attention," he said.

Shortly after the Littleton shootings, Georgia's state school superintendent, Linda C. Shrenko, renewed her call for increased security financing and suggested that school boards be given the authority to allow principals to carry Mace, pepper spray or stun guns. In North Carolina, where there were 42 bomb threats at schools in the three weeks after the Littleton shootings, the state school superintendent, Michael E. Ward, has proposed increased penalties for students who make such threats: an automatic one-year suspension and a maximum jail term of 13 months instead of six months. "This was driven almost entirely by Columbine," he said.

Inspired by the school shootings that preceded those at Columbine, the public schools in Boston this week joined several other systems that have anonymous toll-free telephone lines for tips and warnings about threats of violence. Kathleen M. Johnston, the system's school-safety coordinator, said school officials recognized that the tip line could be abused by students.

"That's a chance you take," she said. "But people very much want this type of outlet. People are becoming more aware of what's going on around them, what people are saying, what people are writing, what people are doing."

Clearly, the recent shootings have had a direct impact on gun-control legislation being debated—and passed—in Congress, and they have prompted many governors to promise disciplinary crackdowns in schools and to propose study commissions on youth violence.

But the shootings also have inspired legislation aimed at curbing what minors can view on the Internet, in video games and in rock concerts, all of which are said to have influenced the two teen-agers who killed 12 classmates and a teacher at Columbine before killing themselves.

In Washington, State Representative Michael J. Carrell, a Republican who is chairman of the Judiciary Committee, introduced a bill after the Littleton shootings that would make it a misdemeanor for anyone to provide information about bomb-making—either through the Internet or the sale or loan of a book—to a minor who then builds a device that injures someone.

Taking an almost parental approach, the Senate in Louisiana passed a measure on May 12 that would require elementary school students to address teachers and school administrators "by using the respectful terms 'Yes, Ma'am' and 'No, Ma'am' or 'Yes, Sir' and 'No, Sir.'"

The legislation, which passed by a 34-to-5 vote, was proposed by Gov. Mike Foster, a Republican, who conceived of the bill before the Littleton shootings, said his spokeswoman, Marsanne Golsby. But the bill's sponsor in the Senate, Donald R. Cravins, Democrat of Lafayette, said the shootings had influenced the timing of the bill's introduction, and Ms. Golsby said the Colorado incident probably expanded its margin of passage.

Supreme Court precedents allow modest restriction of student speech and give school officials significant leeway to conduct random searches. But the American Civil Liberties Union has grown concerned in recent weeks about several measures taken in reaction to the Littleton shootings, particularly stringent disciplinary actions against students for wearing or saying things that school officials deemed inappropriate.

> *"Every time there is a violent or tragic incident, the first reaction of public officials is to scapegoat civil liberties."*
> —**Nadine Strossen, president of the A.C.L.U.**

In Wilmington, N.C., a high school student spent three days in jail this month after being charged with communicating a threat because he wrote the phrase "the end is near" on his computer's background wallpaper. And in Brimfield, Ohio, 11 high school students were suspended after contributing to an off-campus Web site about the Gothic subculture.

"Every time there is a violent or tragic incident, the first reaction of public officials is to scapegoat civil liberties," said Nadine Strossen, president of the A.C.L.U.

Paul D. Houston, the executive director of the American Association of School Administrators, agreed that there had been some overreaction. But he said he understood the instinct of school officials and politicians to respond to the fears of students, teachers and parents.

"It's not the same world as it was before," Mr. Houston said. "It's finally come home that these things can happen anywhere."

Since the rash of school shootings began, that has certainly become the reality here in Newnan, a sleepy town of

12,500 people that likes its distance from the big-city problems of Atlanta. Its high schools now feature security cameras, on-campus police officers, random searches by contraband-sniffing dogs and investigators wielding hand-held metal detectors—measures mostly instituted over the last two years. When a dog became particularly interested in a book bag during a recent search at Newnan High, school officials were relieved to find only a soggy chicken biscuit.

"We're playing by a different set of rules now," said Alan D. Wood, the principal. "'To serve and protect' has become our motto. It used to be on the sides of police cars."

Not surprising, most students at the school object to the new policy on book bags, which will take effect next year. Karen Hembree, a senior, said that the mesh bags, which cost about $15, would do little to impede a determined gunman, would impose on privacy, would pose a financial burden on some students and would fail to protect books and papers in rainstorms.

Her friend Flynn K. Tracy, this year's valedictorian, said she felt much the same way until Thursday's shootings in Conyers, about an hour's drive away.

"I didn't think it would make much difference," Ms. Tracy said. "But now after what happened in Conyers, whether they take minor steps or major steps, schools should do anything they can to make themselves safer."

The Loud Echo of Littleton's Gunfire[3]

The Killings Shifted America's Attitude about Guns and Violence-for Now

BY ANGIE CANNON WITH MAJOR GARRETT AND JEFF KAS
U.S. NEWS & WORLD REPORT, JUNE 21, 1999

As House Republicans—and a few Democrats—anxiously grappled with an upcoming vote on gun restrictions, President Clinton saw an opening–and jumped on it. Lawmakers' unease, he declared, shows how out of touch Washington is with the rest of the country. "If we can still remember Littleton—it hasn't even been two months—then we ought to speak up and be heard," the president proclaimed.

Clinton knows his business. The Columbine High shootings are still echoing across the country, reshaping the nation's guns-and-violence debate. According to the *Pew Research Center*, the student massacre was the third-most closely watched news story of the '90s. It left parents panicked, students uneasy, and children confused. And from legislation on Capitol Hill—including a big vote on gun laws this week—to voluntary restrictions by the entertainment industry, there is the beginning of a movement to limit the marketing of violent wares, especially to kids.

Even a recent GOP poll informed party leaders that strong support exists for a reassessment of gun laws and America's culture of violence. Some 80 percent of respondents back raising the legal age to buy a gun from 18 to 21 and conducting background checks for firearms purchased at gun expos. More than two thirds support a rating system for violent video games and believe that pols are "playing politics" with gun control. Hollywood, those polled said, is "at least partially" to blame for the school killings.

Parental panic. "We have been unable to leave Littleton," says Sen. Joseph Lieberman, a Connecticut Democrat. "We saw ourselves there. A good school in a lovely town with well-off parents. We are all terrified this might happen in our school and our home." Adds E. Mark Warr, a Univer-

---

sity of Texas criminologist: "The effect of Littleton may last longer than most criminal events do because it taps into an intense fear for our children."

And so, months later, politicians are still trying to find ways to calm the nation's fears, scrambling for answers that may not exist. What has emerged is an unusual, complicated merger of liberal and conservative planks: toughness on guns, violent culture, and criminals. But there are no guarantees that any of the proposals will pass or make a big difference.

Last week, Rep. Henry Hyde unveiled a proposal to outlaw the sale of explicit, violent material. Hyde aides admitted the proposal was sailing into uncharted waters by seeking to put some violent movies, video games, books,

> *What has emerged is an unusual, complicated merger of liberal and conservative planks: toughness on guns, violent culture, and criminals. But there are no guarantees that any of the proposals will pass or make a big difference.*

and recordings into the realm of obscenity. The penalty for retailers who peddle such goods to kids: a $1,000 fine or a maximum five-year prison sentence. Whether it can pass Congress or stand up in court are separate questions." Littleton has become the excuse for everything," says Rona M. Fields, a sociologist and psychologist who has written books on violence and social change. "All these medieval remedies are being given an urgency and aren't being examined rationally."

Clinton, meanwhile, last week announced that theater owners would get tough and check the IDs of kids who show up without adults to see R-rated movies. Television networks have continued to keep some of their more violent programming off the air. And Hyde called on music stores to make lyrics packaged with CDs or tapes available to parents for review. In his sweeping bill, the Republican from Illinois also proposed stiff sentences for school shooters: life in prison for 16- and 17-year-olds who intentionally fire guns at school and kill and 10 years for any youth tried as an adult who deliberately shoots a gun at school.

Risky politics. The post-Littleton gun control debate is proving chaotic, especially for the GOP. House Republicans last week appeared headed toward the same fate as their brethren in the Senate, who weeks ago lost face over modest gun control measures. New gun restrictions, drafted with the imprimatur of the National Rifle Association, would dilute Senate-passed back ground checks for all firearms purchased at gun shows. That backsliding goes against the wishes of House Speaker Dennis Hastert, who supports more-rigorous gun show checks. But by week's end, Hastert had thrown up his hands and called for a "free vote"—sparking criticism of his leadership. In the House, gun politics are competing with re-election politics for some Republicans and conservative Democrats who worry antigun votes will hurt them in the 2000 elections. Members fear a repeat of 1994, when pro-gun voters were the ones who showed up at the polls after the assault weapons ban to punish many Democrats, while gun opponents stayed home.

Littleton lives on in other ways, too. Seventeen-year-old Cassie Bernall, who was fatally shot after answering "yes" when the Columbine shooters asked if she believed in God, has been transformed into a martyr, igniting a massive revival among Christian youth. But in Colorado, the tragedy for some has turned to bitterness. Black leaders denounced state officials for scheduling a youth summit for June 19, coinciding with Juneteenth, which celebrates news of the Emancipation Proclamation. And there is tension over how to spend millions of dollars in contributions that have poured into the community, raising hard questions still to be answered—questions like how much of the money should go to families who lost children, how much for families with injured children. "We don't want to have to say whose grief is greater," says Pam Russell, a spokesperson for the district attorney. But in the end, they may have no other choice.

Schools Tightening Standards
After Columbine[4]

By Kenneth J. Cooper and Dale Russakoff
Washington Post, May 27, 1999

When 12-year-old Michael Jukes began tapping his pencil on the chair of the girl in front of him in his sixth-grade classroom, he was trying to annoy her. And he succeeded: She turned around and slapped him. Later, at lunch, Michael got irritated standing in the cafeteria line behind a bunch of fifth-graders. He warned them to hurry up and not to eat all the potatoes, or "I'm going to get you."

That afternoon, Michael was summoned to the principal's office of his Catholic elementary school in Ponchatoula, La., and suspended for two days.

But that was not the end of it. After the infractions, the principal began asking other students about Michael's behavior. Michael, who had been diagnosed with attention deficit hyperactive disorder and was on the stimulant Dexedrine, had a history of trouble getting along with classmates, and one or more of the students the principal spoke to said that earlier in the year Michael had threatened to bring a gun or a knife to school.

Within a week, Michael was called before a judge and locked up for making "terroristic threats." He has been held in a juvenile detention center for two weeks—even though he has not been formally charged with a crime and has not hurt anybody.

"It's Columbine hysteria," said Tracey Lingo, Michael's distressed mother. "It's so insane."

Her son's case is not an isolated one. In the month since the shooting rampage at Columbine High School in Littleton, Colo., school administrators and police across the country have faced increased pressure to crack down on student misconduct in an effort to increase school safety. One result, according to civil liberties lawyers, has been a rash of complaints from upset parents whose children have been suspended, expelled or arrested for alleged misconduct involving vaguely threatening speech, Web sites or

---

4. Copyright © 1999 *Washington Post*. Reprinted with permission. Staff reporter Anita Huslin contributed to this report.

clothing. The lawyers cite examples from around the country:

A 14-year-old girl was strip-searched and suspended for two weeks from her school near Harrisburg, Pa., because during a classroom discussion about the Colorado shootings she said she could understand how unpopular students could be pushed so far that they would lash out violently.

A South Carolina student whose Web site said members of his ROTC unit "can eat feces and die" was suspended for four days because his high school near Aiken took the statement as a violent threat.

A 9-year-old boy in Anne Arundel County was given an in-school suspension for waving a drawing of a gun in his

---

A 14-year-old girl was strip-searched and suspended for two weeks from her school... because... she said she could understand how unpopular students could be pushed so far that they would lash out violently.

---

classroom. His parents said the principal told them the boy's actions were inappropriate in light of the Colorado shootings.

Four fifth-graders overheard talking about bringing guns to their elementary school outside Little Rock were taken to a police station, strip-searched and asked to waive their right to remain silent—all without their parents being notified. Even though their gun talk was not directed at anyone in particular, the boys were charged with terroristic threatening. Three were expelled, and the fourth was suspended for the rest of the year.

In Virginia Beach, Chris Bullock was arrested and charged with "threatening to bomb or burn" for writing an essay on the Standards of Learning test that ends with a fictional student announcing he has a nuclear bomb strapped to his chest. A spokesman for the school system suggested the scene violated a "zero tolerance" policy adopted three years ago.

Three students who wore black trench coats to a West Columbia, S.C., high school had their belongings searched by police and were sent home for the day. Rummaging through one student's book bag, a police officer grilled him on why he had a chemistry book—implying it might be for bombmaking research rather than homework.

"The whole thing is this spiraling, out-of-control situation," said Ann Beeson, a staff lawyer at the American Civil Liberties Union. "I thought at first it was the schools overreacting, but they're having these parents call and insist that things be done about incidents that normally wouldn't come to the parents' attention."

Free-speech advocates say students who may have been unfairly disciplined have lost constitutionally protected rights as well as learning time—without their schools being made any more secure. "Lots of kids are angry and feel disaffected," said Joan Burton of the National Coalition Against Censorship, an advocacy group based in New

---

Free-speech advocates say students who may have been unfairly disciplined have lost constitutionally protected rights as well as learning time— without their schools being made any more secure.

York, "but they don't go blow their classmates away."

But school administrators find vindication for tough policies in the shooting last Thursday at a high school in Conyers, Ga., and the discovery earlier this month of a bomb at a school in Port Huron, Mich.

"Schools are less likely to take chances at this point, and I think their communities in large part would prefer they not take chances," said Gary Marx, spokesman for the American Association of School Administrators. "I think there are as many or more people who think schools should not take any chances in the short term as there are those concerned with student rights."

Most complaints reaching state ACLU affiliates about overwrought disciplinary actions have come from suburbs and small towns where, before Columbine, residents believed they inhabited safe, secure worlds. Now, just contemplating a possible risk of violence in the neighborhood school has left many parents terrified and has put pressure on administrators to be hyper-vigilant—such as those in Vermont who had police blow up a clarinet case believed to contain explosives. (The case contained a clarinet.)

"This is an upper-middle-class, suburban phenomenon," observed Raymond Vasvari, legal director of the Ohio ACLU, which has received about 40 complaints. "What they see coming from TV [about Columbine] is a mirror image of themselves. It becomes very easy for people to imagine it happening here, because here looks so much like there."

One group that has found itself under heightened suspicion is Web-savvy students, whose profiles resemble Colorado assailants Eric Harris and Dylan Klebold. In the case of the South Carolina student suspended for his anti-ROTC Web site, the punishment was a reflection of the disruption the Web site had caused at the school, said Bill Burkhalter, counsel to the school system. "The whole thing, the tenor of it, seemed threatening," Burkhalter said. "In another context, this would be poor taste, vulgar slang. Coming three days after what happened in Colorado, people started looking at it in another way."

Other principals have been more restrained in dealing with cyber-skilled students. A South Florida student who copied the Web site of one of the Columbine assailants attracted the interest of the FBI, but Principal Doug Parrish said South Plantation High School took no disciplinary action because no school rules had been broken.

Burton of the anti-censorship group said the few court cases involving student Web sites have upheld disciplinary action only if the sites were created or maintained in school.

In southern states that outlaw "terroristic threats," vague warnings that under other circumstances might be considered harmless have given police cause to detain students such as the four boys in Jacksonville, Ark. "Coming in the aftermath of the Columbine shootings, you take things a little more seriously than you would before," said Susie Roberts, spokeswoman for the school district, noting that the boys had allegedly discussed bringing the guns to school on a specific day and that one had said he could get a gun from his uncle.

Rita Sklar, executive director of the Arkansas ACLU, dismissed the boys' gun talk as "schoolyard chatter" and criticized the Arkansas law under which they were charged for not distinguishing between "what's a threat or what's a fantasy."

Other students have faced school discipline not for what they said, but for what they wore.

"It's not an issue of a trench coat, it's an issue of a disturbance," said Randy Counts, the principal who sent three students home from Airport High School in South Carolina. "It created a disturbance we didn't need here."

But Andy Brumme, staff counsel with the South Carolina ACLU, maintained that many schools simply have been "looking for anybody who could be the next" Harris or Klebold. "Anybody who has done anything over the course of the school year is suspect," he said, "even if it was just words."

It's a profile that fits Michael Jukes.

Michael's mother said other students at St. Joseph's School in Ponchatoula constantly picked on her son after they found out that he wet the bed. "I know that at one time or another he said to kids, 'Leave me alone, or I'll kill you,'" she said. "Adults say that all the time."

Michael has denied he ever threatened to bring weapons to school, but a psychiatrist who examined him last week questioned whether these denials were truthful.

Bob Furlow, spokesman for the Catholic Diocese of Baton Rouge, said diocese policy requires the immediate removal from class of a student who threatens bodily harm to another. Citing privacy concerns, Furlow declined to discuss Michael's case, but he defended administrators at St. Joseph's.

"If they did not respond, with the seriousness of the threats, they would be seriously negligent in their responsibility to other students," Furlow said.

Local police and juvenile court officials did not respond to telephone messages from the *Post*. Michael's mother suspects they are trying to delay a resolution of the situation until after the school year ends this Friday.

In the meantime, Michael is taking classes at the juvenile detention center.

The Crackdown on Kids[5]

The New Mood of Meanness Toward Children— To be Young is to be Suspect

By Annette Fuentes
The Nation, June 15/22, 1998

When Kipland Kinkel, Mitchell Johnson and Andrew Golden reportedly unloaded mini arsenals of guns at their classmates, they fulfilled the worst fears about young people that now dominate the nation's adult consciousness. Kinkel, 15, of Springfield, Oregon, allegedly is responsible for the deaths of two students as a result of an incident on May 21, as well as for the deaths of his parents. Johnson, 13, and Golden, 11, were charged in connection with the March 24 deaths of four students and a teacher in Jonesboro, Arkansas. All were instantly transformed from average American boys, perhaps a bit on the wild side, into evil incarnate. Forget that Mitchell sobbed next to his mother in court, or that Drew learned to sling a shotgun from Dad and Grandpa the way many boys learn to swing a bat. "Let 'em have it" was the sentiment, with catchy phrases like "adult crime, adult time."

After the Arkansas incident, Attorney General Janet Reno scoured federal laws for some way to prosecute Johnson and Golden so they could be locked up till age 21 if convicted, a stiffer sentence than the state could mete out. One *Washington Post* Op-Ed called for states to adopt a national uniform minimum age for juveniles to be tried as adults for violent crimes.

The three boys are believed to have committed terrible deeds, no question. But twenty years ago, a Greek chorus would have been clamoring to understand why they went bad. The events themselves would have been seen as aberrations. Redemption might have been mentioned, especially since these were not career delinquents. Instead, we have proposals like the one from Texas legislator Jim Pitts, who wants his state to use the death penalty on children as young as 11. And he's got plenty of support, because this is the era of crime and punishment and accountability for all

---

constituencies without wealth or power to shield them. And the young are such a class of people.

In the past two decades, our collective attitude toward children and youth has undergone a profound change that's reflected in the educational and criminal justice systems as well as in our daily discourse. "Zero tolerance" is the mantra in public schools and juvenile courts, and what it really means is that to be young is to be suspect. Latino and black youth have borne the brunt of this growing criminalization of youth. But the trend has spilled over racial and ethnic boundaries—even class boundaries, to a degree. Youth, with all its innocence and vulnerability, is losing ground in a society that exploits both.

In fact, youth crime has not changed as dramatically as our perceptions of it. Data from the National Center for Juvenile Justice show that between 1987 and 1996, the number of juvenile arrests increased 35 percent. Juvenile violent-crime arrests

> *Youth, with all its innocence and vulnerability, is losing ground in a society that exploits both.*

were up 60 percent, but they represent a sliver of all juvenile arrests—about 5 percent of the 1996 total of 135,100. A 1997 study by the center found that "today's violent youth commits the same number of violent acts as his/her predecessor of 15 years ago." As to whether criminals are getting younger, a 1997 report from the Justice Department answers clearly: "Today's serious and violent juvenile offenders are not significantly younger than those of 10 or 15 years ago."

What's more, from 1994 to 1995 there was a 3 percent decline in juvenile arrests for violent crime, and from 1995 to 1996 there was a 6 percent decline. "I have people call me up and ask, 'Why is juvenile crime down?'" says Robert Shepherd Jr., a law professor at the Universiy of Richmond in Virginia. "I say, 'Why was it up?' It could be just one of history's cycles. Over the thirty years I've been involved in juvenile justice issues, I've seen very little change in the incidence of violent crime by kids."

One thing that has changed is the prominence of guns and their role in violence. A 1997 Justice Department report looked at homicides by youths aged 13 and 14 with and without guns. In 1980 there were 74 murders committed with guns and 68 without by that age group. In 1995 gun-related murders totaled 178; there were 67 nongun murders.

Exaggerated claims about juvenile crime would be a hard sell if people weren't ready to believe the worst about young people. A 1997 report from Public Agenda, a non-profit policy group, called "Kids These Days: What Americans Really Think About the Next Generation," found that 58 percent of those surveyed think children and teens will make the world a worse place or no different when they grow up. Even kids aged 5 to 12 weren't spared, with 53 percent of respondents characterizing them in negative terms. Only 23 percent had positive things to say about children. What America really thinks about its kids, in short, is: not much.

The generation gap is old news, but this sour, almost hateful view of young people is different. Adults aren't merely puzzled by young people; they're terrified of them.

The generation gap is old news, but this sour, almost hateful view of young people is different. Adults aren't merely puzzled by young people; they're terrified of them. It can't be a coincidence that the shift in adult attitudes began roughly a generation after the height of political and social movements created by young people of all colors. Policy-makers now propelling anti-youth agendas remember how effective young people can be as a force for change. Demographics and the shifting nature of U.S. families also foster the anti-youth bias. According to census statistics, the number of people under age 65 has tripled since 1900, while the population aged 65 or over has increased elevenfold. One quarter of all households are people living alone. And children are no longer integral to family structure: In 51 percent of all families there are no children under 18 living at home. Young people are easily demonized when their worlds don't coincide with ours. The sense of collective responsibility in raising children disappears as the building blocks of community change.

To an older America in a postindustrial world, children have become more of a liability than an asset. Middle-class parents calculate the cost of raising kids, including an overpriced college education, as they would a home mortgage. Low-income parents are bludgeoned by policies designed to discourage having children, from welfare reform to cuts in higher-education assistance. Young people's place in the economic order is uncertain, and a threat to those elders who are scrambling for the same jobs at McDonald's or in Silicon Valley. Says Barry Feld, professor at the University of Minnesota Law School and author of the upcoming *Bad Kids: Race and the Transformation of Juvenile Court*, "Parents raised kids so they could take care of them when they're old. As caring for the old has shifted to the public sector, the elderly no longer have that fiscal investment in their kids. They know Social Security will be there for them."

Another reason adults are willing to condemn children is that it saves them from taking responsibility when kids go wrong. Take this statistical nugget: From 1986 to 1993, roughly the same period of the youth crime "explosion," the number of abused and neglected children doubled to 2.8 million, according to the Justice Department. And just three years later, the total of all juvenile arrests was 2.8 million. What goes around comes around.

Historically, U.S. criminal law followed the definitions of adulthood and childhood laid down by William Blackstone in his *Commentaries on the Laws of England* (1765-69). Children up to 7 were considered incapable of criminal responsibility by dint of their immaturity. At 14, they could be held as responsible as adults for their crimes; the years in between were a gray area of subjective judgment on culpability. But by 1900, reformers had created a separate system of juvenile courts and reform schools based on the principles that delinquency had social causes and that youth should not be held to adult standards. Eighteen was generally held as the entryway to adulthood.

From 1992 to 1995, forty-one states passed laws making it easier to prosecute juveniles in adult criminal court, and today all fifty states have such laws.

The current transformation in juvenile justice is no less radical than the one 100 years ago. This time, though, we are marching backward to a one-size-fits-all system for youth and adults in which punishment, not reform, is the goal. From 1992 to 1995, forty-one states passed laws making it easier to prosecute juveniles in adult criminal court, and today all fifty states have such laws. In more than half the states, children under 14 can be tried in adult court for certain crimes. In thirteen states, there is no minimum age at which a child can be tried in adult court for felonies. New York permits prosecution of a 7-year-old as an adult for certain felonies. The Hatch-Sessions bill now in the U.S. Senate continues the assault on youthful offenders. It would use block grants to encourage states to toughen further their juvenile justice procedures. One provision eliminates the longstanding mandate to separate incarcerated juveniles and adults. "You're going to see more suicides and assaults if that happens," says Robert Shepherd.

Violent crimes like those in Oregon and Arkansas are a rarity, but they've become the rationale for a widespread crackdown on youth at school and on the streets. If Dennis the Menace were around, he'd be shackled hand and foot, with Mr. Wilson chortling as the cops hauled his mischievous butt off to juvenile hall. In Miami recently, a 10-year-old boy was handcuffed, arrested and jailed overnight because he kicked his mother at a Pizza Hut. His mother protested the police action—it was a waitress who turned him in. The boy now faces domestic battery charges in juvenile court.

Last October at the Merton Intermediate School in Merton, Wisconsin, four boys aged 12 and 13 were suspended

---

In Miami recently, a 10-year-old boy was handcuffed, arrested and jailed overnight because he kicked his mother at a Pizza Hut.

---

for three days and slapped with disorderly conduct citations and fines (later dropped) by the local sheriff after they yanked up another boy's underwear "wedgie style." "The boys were playing, wrestling around in the schoolyard, and there was a pile-on," says Kevin Keane, an attorney who represented one of the boys. "One kid was on the ground and the others gave him a wedgie. He wasn't hurt or upset, and they all went back to class." But the principal learned about the incident and termed it a sexual assault.

Anti-youth analysts prefer to think more juvenile arrests means more kids are behaving recklessly. But it's just as plausible to argue that the universe of permissible behavior has shrunk. Look at curfews, which were virtually unknown twenty years ago. Curfews generated 185,000 youth arrests in 1996—a 113 percent increase since 1987. Disorderly conduct arrests of youth soared 93 percent between 1987 and 1996, with 215,000 arrests in 1996 alone.

Public schools are at ground zero in the youth crackdown. A report released in March by the National Center for Education Statistics surveyed 1,234 public schools on crime and security measures. Three-fourths have "zero tolerance" policies on drugs, alcohol and weapons, which means ironclad punishment for any transgression. Six percent of the schools surveyed use police or other law enforcement on campus at least thirty hours a week, while 19 percent of high schools have stationed cops full time. Public schools are even using dogs to search for illegal drugs. The Northern California A.C.L.U. filed suit in March 1997 against the Galt, California, school district on behalf of two students and a teacher who were subjected to dog searches during a course on criminal justice. "It's a real state police-prison element introduced into the schools," says A.C.L.U. lawyer Ann Bick. "It tells kids, 'We don't trust you.' And they'll live down to those expectations."

If the goal is to change behavior, draconian policies aimed at young people have been a dismal failure. Half a dozen studies have shown that transferring juveniles to adult courts not only doesn't deter crime, it's more likely to spur recidivism. But if the goal of the crackdown on youth is to divert attention from the real crimes plaguing the nation— child poverty, failing educational systems, 15 million kids without health insurance—then it's a success. New York City Mayor Rudolph Giuliani uses that strategy brilliantly: In January a child was killed by a brick falling from a badly managed school construction site, and reading scores were once again abysmally low. What were Giuliani's issues? Uniforms for students and deployment of police in the schools.

The criminalization of young people makes no sense, of course. Kids are a national treasure and natural resource, the bearers of our collective dreams and hopes. But logic and humanity don't often determine public policies or opinion. We are sowing the seeds, the dragon's teeth, of our own comeuppance. Erasing the line between youth and adulthood without granting youths the same constitutional protections and rights of citizenship as adults sets up a powerful contradiction. And sooner or later, to paraphrase Malcolm X, the chickens will come home to roost.

Zap Zero Tolerance[6]

BY RUSS SKIBA AND REECE PETERSON
EDUCATION DIGEST, APRIL 1999

Recent, seemingly random school violence in communities heretofore immune to it means renewed calls for increasingly severe penalties for any kind of school disruption, a stance that has led to widespread "zero tolerance" discipline policies. Already many districts have decreed any sort of threat as resulting in automatic expulsion. Some have suggested that principals be armed to deter—or perhaps outshoot—students who bring firearms to school.

Though extreme and unlikely to be implemented, this approach is simply the far end of a continuum of responses to the largely unquestioned assumption that school violence is accelerating at an alarming rate, necessitating increasingly draconian disciplinary measures for school safety. Before continuing down a path that may well turn principals into town marshals and cafeterias into free-fire zones, let's examine the track record of zero tolerance.

The term "zero tolerance"—policies that punish all offenses severely, no matter how minor—grew out of 1980s state and federal drug enforcement policies. From the outset, the harsh punishments meted out under them engendered considerable controversy. By 1990, the U.S. Customs Service quietly discontinued its initial zero tolerance program after it led to seizure of two research vessels on which a small amount of marijuana was found.

Just as the programs were being phased out, the concept was beginning to catch on in public schools. In late 1989, school districts in Orange County, California, and Louisville, Kentucky, promulgated zero tolerance policies that called for expulsion for possession of drugs or participation in gang-related activity.

In New York, Donald Batista, of Yonkers public schools, proposed a sweeping zero tolerance program to act against students who caused school disruption. With its restricted school access, ban on hats, immediate suspension for any school disruption, and increased use of law enforcement,

---

the program contained many elements of zero tolerance approaches of the past decade.

Broadening Nationally

By 1993, the policies were being adopted by school boards across the country, often broadened to include not only drugs and weapons but also tobacco-related offenses and school disruption. In 1994, the federal government stepped in to mandate the policy nationally when President Clinton signed into law the Gun-Free Schools Act, mandating an expulsion of one calendar year for possession of a weapon and referral of students who violate the law to the criminal or juvenile justice system. It also provides that the one-year expulsions may be modified by the "chief administrative officer" of each local school district on a case-by case basis.

But what is the reality of school violence and drug use? Some data suggest we are overreacting. In *Violence and Discipline Problems in U.S. Public Schools, 1996-1997*, the National Center for Education Statistics (NCES) surveyed a nationally representative sample of 1,234 school principals or disciplinarians at elementary, middle, and high school levels. Asked to list serious or moderate problems in their schools, the most frequently cited problems at all levels were the less violent behaviors such as tardiness (40%), absenteeism (25%), and physical conflicts between students (21%). The critical incidents typically the focus of school safety debates were reported to be at least "a moderate problem" only relatively infrequently: drug use (9%), gangs (5%), possession of weapons (2%), and physical abuse of teachers (2%). The report found that violent crimes occurred at an annual rate of only 53 per 100,000 students.

The evidence seems to contradict our gut feelings. Comparing the current NCES survey with a 1991 survey of public school principals shows virtually no changes across minor misbehavior or more serious infractions. Noted school violence researcher Irwin Hyman tracked indicators of school violence over the past 20 years and concluded, "As was the case 20 years ago, despite public perceptions to the contrary, the current data do not support the claim that

> *"As was the case 20 years ago, despite public perceptions to the contrary, the current data do not support the claim that there has been a dramatic, overall increase in school-based violence in recent years."*
> —Violence Researcher Irwin Hyman

there has been a dramatic, overall increase in school-based violence in recent years."

Can it be that there are so few incidents of truly dangerous behavior and that things are not necessarily getting worse? Perhaps some behaviors just shake us up, whatever their frequency. School shootings of multiple victims are extremely rare statistically. However, statistics are hardly reassuring if the possibility exists that it could happen in our school, to our children. It is probably healthier that a single shooting on school grounds be viewed as one too many than that we become inured to violence.

Yet this fear of random violence is the prime motivator for zero tolerance to school discipline. Zero tolerance has cast a broad net, by definition treating both minor and major incidents with equal severity to "send a message" to potential violators.

Near Epidemic

Indeed, infractions that fall under zero tolerance seem to multiply as the definition of what will not be tolerated expands. Test cases of school district zero tolerance policies reported in the media from 1988 to 1993 did involve difficult judgments about the severity of the punishment, but they were also clearly concerned with weapons and drugs. Over time, however, increasingly broad interpretations of zero tolerance have resulted in a near epidemic of suspensions and expulsions for seemingly trivial events.

The reaction to these cases has created sharp divisions in schools and communities. In some incidents, parents filed lawsuits against the school districts, mostly unsuccessfully. A number of states have amended zero tolerance policies to allow more flexibility for individual cases, while the Office for Civil Rights in the U.S. Department of Education began advocating a less comprehensive interpretation of sexual harassment after the suspension of a 6-year-old boy for kissing a classmate made national headlines.

Yet in many cases, school administrators and school boards have not backed down even in the face of public clamor. They claim their hands are tied by federal or state law (despite language in the federal law that allows local review on a case-by-case basis), or assert that zero tolerance is needed to send a message to disruptive students.

If the NCES data on school violence are correct, it is not surprising that the broad net of zero tolerance will catch a host of minor misbehaviors. Since there are few incidents of serious violence and many of minor disruption, policies that set harsh consequences indiscriminately will capture a few incidents of serious violence and many incidents of minor disruption.

In fact, suspension and expulsion data suggest that the incidents the media bring to national attention are not all that inaccurate in describing the types of behavior that lead to exclusion from school. Suspension data consistently show that, as NCES has reported, referrals for drugs, weapons, and gang-related behaviors constitute but a small minority of office referrals leading to suspension. Fighting among students is the single most frequent reason for suspensions, but the majority occur in response to relatively minor incidents that do not threaten school safety.

Unlike the domain of academic achievement, there has been no concomitant pressure to test the efficacy of interventions that target school behavior.

At the middle school level, disrespect and disobedience are among the most common reasons for suspension, and a significant proportion of suspensions are for tardiness and truancy. A study of school expulsion in American education reported that the majority of offenses were committed by students who would not generally be considered dangerous to the school environment. In this study, as in many on suspension and expulsion, poor academic skill was a strong predictor of school exclusion.

It has been almost a decade since school districts began zero tolerance policies, and four years since the policy was institutionalized nationally in the Gun-Free Schools Act. How well did it work? We don't really know. Unlike the domain of academic achievement, there has been no concomitant pressure to test the efficacy of interventions that target school behavior. Perhaps as a result, there are almost no studies that evaluate the effectiveness of zero tolerance strategies.

Of course, the media have reported claims by school districts that zero tolerance approaches have curtailed guns, gangs, or fighting in their schools. The most comprehensive, controlled study of zero tolerance policies, however, appears again to be the NCES study of school violence.

The NCES survey asked principals to identify which possible components of a zero tolerance strategy (e.g., expulsions, locker searches, use of metal detectors, school uniforms) were employed at their school. Of responding principals 79% reported having a zero tolerance policy for violence. Schools with no reported crime were less likely to have a zero tolerance policy (74%) than schools that reported incidents of serious crime (85%). From one perspective, the relationship is unsurprising, since unsafe schools might well be expected to try more extreme measures. Yet after four years of implementation, the NCES found that schools that use zero tolerance policies are still less safe than those without such policies.

As time has allowed us to gain some perspective on the recent school shootings, the media have begun to report data showing that school violence has remained fairly level since the early 1990s. One overlooked implication of these figures is their evaluative significance for the Gun-Free Schools Act.

Almost No Data

In an era of accountability, is it unfair to expect that a national policy implemented consistently, one might even say aggressively, over four years should demonstrate some measurable effect on its target: school disruption and violence? Virtually no data suggest that zero tolerance policies reduce school violence, and some data suggest that certain strategies, such as strip searches or undercover agents in school, may create emotional harm or encourage students to drop out. When the lives of school children and staff continue to be claimed in random shootings after extensive implementation of the most extreme measures in our schools, is it wise to push these strategies harder?

Our concerns about long-term effects of zero tolerance multiply when we look more closely at one of its central components: school exclusion. In the 1980s, national concern over children termed "at risk" led to extensive investigations of the causes and correlates of dropping out. Consistently, school suspension was found to be a moderate to strong predictor of a student's dropping out of school. Over 30% of sophomores who dropped out of school had been suspended, a rate three times that of peers who stayed in school.

Indeed, the relationship between suspension and dropping out may not be accidental. In ethnographic studies, school disciplinarians report that suspension is sometimes used as a tool to "push out" particular students, to encourage "troublemakers" or those perceived as unlikely to succeed in school to leave.

Growing Alienation

Recent advances in developmental psychopathology suggest other explanations for the relationship between suspension and dropping out. In the elementary school years, students at risk for developing conduct disorders exhibit disruptive behavior, below-average achievement, and poor social skills. Together, these deficits cause them to become increasingly alienated from teachers and peers.

As they reach middle school, they become less interested in school and seek the company of other antisocial peers, perhaps even gangs. Their families often fail to monitor their whereabouts, allowing more unsupervised time on the streets. In such a context, it seems unlikely that suspension will positively influence the behavior of the student. Rather, it may simply accelerate delinquency by giving a troubled youth with little parental supervision a few extra days to "hang" with deviant peers.

In the face of an apparent inability to influence violence in schools, harsh measures are intended to send a message that the administration is still in charge.

Whether and how to provide services to students who are suspended and expelled may be our next pressing national discussion. Without such services, school personnel may simply be dumping problem students out on the streets, only to find them later causing increased violence and disruption in the community. In sum, we lack solid evidence to support the effectiveness of harsh policies in improving school safety, and we face serious questions about the long-term negative effects of one of the cornerstones of zero tolerance, school exclusion.

Indeed, the popularity of zero tolerance may have less to do with its actual effects than with the image it portrays. Writing in the *Harvard Educational Review*, Pedro Noguera argues that the primary function of harsh punishment is not to change the behavior of the recipient, but to reassert the power of authority. Seemingly random violence poses a profound threat to schools and to the authority of those who administer those schools. In the face of an apparent inability to influence violence in schools, harsh measures are intended to send a message that the administration is still in charge. Whether it is effectively received or actually changes student behavior may be less important than the reassurance that sending it provides to administrators, teachers, and parents.

In his recent book, *The Triumph of Meanness*, Nicholas Mills argues that a culture of meanness has come to characterize many aspects of our nation's social policies: "Meanness today is a state of mind, the product of a culture of spite and cruelty that has had an enormous impact on us."

The zeal with which punitive policies are sometimes implemented suggests that zero tolerance discipline may be yet another example of what Mills is referring to. Whether such policies work or how they affect the lives of students may be less important than providing harsh punishment for offenders as a form of generalized retribution for a generalized evil.

In any institution, preservation of order demands that boundaries be set and enforced. Children whose families

> *If we rely solely, or even primarily, on zero tolerance strategies to preserve school safety, we accept a model of schooling that implicitly teaches students that preservation of order demands suspension of individual rights and liberties.*

set no limits for them soon become uncontrolled and uncontrollable. In the same way, schools and classrooms where aggressive, dangerous, or seriously disruptive behaviors are tolerated will almost inevitably descend into chaos.

Yet indiscriminate use of force without regard for its effects is the hallmark of authoritarianism, incompatible with democracy and with transmission of democratic values to children. If we rely solely, or even primarily, on zero tolerance strategies to preserve school safety, we accept a model of schooling that implicitly teaches students that preservation of order demands suspension of individual rights and liberties.

As we exclude ever higher proportions of children whose behavior does not meet increasingly tough standards, we will inevitably meet many of those disruptive youths on the streets. In choosing control and exclusion to deal with school disruption, even as we refrain from positive interventions, we increase the likelihood that the correctional system will become the primary agency responsible for troubled youths. Ultimately, as we commit school discipline, we may also need to resign ourselves to increasingly joyless schools, increasingly unsafe streets, and dramatically increasing expenditures for detention centers and prisons.

Serious, Not Extreme

Seriousness of purpose to avert school violence does not necessarily demand rigid adherence to harsh and extreme measures. Alternatives to politically facile get-tough strategies rely on a comprehensive program of prevention and planning. However, prevention is not a politically popular approach to solving problems of crime and violence in America. A recent task force on prevention research, commissioned by the National Institutes of Mental Health (NIMH), found wide gaps in our knowledge, noting that "virtually no preventive services research of any kind" was found under NIMH sponsorship.

Yet, if we are to break the cycle of violence in American society, we must begin to look beyond a program of stiffer consequences. We must begin with long-term planning aimed at fostering nonviolent school communities.

First, programmatic prevention efforts such as conflict resolution and schoolwlde behavior management can help establish a climate free of violence. Conflict resolution has been shown to have a moderate effect on student aggression in schools, but more important, it teaches students to consider and use alternatives to violence in solving conflicts. Schoolwide discipline plans and the planning process required to develop and implement them help ensure that school staff have both the consistent philosophy and the consistent procedures critical to effective behavior management.

Second, screening and early identification of troubled young people appear critical in preventing the eruption of violence. In a number of the recent multiple-victim shootings, the shooter left warning signs, cries for help unheeded. There is at least one widely available, well-researched measure to screen for troubled students, whether the concern is acting out behavior or social withdrawal: Hill M. Walker and Herbert H. Severson's *Systematic Screening for Behavior Disorders (SSBD): User's Guide and Administration Manual*, published by Sopris West, in Longmont, California, in 1992. With such screening and with knowledge of the early warning signs in the President's guide for preventing violence (published as *Early Warning, Timely Response: A Guide to Safe Schools*, by the U.S. Department of Education, Washington, D.C., in 1998), we are beginning to have the capability of identifying students with serious problems while they can still be helped.

Finally, schools with effective discipline have plans and procedures in place to deal with the disruptive behaviors that inevitably occur. School safety teams or behavior support teams—composed of regular and special education teachers, personnel from related services, administrators, and parents—ensure a consistent, individualized response to disruptive students. Individual behavior plans and a functional assessment process for developing those plans provide consistent consequences for offenders and teach disruptive youngsters alternatives to aggression. Emergency and crisis planning before serious incidents occur can help ensure that, if violence erupts, its negative short- and long-term effects will be minimized. In short, effective intervention emphasizes building positive pro-social behaviors rather than merely punishing inappropriate behaviors. Whether at the school or individual level, it requires a wide spectrum of options that extend significantly beyond a narrow focus on punishment and exclusion.

Such a program demands complex and careful planning. But our problems are highly complex and will not abide simplistic solutions. Zero tolerance strategies have begun to turn schools into supplemental law enforcement agencies, but demonstrate little return despite a decade of hype. Long-term, comprehensive planning and prevention can build safe, responsive schools over time by emphasizing what American education has always done best: teaching.

Taking Aim at Violence[7]

BY MICHAEL EASTERBROOK
PSYCHOLOGY TODAY, JULY/AUGUST 1999

Tension in the classroom had been building all year. The English teacher was fresh out of college and her pupils, about 15 of them, were seniors on the advanced-placement track at South Fayette High School outside of Pittsburgh, Pennsylvania. These stellar students weren't accustomed to pulling grades below an A, but the teacher was infuriatingly tough, frequently returning papers marked C and D. "It was kind of like a little war," says Matt Welch, the class president and one of the students. "It just seemed like she was out to get us."

If there was one person the teacher really seemed to have it in for, it was Aaron Leese. A bold 18-year-old with short red hair, Leese was popular with his classmates, if not exactly your model student. Police had busted him in the park with a bottle of bourbon. In school, he had a habit of embarrassing the teacher by asking her questions in front of the class that she found hard to answer. Leese also didn't take kindly to low marks on his assignments. Once, he was so riled by a grade that the teacher asked him to leave. As he was walking out he muttered something like "troglodyte bitch," which earned him a three-day suspension.

The relationship between the two became increasingly strained. One morning in spring, she handed back one of the year's last big assignments, a 10-page essay on a book of one's choice. Leese had written his on Thomas Moore's *Utopia*. He needed an A to pass the class, but he received a D. "I said, 'Man, if I don't pass this class, I'm going to be mad enough to kill,'" Leese recalls. "It was something I said out of frustration. After that the teacher said, 'That could be misinterpreted, you know?' I said, 'Yeah, my bad. I take it back.'"

The exchange went so quickly that a student who sat directly behind Leese didn't even catch it. But it made a distinct impression on the teacher. After class ended, she reported it to the principal, who pulled Leese into his office and phoned the police. By noon, Leese was being escorted off school grounds by two officers from the South Fayette Township Police Department. He was now facing criminal charges. "I was in tears," Leese says.

Had Leese made his comment just five years ago instead of in spring 1998, it might well have gone unnoticed. But a string of deadly shootings at schools around the country is radically altering how these institutions interact with their students. Since February 1996, the massacres, seven in all, have left a total of 35 students, teachers and principals dead. In the latest tragedy at Columbine High School in Littleton, Colorado, two youths killed 13 before taking their own lives.

> *Reporters delving into the lives of the young killers invariably have surfaced with tales of suspicious remarks made before the carnage.*

Alarmed by such incidents, educators are changing the way they go about their mission—and the steps some are taking go far beyond a heightened sensitivity to violent language. They're installing spiked fences, metal detectors, emergency alert systems. They're hiring security guards and imposing searches of students' bags, lockers and desks. And they're insisting that teachers learn skills not included in any syllabus: how to run lock-down drills, how to strip a student vigilante of his weapon.

No one would deny that educators have a right—make that an obligation—to do all they can to protect themselves and their charges from what has become a prime threat to their safety: students themselves. But worrisome questions have arisen about the effects such measures are having on the education which is the schools' purpose to provide. More disturbing still are suggestions that the efforts may not be effectively preventing trouble—and may even be promoting it.

The change most immediately apparent to students has been the move to punish those who use violent language. It's hard to fault administrators for paying close attention to such outbursts. Reporters delving into the lives of the young killers invariably have surfaced with tales of suspicious remarks made before the carnage. Like Barry Loukaitis, the 14-year-old who killed two students and a teacher at Frontier Middle School in Moses Lake, Washington, who told a friend how cool it would be to go on a shooting spree. Or Kip Kinkel, accused of killing four people at Thurston High School in Springfield, Oregon, who talked frequently of shooting cats, blowing up cows and building bombs. And more recently still, Eric Harris, one of the Columbine shooters, who posted a message on the Internet saying, "You all better hide in your houses because I'm coming for everyone, and I will shoot to kill and I will kill everyone."

Remarks like these, recalled with remorse after the fact, have led principals and teachers to be on the lookout for more of the same. But when do such comments represent an actual intent to kill, and when are they merely the product of an active fantasy life?

Robby Stango, for example, was a 15 year-old freshman at Kingston High School in upstate New York in May 1998 when school officials were alerted to a poem he had written for a class assignment. Titled "Step to Oblivion," the poem is about a divorced man who decides one night to jump off a cliff and end his life. "Here I am/ Standing here on this gloomy night/ Minutes away from my horrid fate," the verse begins. The precipice is only seven feet high, however, and the man survives the fall. "Maybe my prayer was answered/ Or it could have been just luck/ But I was given a second chance at life," the poem concludes.

... when do ... comments represent an actual intent to kill, and when are they merely the product of an active fantasy life?

Despite its positive ending, the verse convinced school officials that Stango was headed for trouble. Although the teen was seeing a counselor at the time about problems he was having at home, he didn't pose a danger to himself or others, according to therapists familiar with his case. Yet the school's discovery of the poem set off a chain of events that resulted in Stango being forced, against his mother's wishes, into a five-night stay in a psychiatric ward. Alice Stango has since filed a lawsuit against the school district and the county.

It was also writing assignments for English class that got eighth-grader Troy Foley, from the California coastal town of Half Moon Bay, in trouble. In an essay titled "The Riot," Foley, then 14, wrote of a kid who is so enraged with school rules, especially the ones forbidding him to wear a hat and drink soda during class, that he incites a student riot that ends with the principal getting bludgeoned to death. Two weeks later, Foley handed in "Goin' Postal," an equally violent tale about a character named Martin who sneaks a pistol into school and kills a police officer, the vice principal and principal. Though he had no history of violent or even disruptive behavior, Foley was suspended for five days for making a terroristic threat. Foley's mother, assisted by the American Civil Liberties Union, managed to have the record changed to state that Foley was suspended for two days for using profanity in school assignments. Foley has since skipped high school and is enrolled at a two-year community college.

Parents and lawyers of both boys contend that the schools overreacted in these cases, punishing children whose only crime was a vivid imagination. But even if that's so, it leaves an important question unanswered: how do principals and teachers know when a violent story or remark signals a real threat? Those who turn to psychological research will find only equivocal answers at best.

> *"I don't know of any study that has empirically examined whether the use of violent language in creative writing can actually predict those who are going to commit a crime."*
> —Edward Taylor, professor of social work at the University of Illinois

"These things may be indicators, and they may not," says Kevin Dwyer, Ph.D., president-elect of the National Association of School Psychologists. "To try to predict an individual's future behavior based on what they say or write isn't really possible." His view is shared by Edward Taylor, Ph.D., professor of social work at the University of Illinois at Urbana-Champaign and an expert on childhood mental illness. "I don't know of any study that has empirically examined whether the use of violent language in creative writing can actually predict those who are going to commit a crime," declares Taylor. Such language so permeates American popular culture, he notes, that its use doesn't necessarily indicate a predilection for the use of force.

Mindful of the complexities involved in predicting which students will become violent, many school districts are attempting to circumvent the threat entirely by altering their physical landscapes. Located in the small town of West Paducah, Kentucky, on the banks of the Ohio River, Heath High School was dragged into the national spotlight in the winter of 1997 when 14-year-old Michael Carneal

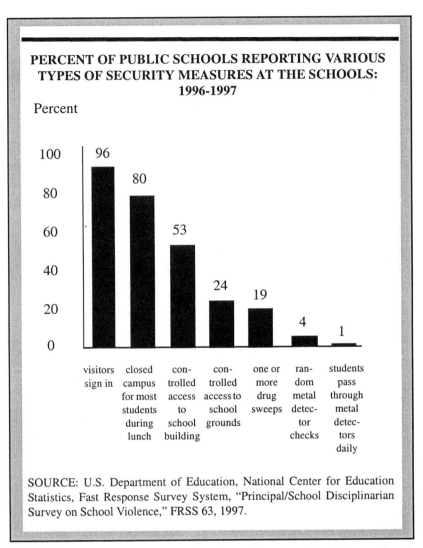

PERCENT OF PUBLIC SCHOOLS REPORTING VARIOUS
TYPES OF SECURITY MEASURES AT THE SCHOOLS:
1996-1997

Percent

visitors sign in	closed campus for most students during lunch	controlled access to school building	controlled access to school grounds	one or more drug sweeps	random metal detector checks	students pass through metal detectors daily
96	80	53	24	19	4	1

SOURCE: U.S. Department of Education, National Center for Education Statistics, Fast Response Survey System, "Principal/School Disciplinarian Survey on School Violence," FRSS 63, 1997.

gunned down classmates, killing three girls. The school quickly convened a security committee, which authorized a $148,000 security plan.

Today, Heath requires visitors, teachers and students to wear identification tags around their necks at all times, like soldiers. It has students sign consent forms authorizing staff to rummage through backpacks and cars for weapons; each morning before entering school, students line up to have their bags searched. Heath also has hired a uniformed, armed security guard. Officials have prepared should a weapon slip by security. They've purchased two-way radios for staff members to wear on their belts, in case they need to communicate during an attack. And they've placed emergency medical kits and disaster-instruction manuals in each classroom.

The new environment at Heath High School dismays many parents and students. "They made my son sign papers so they can search his possessions, his locker, anything, anytime," says one unhappy parent. "From what I understand, the Constitution is still in effect. I don't like the idea of my child going to school and having school officials search him at their discretion. They're trying their best, but they don't seem to be getting it right."

Heath's principal Bill Bond defends the measures. "We have restrictions on everything we do," he points out. "I've never thought about carrying a bomb on an airplane, but I

In April 1998, an Indiana school district became the first in the country to install metal detectors in its elementary schools, after three of its students were caught bringing guns into the buildings.

---

pass through airport security just like everybody else. The very concept of security is always going to reduce freedom. That is a trade-off people have been dealing with since the beginning of time."

Schools around the country are following Heath's lead. In April 1998, an Indiana school district became the first in the country to install metal detectors in its elementary schools, after three of its students were caught bringing guns into the buildings. This past January, the U.S. Department of Education reported that nearly 6300 students were expelled in the 1996-1997 school year for carrying firearms: 58% had handguns, 7% rifles or shotguns and 35% other weapons, including bombs and grenades.

Faced with such statistics, more schools than ever before are buying security devices like spiked fences, motorized gates and blast-proof metal covers for doors and windows. Administrators are also signing up in droves for the services of security experts. Jesus Villahermosa Jr., a deputy sheriff in Pierce County, Washington, expects to run 65 sessions for educators this year, double the number held in 1997. "I'm completely booked," says Villahermosa, whose curriculum includes how to disarm students and how to run lock-down drills.

Such measures may make schools feel less vulnerable, but how do they affect the learning that goes on inside? Here again, research provides only tentative answers. Citing neurological and psychological research, Renate Nummela Caine, professor emeritus of educational psychology at California State University-San Bernadino, maintains that when students feel threatened or helpless, their brains "downshift" into more primitive states, and their ability to think becomes automatic and limited, instinctive rather than creative.

Regimented classrooms, inflexible teachers, an atmosphere of suspicion, can all induce feelings of helplessness, contends Caine, author with her husband Geoffrey Caine, a law professor turned educational specialist, of *Making Connections: Teaching and the Human Brain* (Addison-Wesley, 1994). "What schools are doing is creating conditions that are comparable to prisons," she declares. "Where else are people searched every day and watched every minute? They want to clamp down and they want control. It's based on fear, and it's an understandable reaction given the circumstances, but the problem is that they're not looking at other solutions."

> *Psychologists say that surrounding troubled young people with the accoutrements of a police state may only fuel their fascination with guns and increase their resistance to authority.*

Psychologists say that surrounding troubled young people with the accoutrements of a police state may only fuel their fascination with guns and increase their resistance to authority. Likewise, punishing young people for talking or writing about their violent musings may just force the fantasies underground, where they may grow more exaggerated and extreme. "It's a response that says, 'We don't know how to react, so we're going to respond harshly,'" says Patrick Tolan, Ph.D., professor of adolescent development and intervention at the University of Illinois-Chicago. "If you're a child, would you come forward and say you're troubled in that atmosphere? Are you going to rely on adults if that is how simplistically they think about things? Rather than saying something to a counselor, you might well keep quiet."

Suspending or expelling a student, moreover, strips him of the structure of school and the company of people he knows, perhaps deepening his alienation and driving him to more desperate acts. Kip Kinkel, for example, went on his rampage after being suspended from school for possessing a stolen handgun.

Yet there are punishments more severe and alienating than suspensions and expulsions. As schools begin to resemble police precincts, school officials are abdicating their duty to counsel and discipline unruly students and letting the cops down the hall handle the classroom disruptions, bullying and schoolyard fights. And the cops aren't taking any chances. They're arresting students and feeding them into a criminal justice system that sees little distinction between kids and adults. "Once that police officer is on the scene, the principals and teachers lose control completely," says Vincent Shiraldi, executive director of the Justice Policy Institute in Washington. "I think it will make students a more litigious group and much less able to solve their problems peacefully and reasonably."

There may be a better way, and educators are beginning to look for it. Instead of building schools like fortresses, architects are experimenting with ways to open them up and make them more welcoming. Designers are lowering lockers to waist-height and in some cases eliminating them entirely, so students can't hide behind them or use them as storage spaces for guns. Instead of being built on the outskirts of a school, administrative offices are being placed in the middle, enclosed in glass walls so officials can see what's going on. Gymnasiums and auditoriums are being opened to the public, serving as meeting places for the local chamber of commerce or performing arts group. "The kids feel nurtured by this," says Steven Bingler, a school architect in New Orleans who participated last October in a symposium on making schools safer that was sponsored by the U.S. Department of Education and the White House Millennium Council. "School doesn't feel like a prison to them anymore."

On a more personal level, some schools are offering increased access to counselors; others have hired a "violence prevention coordinator" to whom students can give anonymous tips about classmates in trouble. In accord with this less punitive, more therapeutic approach, students who use threatening language are being steered into anger-management programs, intensive therapy and to other support services.

As for Aaron Leese, he was charged with making a terroristic threat and thrown in a holding cell for the afternoon. "My thought was that they wanted to scare me a bit so that I would bend to the system," he says. The charge was dropped after he submitted to a 90-day probation and a psychiatric evaluation. Leese was ordered to stay off school property, forcing him to miss all the senior activities planned for the end of the year—a banquet, a picnic, a dance. Then his principal, Superintendent Linda Hippert, relented. "I felt that Aaron needed to be punished, but my assumption after the investigation was that the punishment did not fit the crime," says Hippert. "I know Aaron very well, and what he was denied was above and beyond what he had done." With her blessing, Leese was allowed to graduate with his class.

IV.
Media Coverage of
Violence

Editor's Introduction

As one of the central targets in any teen violence debate, the media have been placed under tight watch by a number of groups, not the least of which are politicians hoping to find fuel for their legislation proposals to limit the entertainment industry's portrayal of violence. Still, there is evidence that certain portions of the media are heeding the call to tread carefully through controversial material. This fourth section of the book attempts to look at the issues surrounding media coverage of violent events such as the Columbine massacre.

Peter Applebome's article for the *New York Times* starts off this section, delving into the issue of media interpretation of tragic events. Applebome questions whether the media should be trying to find explanations for incidents in which there may not be clear reasons. Instead of offering "pat explanations" that fall flat, the author states that the media must move to find deeper answers for complicated situations like teen violence.

Next is an account of a controversial newspaper decision made after the Columbine shooting. The *Chicago Sun-Times* decided not to run the massacre on the front page of its newspaper, making it one of the few papers in the country not to do so and causing a wave of controversy to emerge in the publishing industry. The authors of this *Editor & Publisher* article look at the key issues involved in the *Chicago Sun-Times's* decision, and the response the action received from newspaper pundits.

The third selection is an article for the *Village Voice* by Jason Vest entitled "Paper-Thin Reporting." This article examines the role of the "expert" advisor in media coverage, and questions whether some news organizations, in their rush to publish the story, did not contact proper authorities on the subject of mass shootings. Vest also looks into key information that was omitted in the reports on Columbine and similar school shootings, namely that they are not a uniquely American phenomenon, and that the incidents were not very different in nature from adult mass shootings.

The next article in this section comes from Mari Margaret McLean, and it looks into the role of negative reporting on school violence. In particular, McLean examines media exaggeration and questions the extent of the damage to urban schools when they are "bashed" in both the news and entertainment arenas. McLean puts forth the argument that such disparaging accounts of the public educational system only reinforce the notion that inner-city schools are a source of violence, rather than simply a reflection of societal violence. The writer does acknowledge a problem with violence in schools but advocates a reformation where responsibility is shared by educators, officials, and parents, and where children do not perceive their schools as prisons.

In the final article, Fred McKissack, writes in *The Progressive* that the tragedy at Columbine caused producers and advertisers to engage in a "PR retreat" whereby the hot-button issues of guns and violence were suddenly shelved. McKissack comments on several instances where groups targeted by the media after the massacre (namely gun rights advocates and entertainment insiders) choose to backtrack under the cover of bad timing, rather than face a public backlash. The author goes on to suggest that these groups should have stood by their ads and television shows, thereby opening up a public discourse, but that a public relations mindset suffocates this kind of deep discussion.

Round and Round in the Search for Meaning[1]

BY PETER APPLEBOME
NEW YORK TIMES, MARCH 29, 1998

Almost from the moment the bullets stopped flying outside Westside Middle School in Jonesboro, Ark., the explanations and analysis began whizzing by. It was guns. It was the violent culture of the South. It was the violent culture of American media. It was bad parenting. It was the breakdown of the family caused by liberal politics or economic stress. It was violence against women. It was lax juvenile justice laws.

There was much that was true and valid in the instantaneous groping for meaning that followed the horrendous shooting incident in which two young boys are accused of killing four girls and one teacher, and wounding 10 others. But to many students of American culture, there can be something sadly diminished, and ultimately misleading, in the ritualized rush to instant judgment—or the rush to instant spin and advocacy—that now follows each cataclysmic lurch of the news cycle. And it is worth asking amid the flood of questions that the shootings leave in their wake whether the babble of interpreters provides insight or just sows more confusion and cynicism.

"Not only in the media but in the so-called helping services—the shrinks and social workers and counselors and the proliferation of support groups—we now have a mob of meaning makers and interpreters of why things happen," said Larry Rasmussen, a professor of social ethics at Union Theological Seminary in New York. "There was a time when the religious community was the locus for that, but now it happens all over the place. The question is whether that provides more clarity or whether something serious is lost amid all the verbiage."

There is, no doubt, something entirely natural and even valuable in the anguished analysis that events like the Jonesboro shootings set in motion. In some ways, it helps fill an intrinsic need for coherence and meaning in the face of unfathomable events. In his book *News Values* (Univer-

---

sity of Chicago Press, 1996), Jack Fuller, the former publisher of *The Chicago Tribune* who is president of the Tribune Publishing Company, argues that at a time of information overload, making sense of events, rather than just reporting them, is an increasingly critical part of the journalistic franchise.

"It can be an invitation to be banal or insufferably preachy, but done well, people need to have some context, need to make sense of an event," Mr. Fuller said. "The more profoundly resonant the event, the more people need to fit it somehow into an emotional or moral context."

But the profound resonance of the Jonesboro shootings has not always lent itself to equally profound responses. Anti-gun groups leaped on the incident as an occasion for

---

> *"Instead of just going there and yanking on the heart strings, we've now got armies of pundits ready to hold forth on a moment's notice with various simplistic notions of what just went down."*
> **—Mark Crispin Miller, media instructor at New York University**

---

activism and spin. "Our children's teddy bears are subject to more regulation than are the firearms causing this public health epidemic," said a spokesman for an anti-gun group sponsoring a day of protest May 2 on behalf of the 50,000 young victims of gun violence over the last 10 years.

On one of the television shows endlessly dissecting the event, Oliver L. North, the former Iran-Contra figure-turned-politician-turned-radio-personality, said it was "unconscionable" for gun-control advocates to try to make political hay out of the tragedy. Then he substituted his own spin, saying that as a life member of the N.R.A. and as someone who grew up "with a .22 rifle in one hand and a fishing rod in the other," the tragedy proved that the responsibility for raising kids rests with parents, not Federal, state or local governments.

It is a reminder how much of what passes for analysis is really little more than advocacy. "Instead of just going there and yanking on the heart strings, we've now got armies of pundits ready to hold forth on a moment's notice with various simplistic notions of what just went down," said Mark Crispin Miller, who teaches courses on the

> # Facts About Violence Among Youth and Violence in Schools
>
> Less than 1% of all homicides among school-aged children (5-19 years of age) occur in or around school grounds or on the way to and from school
>
> 65% of school-associated violent deaths were students: 11% were teachers or other staff members; 23% were community members who were killed on school property
>
> 28% of the fatal injuries happened inside the school building; 36% occurred outdoors on school property; 35% occurred off campus
>
> 85% of homicide victims 15 to 19 years of age were killed with a firearm
>
> The rate of homicide among males 15 to 19 years of age declined 12.7% over a one year period
>
> SOURCE: Statistics taken from a 1996 CDC National Center for Injury Prevention and Control (NCIPC) study

media at New York University. "We don't use the word 'propaganda' much anymore, but the constant heavy drone of knowing voices out there is largely a chorus of propagandists talking at us."

The Long View

And while the Arkansas shootings struck many as an entirely appropriate vehicle for examining important issues, particularly gun use and violence, many of the pat explanations fell flat.

The South may in fact have more guns than the rest of the nation. But given that the legacy of guns and violence dates from colonial times, that does little to explain the recent rash of shootings in Jonesboro or Pearl, Miss., or Paducah, Ky.

And just as House Speaker Newt Gingrich drew much criticism with his pronouncements that Susan Smith killing her children in South Carolina or a gruesome killing in Chicago a few months later were arguments for electing Republicans, many observers said the search for quick meanings in complicated events can get in the way of the search for deeper ones.

"One thing religion has, which is not very popular in the media, is the long view of history," said Donald W. Shriver, president emeritus of Union Theological Seminary, who teaches a course on religion and the media at Columbia University. "Jews, Christians and Muslims rely on docu-

> *"We need to make sense of things, but that doesn't give you a license to be simpleminded or leap to cosmic conclusions based on virtually nonexistent facts."*
> —**Former Chicago Tribune Publisher Jack Fuller**

ments 2,000 and 3,000 years old, not on today's headlines. I wish news people were able more often to raise serious questions about the long-range meaning of events without trying to answer them. That would be a better contribution to moral and religious reflection than premature moralizing."

Others say that in the rush to instant judgment, it's not just the answers that fall short, it's also the questions.

It's Noisy Out There

June Jordan, a professor of African-American studies at the University of California at Berkeley, notes that the overall frame for the coverage in Jonesboro—How could it happen in a nice small town like this?—differs sharply from similar inner-city tragedies, where the context is often the inherent depravity of the urban environment and its inhabitants. "So much of what we hear through the media, comes through such a racialized prism," Professor Jordan said.

Mr. Fuller and many journalists argue that the noise level of contemporary society is so high and the quantity of information so heavy that the question is not whether those in the media and elsewhere should struggle to make sense of it, but how well they do it.

"We need to make sense of things, but that doesn't give you a license to be simpleminded or leap to cosmic conclusions based on virtually nonexistent facts," Mr. Fuller said. "The way to do this properly, and the way it's done by people who do it best, is to take a situation as it is, complete with the elements of uncertainty, and deal with it on that level. It's not to make sweeping generalizations based on trivial pieces."

It may well be that people are perfectly capable of sifting out what is spin and what is more important and seeing an episode like Jonesboro both as an occasion for valid—even essential—arguments about gun control and a case with broader dilemmas beyond knowing.

Many people are skeptical about putting concise meanings on very complex events. Thus, when asked the inevitable—"Why?"—Karen Curtner, the principal of Westside responded, "That is a hard question, and I don't think there is an answer out there that we are looking for." This rush to quick judgment is unlikely to end. In a society addicted to fast-food, E-mail and ever-faster computer chips, a demand for instant analysis seems inevitable, even logical. The real question is whether that coexists with a more questioning scrutiny that realizes the pat answers and spin are only part of a much bigger picture.

George Steiner, the literary critic and classicist, is one who is doubtful.

"I think the sound-bite mentality cheapens thought," he said. "Imagine Dostoevsky. There are some incidents like this, two boys killing other children, in his famous diary. Imagine what Dostoevsky would do with that. He would deal with the transcendentally important question of evil in the child. Today the editor would say 'Fedor, tomorrow, please, your piece. Don't tell me you need 10 months for thinking. Fedor, tomorrow.'"

H.S. Shooting Kept off Page One[2]

Chicago Sun-Times decides to put horrific inside for children's sake

BY MARK FITZGERALD, LUCIA MOSES AND JOE STRUPP
EDITOR & PUBLISHER, APRIL 24, 1999

For the second time in a year, the *Chicago Sun-Times* was alone among big-city newspapers in keeping a horrifying school shooting off its tabloid front pages.

In a front-page editor's note in its April 21 edition, editor-in-chief Nigel Wade says the paper did not play the Littleton, Colo., shooting on its front page "because we are concerned that such treatment could harm or frighten vulnerable children. We see a danger that publicity surrounding such attacks could be contributing to the phenomenon."

The *Sun-Times* gave full coverage to the story on pages 2, 3, and 4, with four locally written sidebars including one by television critic Phil Rosenthal chastising Denver television station KUSA for broadcasting live a cell phone interview with a student hiding from the two alleged "Trenchcoat Mafia" gunmen.

While other U.S. dailies gave the story prominent play, ethical considerations played a role in choice of photos, story placement, and headline picks and feelings were mixed on how to present the story about the latest, most violent of school shootings in recent years.

Some newspapers went for the most shocking photos, while others avoided them, citing concerns about copycats.

For the Raleigh, N.C., *News & Observer*, the issue wasn't whether to put the story on Page One but which photos to use. The newspaper picked an overhead photo of the school scene instead of an image of screaming kids that was widely used elsewhere but which executive editor Anders Gyllenhaal considered "voyeuristic." But he disagreed with the *Sun-Times*' decision to keep the story off Page One.

"I think what you're saying is, you're going to wish it didn't happen, we're going to control based on what you do and do not like," he says.

The *Columbus* (Ohio) *Dispatch* heard from some offended callers after running a wire photo of a dead student on its front page, says Ben Marrison, managing editor for news. "No one likes to see dead kids, but this is a case where reality hurts."

While the Colorado shooting may have been an obvious front-pager, many editors say they have used restraint when reporting teen suicides and bomb threats, stories that have been linked to copycat incidents.

Anecdotal evidence supports the copycat phenomenon, says Deni Elliott, director of the University of Montana's Practical Ethics Center, who has written on the subject.

While supporting the *Sun-Times*' decision, she says. "It's a hard call because we desperately need to understand why these tragedies happen."

Sue Carter, journalism professor at Michigan State University, also lauded the newspaper's decision. "They have not backed off the coverage yet they considered the totality of the audience. The coverage is there, but it's not used to sell the paper."

Wade first took this contrarian journalism stance for the paper's coverage of the May 21, 1998, shooting at a high school in Springfield, Ore. That shooting—in which a 15-year-old allegedly killed his parents, then went to the school and killed four students and a teacher while wounding 10—climatized a bloody school year in America that saw similar killings in Bethel, Ark.; Pearl, Miss.; and West Paducah, Ky.

Readers of all kinds—parents especially—warmly greeted that decision then and now, Wade says in an interview.

While the Colorado shooting may have been an obvious front-pager, many editors say they have used restraint when reporting teen suicides and bomb threats, stories that have been linked to copycat incidents.

"Reader reaction is absolutely the same: My voice mail was full when I got here. The calls are running 20 to 1 in favor of what we did," Wade says. "There is very strong support. . . . Parents tell us this gives them a choice of whether to let their children see this."

While the Littleton shootings didn't appear on the *Sun-Times* front page, a headline nevertheless referred to horrific violence. "NATO reveal atrocities," read the page-wide head over a story about Kosovo.

"As I have said, we are not going to keep wars and disasters off the front page," Wade says. "But there is particular psychosis at work with these school shootings. We're not dealing with the likes of Milosevic with his reprehensible deeds. We are talking about unstable teenagers taking frightening actions because of some impression they've been wronged. It's part of a cycle we don't want to feed into."

Trying to minimize harm may interfere with good news coverage, warns Bob Steele, director of media ethics at the Poynter Institute. "The front page . . . carries particular weight," he says. "What the *Sun-Times* is doing by not placing it up front is potentially minimizing its importance."

Story placement, of course, is only one of many criteria— and, some argue, one of the more minor ones—of responsible story play. Headline, photo choice, design and story content, are more important to the story's impact than where it appears, says Bob Giles, executive director of the Media Studies Center, which is funded by The Freedom Forum.

> *"The front page . . . carries particular weight . . . What the Sun-Times is doing by not placing it up front is potentially minimizing its importance."*
> —Bob Steele, director of media ethics at the Poynter Institute

With ironic timing, The Freedom Forum released a report the day after the Colorado shooting examining news coverage of tragedy. Based on an examination of an earlier school shooting in Jonesboro, Ark., the report recommended, among other things, that newspapers avoid demonizing suspects or glorifying victims, stick to simple language and know when to move the story off Page One.

Bill Babcock, director of the Silha Center for the Study of Media Ethics and Law at the University of Minnesota, says the Colorado case is a good time to tone down graphics and reject gory photos. While he thought the story needed to be on Page One, he criticized the use of another widely played photo that showed a bloody victim on the ground, tended to by emergency workers.

John Walter, managing editor of the *Atlanta Journal and Constitution*, points out that readers had been hit with so much TV coverage that some bloody photos in the newspaper were not likely to be offensive.

"After America watched it for six long hours, no warnings were needed," says Walter, whose paper put out a special eight-page section on the shooting. "No picture we were going to use or language we were going to print could match what people saw on TV."

The fact that the Littleton shootings were the most lethal ever in an American school made the decision to keep it off the front page harder, Wade says. "It goes against all of your instincts. One wants to take the strongest story to the top," he says.

Inside the *Sun-Times* newsroom, some staffers felt hampered by the newspaper's policy, columnist Richard Roeper says.

"We all knew, from the start, that this was not going to be on the front page because of the pledge by editor-in-chief Nigel Wade," Roeper said in an interview on the Chicago TV show *Fox Thing in the Morning*. "In another aspect, we've painted ourselves into the corner [with the policy] because this was such a big story." Which is how the paper played it, Wade says. "I want to emphasize this was an issue of presentation. The full story was there. This was not censorship by any means."

Paper-Thin Reporting[3]

By Jason Vest
The Village Voice, May 11, 1999

In the days after the Littleton shooting, Robert Giles, director of the Freedom Forum's Media Studies Center, issued a press release decreeing that—a year after the utterly excessive and inane coverage of the school yard massacre in Jonesboro, Arkansas—news organizations were being "more fair" than the previous year. They had taken a "more sensitive approach to interviewing students," he said, and had "avoided jumping to conclusions" about the causes of the tragedy. Only one real failing, the release noted: "news outlets still seem overeager in reporting the number of casualties." Otherwise, all was well. "These observations reflect a recognition that the public increasingly holds the press accountable for its performance and at least in early reporting, the press appears to be responding by being more responsible."

Press Clips wonders if Giles is, as one of our colleagues suggested, "on the pipe."

It's a bit much to consider it "fair and sensitive" of MSNBC to cut from an interview with a surviving student who described tending to a mortally wounded teacher, to commentator-cum-opportunist Pat Buchanan, who blasted American youth culture as debased. It seems at least in bad taste, if not offensive, for networks to crow over ratings spikes for such a tragedy. And when *The Washington Post* reports that "in political tracts and other elements of the conspiratorial imagination, trench coats serve as a symbol for things from Hitler and the Nazis to mass murder to suicidal fantasies," one really has to wonder whether it could lead to errant conclusions about youth who hide nothing more malignant than quiet affinities for thrift stores or a John Woo-inspired milieu.

But what astounds most about Giles's assessment is his failure to mention that for the most part, news organizations haven't bothered to talk to any of the nation's actual expert researchers on the subject of mass murder, nor have they done the responsible thing based on a finding on

---

which those researchers agree—that when it comes to the causes of mass murder, while culture is undeniably a factor, the most salient media isn't entertainment, but news.

When workplace mass murders began to rise about 10 years ago, reporters like *The Washington Post*'s Curt Suplee and *The New York Times*'s Fox Butterfield sought out the handful of people who have devoted their professional lives to studying these morbid occurrences. As journalists discovered, researchers had found that mass murderers could be categorized: those who killed their families, those who turned on their workplaces, and paramilitary enthusiasts who took out random citizens in public places. Despite the categorical differences, the investigators found the offenders were essentially the same—socially isolated men whose myriad frustrating experiences were complemented by mental disorders. Legitimate feelings of marginalization and being pushed around were exacerbated by an externalizing of responsibility. Almost all manifested outward signs of deterioration—and even openly planned their crime—but weren't taken seriously; almost all either turned their guns on themselves or opted for "suicide by cop."

> *"...by spending so much time interviewing psychiatrists who work with kids, we emphasize an individual-level explanation for something that's more complex."*
> **—Jack Levin, professor and mass murder researcher, Northeastern University**

In this case, however, the likes of Suplee and Butterfield weren't anywhere near Littleton, and *Post* and *Times* editors apparently didn't bother to do a quick Nexis search. If they had, according to Northeastern University professor and mass murder researcher Jack Levin, they would have grasped that in the context of what's known about mass murder, the Klebold-Harris rampage was par for the course. "They were just like their older counterparts—this was the teenage equivalent of a workplace massacre," says Levin, who's concerned that the coverage of the Littleton shootings is lending itself to scapegoating youth and perpetuating false notions about the causes of this and similar shootings. "I'm getting tired of people blaming popular culture, and by spending so much time interviewing psychiatrists who work with kids, we emphasize an individual-level explanation for something that's more complex."

Indeed, it's not as if mass murder—adolescent or otherwise—is a uniquely American phenomenon; according to journalist Antonio Mendoza, reporters have missed the opportunity for perspective thanks to international myopia. "Not only are all these killers similar, despite their ages, but they're all over the world. I haven't seen anyone reference a number of recent young mass murderers in Russia," says Mendoza, who relentlessly tracks and reports on global mass murders and serial killings for his Internet Crime Archives (www.mayhem.net). "And guess what the deal is with those kids? Russian army conscripts who crack after being jazzed and humiliated by their peers. I've noted in a lot of cases Hitler-Nazi obsessions—not really out of political neo-Nazi beliefs," he says, but based on the twisted mix of outcast-turned-*übermensch* that Hitler embodies.

> *"Not only are all these killers similar, despite their ages, but they're all over the world."*
>
> **—Journalist Antonio Mendoza**

Mendoza adds that press examination of mass murders in Australia and New Zealand might have been useful as well. "But instead of focusing on what matters, the press focuses on stuff that's of no consequence. There's more talk about how this is all movies' and Marilyn Manson's fault instead of pointing out that, to kids who have no German background, speaking German to one another and going 'heil Hitler' is a pretty recognizable sign of a human time bomb."

But as a wave of copycat incidents and threats spread across the nation's schools, accusations against Marilyn Manson and Hollywood thrived, along with the standard culture-war carping from the Amen Corner. (In one particularly bizarre moment on CNN's Larry King Live, actor Yaphet Kotto—whose sole qualification to sound off on Littleton appears to be his role as a police lieutenant on *Homicide*—blamed the whole thing on the fact that "God is not in the classroom anymore," and repeated the misinformation, sans reality check from King, that students aren't allowed to pray.) While coverage of copycat attempts relied on quotes from educators, psychologists, social workers, politicians, and law enforcement officials, virtually unheard from were people like Park Dietz and David Phillips, whose studies have found that news reports—not movies or video games—are the prime media mover in begetting copycats.

"There's sort of an agreed-to conspiracy on all sides in cases like this: the media needs experts, and experts are willing to pretend to be experts, and everyone feels better after the terrifying thing has been explained," sighs the University of California San Diego's Phillips, who says he's still wondering if anyone will call him. In one pioneering study, Phillips found that not only did single-driver car crashes increase after publicized suicides, and multiple-fatality crashes increase after mass murder-suicides, but the numbers seemed to have a relationship to the style and saturation of media coverage. In another investigation, UCLA's Dietz (arguably the nation's top criminal forensic psychiatrist) found that suicide, product tampering, and mass murder lent themselves to imitation, and that the degree of imitation was inspired by sustained and sensationalized media coverage.

> *"There's sort of an agreed-to conspiracy on all sides in cases like this: the media needs experts, and experts are willing to pretend to be experts, and everyone feels better after the terrifying thing has been explained."*
> —David Phillips, University of California

"I actually wrote a long series of suggested guidelines for the World Health Organization that would make stories like this less likely to be imitated without making it so the stories disappeared from the paper, or how to cover, but reduce," says Phillips. "You have to think of these stories as a sort of advertisement for mass murder. The more alternatives you give in coverage to the act, the less likely you are to see the act imitated."

There were, to be sure, a handful of exceptions in the coverage of Littleton: though *US News & World Report* brutally whittled it down for space, Anna Mulrine's examination of research on bullies was informative and insightful, as was CBS's *60 Minutes II* interview with another juvenile mass murderer. Overall, though, it seems

Klebold and Harris got exactly the postmortem celebrity they wanted. And even though school yard mass murders are comparatively rare and juvenile homicide rates are down, coverage of Littleton—like Jonesboro and others before it—has resulted in calls for metal detectors and security forces to be deployed at schools across the country, something Levin says is "the last thing schools need."

But no matter. As *Seattle Times* TV columnist Kay McFadden astutely observed last week, "In striving to beat the pants off the competition, most seemed to forget that being a news leader incurs responsibility—and sometimes blame."

It's a "Blackboard Jungle" Out There—or Is It?[4]

BY MARI MARGARET MCLEAN
THE EDUCATION DIGEST, JANUARY 1996

A few years ago, a local-TV evening-news report caught my attention: Students and teachers at the high school where I taught had been "terrorized" that day by a gun-toting student. I was amazed, since no one, students or teachers, had mentioned this during the day.

The truth of the story, I found out afterward, was that before school had started, one student had reported that another had a revolver in his book bag. The administrator asked the accused to give him the bag, which he did without incident. A loaded revolver was found, and the police were called to arrest the student. The media, monitoring police calls from schools, heard that a gun had been taken from a student and, essentially, fabricated the rest of the story.

The following day, when I discussed it with my Developmental Reading classes, students expressed surprise. Like me, no one had heard of it before it became news. One student laughingly said that until he'd seen the news story, he hadn't realized that he'd been "terrorized" and was a little sorry he'd missed all the reported excitement in an otherwise boring day!

I think this story is illustrative of much of the problem of school violence in this nation. Many reported "violent" events are, like this incident, not actually violent at all, although the possibility may exist for violence.

Television news, however, in intense competition for the public's attention, does not generally concern itself with the difference between real violence and the perceived threat of it. The measure of a "good story" nowadays seems to be the extent to which it can shock and disturb us, and stories of violence in unexpected places such as schools are calculated to carry maximum shock value.

The background to such a story (the reason the student was carrying a gun), and the context in which the story

---

occurred (the prevalence of guns in American society and/ or the attitude that all individuals must protect themselves), go unexamined and even unmentioned. Actions are divorced from motives, and the public is left with the impression that the schools themselves constitute the entire problem.

The print media are not immune to the need to sensationalize facts to get the public's attention, either. Under the influence of big business, which wants to turn schools into for-profit institutions, and the political conservatives who want to establish the voucher system, newspaper publishers regularly print headlines that scream out how public schools are failing to adequately discipline and educate.

In fact, school-bashing has been a favorite pastime in

> ### *Even respected news magazines rarely present anything but a negative view of American schools, with heavy emphasis on the supposed climate of violence.*

America for so many years that even when works of nonfiction appear that are meant to raise our consciousness about the promises and possibilities overlooked in urban public schools, they only tend, instead, to further convince readers that these schools are the pathology of the educational system.

Even respected news magazines rarely present anything but a negative view of American schools, with heavy emphasis on the supposed climate of violence. The November 8, 1993, issue of *U.S. News and World Report*, for example, devoted considerable space to "Violence in Schools," in which reporters warn that "school violence is on the rise." To prove it, they cited unexamined statistics, and gave brief descriptions—devoid of background, context, or outcome—of incidents of school violence.

Included among the data is the now-infamous "How Times Have Changed" list that purported to compare the top disciplinary problems reported by teachers in 1940 and 1990. On this popularly cited list, items such as "chewing gum" and "cutting in line" (1940) were juxtaposed with "alcohol abuse" and "rape" (1990), comparisons designed to sear the imaginations of most readers, horrify them, and increase the likelihood that they will unquestioningly believe whatever they hear or read about violence in schools.

True Lies

The "facts" in this list were apparently accepted by the authors without question, although the list has been found to be a fabrication of an individual who has admitted making it up: The 1940 portion was composed from his own school memories; the 1990 portion stems from what he reads and hears about schools today. [See *The Education Digest*, April 1995, p. 4. Ed. Note.]

Furthermore, the abundance of statistical data in the article seemed calculated to overwhelm the reader with images of fear (e.g., 16 percent of eighth-graders "fear for their safety") and violence (5 percent of twelfth graders have been "injured by a weapon"). The authors failed to point out, however, that the vast majority of those interviewed in this study (84 percent of eighth-graders, 95 percent of twelfth-graders) do *not* fear for their safety and had not been victimized by someone wielding a weapon. Thus, the statistics that went ignored tell us more about school climate than the ones cited.

The public's willingness to believe the worst about America's schools may have been fueled by the entertainment industry's portrayal of public schools, which, for over three decades, has been anything but flattering. Consider the way American public education has been depicted in such films as *Blackboard Jungle* (1955), *Up the Down Staircase* (196 7), *Teachers* (1984), and *Lean on Me* (1988).

Stereotypes Abound

Stereotypes of urban educators and students abound in these films: Administrators are either bumbling and inept, or are cold and slightly sadistic bureaucrats; teachers are burned out, incompetent, arrogant, and/or fearful; students are tuned out, turned off, cunning, and often vicious, belonging to street gangs and carrying weapons. Most students and teachers are at odds, and characters engage in numerous acts of mental, and even physical, cruelty toward one another.

There is almost always one psychotic personality, usually armed and extremely dangerous, who will terrorize all or some of the school population before the movie ends. The physical condition of the schools is uniformly depressing: dark, threatening hallways, cheerless classrooms filled with broken furniture, offices that resemble a Cecil B.

DeMille crowd scene, and security measures reminiscent of prisons.

In fact, the portrayal of American public schools, particularly urban schools, by both the news media and popular film-makers has contributed to a misunderstanding of what goes on in public schools. The result of media influence on our thinking is that we—teachers, students, and parents—have, just like the general public, begun to expect that violence will occur in schools. Like the media, we have begun to exaggerate what we see and hear and to give credence to gossip and rumor.

> *In a climate of fear, teachers are more likely to see students who are uninterested, uncooperative, or disrespectful as posing a potential physical threat and, consequently, are unlikely to see promise in those students.*

This is not to suggest that school violence is simply a myth. Incidents of real violence in schools are cause for serious concern. But the images presented by the media and the entertainment industry have contributed to the expectation of violence in our schools. Given these images, the public, which includes educators and students, believes that urban public schools are places where anything terrible can, and probably will, happen.

In a climate of fear, as pointed out by *U.S. News and World Report*, people's concern that they might be victimized will make them "more likely to interpret others' intentions as threatening and to respond aggressively." Among students, the fear and aggression are often played out in fights, but among teachers and students, they usually get played out in more subtle ways.

In a climate of fear, teachers are more likely to see students who are uninterested, uncooperative, or disrespectful as posing a potential physical threat and, consequently, are unlikely to see promise in those students. Preoccupied with the fear of violence, most teachers will seek a disciplinary solution to the perceived problem, which only compounds mutual feelings of mistrust and dislike. Rarely, in a climate of fear, will embattled teachers make the effort to examine the problem from an academic perspective, reflecting on the possibility that their own teaching methods, personal style, or the curriculum may need adjustment and change to help students become interested, cooperative, and, occasionally, more respectful.

Perhaps the greatest damage the negative focus on schools has done is to cause people to see schools as places that are the source of violence, rather than as places that reflect the violence of society as a whole. It is unfair and unproductive to single schools out as violent places while educators and students remain at the mercy of political leaders who refuse to place school problems within the larger societal context and who, consequently, refuse to accept responsibility for voting in the types of social reforms and programs that might help curb violence overall.

The cost of such a social agenda would necessitate not only more taxes, but also that everyone assume some responsibility for what has happened in American society—either by voting new taxes, paying those taxes, or taking advantage of the programs themselves. It is easier, especially given the current climate in which almost no one accepts responsibility for anything, even their own behavior, to find a scapegoat for society's ills, and the media and entertainment industry have made urban public schools just that.

When an institution is seen as a violent place, those both inside and outside the institution will act and react to everything that happens there within that frame of reference. Containing potential violence demands strict discipline, unquestioning obedience to authority, and mindless conformity.

When seen as violent institutions, schools become places where the emphasis is on control and punishment rather than on academics and achievement, and educators are, as a result, relieved of the responsibility of finding ways to make schools and education inviting to youth. When students view schools as prisons and teachers and administrators as guards and wardens, they will begin to behave more like prisoners than like students, and violence in schools will become its own self-fulfilling prophecy.

Sound the P.R. Retreat[5]

BY FRED MCKISSACK
THE PROGRESSIVE, JULY 1999

On the same morning a Georgia sophomore shot six of his fellow students, the Senate approved a bill calling for background checks on gun buyers at pawn shops and gun shows and the use of safety devices on guns. "We are all just elated over this victory," declared Vice President Al Gore, who cast the tiebreaking vote. "Finally, the majority is turning the corner and helping to protect the children and families of this country."

The bill is a good thing. It's forward thinking. And yet, neither Congress, nor the gun advocates who lobby there, nor the much-maligned entertainment industry, nor for that matter, the media seem very interested in a deep analysis of what drives teenagers to shoot their classmates. Instead, we have relentless, almost nauseating coverage of the weeping friends and family members of the deceased, plus a lot of glib talk about our violent culture that doesn't lead us anywhere. Forget about Marilyn Manson-the endless media coverage of the mass grieving over the school shootings in Littleton, Colorado, may have contributed more to the shooting by that fifteen-year-old Georgia boy. After carrying out his copycat crime, he put a gun in his mouth, but minutes later, he laid down his weapons and began to cry. A witness heard the boy say, "Oh, my God! I'm so scared, I'm so scared."

Clearly, he can't explain what he was doing. Can we?

The response to the school shootings has been pretty thin. Schools reacted by sending home kids who wear black trench coats or other "menacing" clothes. And purveyors of violent entertainment—Hollywood as well as gun manufacturers were quick to embrace a similarly superficial fix.

Take two articles in *The Wall Street Journal* that appeared the same day as the Georgia shooting but dealt with the aftermath of Littleton, Colorado. Both stories show why it's so hard to find honest debate on difficult issues. GUN INDUSTRY CANCELS ADS, CITING CON-

---

CERNS OVER TIMING was the headline on the far-right column of the B section of the *Journal*. Apparently, six weeks into a new ad campaign, the National Shooting Sports Foundation (NSSF) pulled the plug. The ads, which appeared in upscale publications such as *The Atlantic Monthly* and *The New York Times Book Review*, were canceled because the organization's leaders didn't want to offend anyone after the Columbine shooting.

"We decided the campaign would be seen as inappropriate and insensitive at this time," Robert Delfay, the group's head, told the *Journal*. THE VERY FACT THAT IT CAN BE DANGEROUS IS WHAT MAKES IT SAFE is the headline for one of the ads. "Since the first cave man threw a

> *The problem is too much P.R. The public relations mindset stifles meaningful discussion—in this case, the merits of sport shooting.*

stone," the ad says, "the challenge of hitting a target has been part of human nature." The ads were created by P.R. giant Porter Novelli, which had spent just a half million of a three year, $3 million educational campaign. And this is where things get a bit strained. *The Wall Street Journal* reports that Delfay was told by Porter Novelli executives that because of the shooting, gun advocacy couldn't be done at this time—so "they suggested we table the whole thing."

This is why teenagers don't trust adults. Why should the NSSF—which is far less strident than the National Rifle Association—feels the need to retreat from its position in the face of adversity? Unless the organization doesn't believe its own rhetoric, which is quite possible if you've ever read Christopher Buckley's book *Thank You for Smoking* (HarperPerennial, 1995).

The problem is too much P.R. The public relations mindset stifles meaningful discussion—in this case, the merits of sport shooting. Porter Novelli, which has represented anti-tobacco groups in the past, says that given the current environment, "we do not see a constructive role for an NSSF educational-advertising program as originally intended." Well. What the hell does that mean? This is the perfect time to make their case, unless they don't believe the argument is sound. If Porter Novelli's reasoning for pulling the ads were to be fully extended, then crime conditions in urban areas would mean that the NSSF's campaign should never have seen the light of day. But these ads were not going to be seen in *Jet* or *Ebony* or *The Source* or on billboards in the 'hood. It's only after gun violence comes to the suburbs that we see the gun advocates scurrying to soft-pedal their message—and Congress bestirring itself.

The after-effects of the shooting have television executives running for cover, as well. As with the NSSF, the smell of fear at CBS is tinged with bullshit. Just below the NSSF article in *The Wall Street Journal* is a story entitled CBS SHELVES FALL MOB SERIES AS TOO VIOLENT. The Mob? Violent? Say it ain't say so.

> *It's only after gun violence comes to the suburbs that we see the gun advocates scurrying to soft-pedal their message—and Congress bestirring itself.*

"CBS said last month's shooting at Columbine High School prompted it to shelve the *Falcone* series, at least for now," writes Kyle Pope of the *Journal.* "'It's not the right time to have people being whacked on the streets of New York,' said CBS Television President Leslie Moonves."

Moonves is considered one of the smartest people in Hollywood, and he has made CBS a better network, raising the bar for all news magazines with *60 Minutes.* But his motives for not showing *Falcone,* a show about an undercover FBI agent, seem worse than disingenuous. When is it the right time to have people whacked on the streets of New York? Moonves said that he and other executives viewed the pilot days after the Columbine shooting and decided that the show, in its current form, would not make it on the schedule. One wonders if the shooting had not occurred whether the producers of the show would have been able to make a more persuasive case for airing the series.

Instead of spurring a serious self-examination on the part of the entertainment industry and the gun lobby, Columbine just prompted a P.R. retreat. And many commentators badly overreached by lumping shoot-'em-all-up video games like Quake with thoughtful, albeit violent, television such as HBO's *The Sopranos.*

The tragedy of Columbine is that fourteen kids died in an act of violence so alien to the rest of society that it almost defies reason. Yet we've compounded the tragedy with reactionary measures and rhetoric. Despite the very public grieving period after Columbine, we find ourselves wondering why teenagers seem to be in more pain today than ever before.

V.
Violence and Crime in Higher Education

Editor's Introduction

As a result of the recent mass shootings and appalling crimes committed by adolescents and teenagers, a majority of the attention shown to school violence these past few years has been focused on middle and high schools. There is, however, an area of education still heavily affected by violence and crime that remains quietly on the sidelines. For several years now, colleges and universities have been struggling with crime and more specifically, crime reports, as they attempt to make their campuses safe for students, faculty, and staff. Still, despite requests by students and parents for more public access to crime statistics, university officials are concerned about alarming potential students with graphic facts and figures. In this last section of *School Violence*, the issue of violence in higher education is addressed, including the secrecy and suppression of crime statistics, underreporting of incidents, effectiveness of the campus court system, and the effort to eradicate violent fraternity hazing on campus.

The first article here, by Timothy Quinnan for the *Chronicle of Higher Education*, sets the tone for the section by describing how high school violence is not the only concern of educators and parents. Quinnan acknowledges that although college campuses give the impression of scholarly serenity separate from society's ills, they are, in fact, no more immune to violence and crime than any other institution of learning. The author speaks of his own experiences with possibly troubled students and details ways to curb violence on campus.

Next, Debbie Goldberg looks at crime rates on college campuses in her article "Crime on Campus: How Safe are Students?" The writer evaluates a variety of statistics and investigates the nature of college crimes, a majority of which go unreported by students. In this article, Goldberg also looks at the role of student responsibility and perception of when a "crime" has actually occurred.

In an article for the *New Republic*, Robyn Gearey explores the issue of making college crime statistics public. The writer looks at the tendency for schools to underreport crimes, and the ways in which watchdog groups are attempting to enforce public access to university crime statistics. According to the article, two Congressional acts are pulling schools in different directions. The 1990 Student Right-to-Know and Campus Security Act (CSA) requires schools to compile statistics and distribute them to students, faculty and staff, as well as to prospective students. The 1974 Family Educational Rights and Privacy Act (FERPA), however, stipulates that schools receiving federal funding must not release a student's educational record without his or her permission. Some schools have interpreted this latter act as extending to students' disciplinary records, including criminal acts. Gearey looks at specific schools that have come under fire in this debate, university discouragement of reporting crimes to the police, and potential legislation that would resolve the conflict between the criminal reports and privacy laws.

"Crime on Campus: What Colleges Won't Tell You" by Paul McMasters is the next piece in this portion of the book. The author comments on the 1999 Student Press Law Center's report on the availability of crime statistics from university officials. McMasters asserts that, in addition to students and prospective students, journalists must also have access to crime reports, although many are still hesitant to readily provide facts and figures. The article looks at the movement to have more accurate crime reports made public and examines recent legislation and regulations being enforced to make such information available to students.

In the next article, Dana Hawkins examines the college criminal justice system, questioning whether university tribunals are able to handle violent crime. "Is There Any Justice in Campus Courts?", written for *U.S. News & World Report*, looks at three central areas of the college court system that concern students: the mishandling of evidence by untrained campus police, the inability to invoke severe punishments upon assailants, and the absence of due process in campus court proceedings. Furthermore, Hawkins explains the history of college tribunals and addresses current attempts to revamp the process.

In the last article in this section, "Efforts to End Fraternity Hazing Have Largely Failed, Critics Charge," Ben Gose investigates the well-known problem of college hazing. While fraternity hazing has a long and dubious tradition as a part of campus life, college officials are witnessing more and more violent, and in some instances even deadly, cases of juvenile pranks gone horribly wrong. Gose looks at specific incidents where fraternity hazing turned violent and examines the effects of anti-hazing laws. He also explores the issues of liability which many fraternities and other organizations face when they are implicated in dangerous hazing practices.

Preparing for the Moment When a Student's Rage Turns to Violence[1]

BY TIMOTHY QUINNAN
THE CHRONICLE OF HIGHER EDUCATION, AUGUST 13, 1999

High schools are not the only educational institutions in which violence can occur. Recent events at Littleton, Colo., and elsewhere may provide a preview of what looms on the horizon for higher education.

In the wake of the killings at Columbine High School, everyone seems to have a theory about why adolescents today act out their aggressive impulses in so deadly a manner. Some people blame the darker dimensions popular culture, such as violent video games and movies, "gangsta" rap music, and misanthropic World-Wide Web sites and chat rooms. If our culture's endorsement of violence is a contributing factor to young people's aggression, college students are probably no better equipped to resist it than high-school students are.

Whatever the cause of violence, colleges and universities are not prepared for its eruption on their campuses. A *laissez-faire* attitude permeates academic life: no parents, few rules, little monitoring, a great deal of individual freedom. Unfortunately, it's precisely that attitude that leads us into danger.

Our vision is skewed toward the utopian. We see campuses as islands largely untouched by the social ills outside, as the safest and sanest of all public spaces. Of course, the security officers we employ report a smattering of relatively minor crimes, such as vandalism or theft, but no one worries too much about those. Even crimes such as sexual assault don't happen very often on our campuses, and many of them are not reported, because of the stigma attached to the victim. That apparently idyllic environment lulls us into feeling immune from the kind of premeditated violence that now occurs all too frequently in secondary schools.

---

1. Copyright © 1999 *The Chronicle of Higher Education*. Reprinted with permission.

In the rare cases when college students do shoot their peers or teachers, we quickly look for signs that the killers are mentally or physically ill. We can't imagine that the next carnage will be perpetrated by someone similar to the Columbine killers: volatile and unpopular, perhaps, but functional, by most accounts. It may well be a student who seems quiet and normal who blows up, pushed over the edge and into infamy by something we haven't recognized.

As a student-affairs dean, I often see students who come

> *In the rare cases when college students do shoot their peers or teachers, we quickly look for signs that the killers are mentally or physically ill. We can't imagine that the next carnage will be perpetrated by someone . . . [who is] functional, by most accounts.*

to lodge complaints about their peers or to reply to charges of misconduct made against them. Most of the cases are misdemeanors—one student protests an unfair accusation of plagiarism another files a complaint against a class mate who won't stop talking during lectures and is infringing on her right to learn. We resolve most such cases in fairly short order.

However, about 5 percent of the cases I deal with leave me wondering, and a little anxious. A disgruntled student with smoldering eyes tells me there is no way he'll accept the grade he just got, and if the teacher refuses to alter it, the student is "going to go postal." Another student, referred to me by a professor for hurling insults at a peer during class, tells me that she's going to "get" her antagonist for stealing her boyfriend, and mentions that she has a gun at home.

Ten years ago, I would have counseled such students not to use reckless speech for fear that it would be taken seriously. At the end of the day, however, I would have closed their files and gone home a carefree man, sure that they didn't truly intend to hurt anyone.

Things have changed. Now, when I talk with such students, their words convey a wrath so menacing that it trips an alarm in my head. One of these days, I fear, a student like that will end up doing what he or she threatens.

What has changed is the degree of anger behind the students' statements. Instead of voicing dissatisfaction over an issue, students are making extreme threats against other human beings. Through my counseling sessions, I've watched the hostility intensify over the years. Perhaps part of it does come from a popular culture that devalues life. Causes are elusive. Yet given recent events, my apprehension seems justified.

If you think I'm overreacting, recall the case of the graduate student at Wayne State University in 1998. Distraught over a grade he had received on a final exam in an engineering course, he brought a rifle to a classroom where the professor who had given him the grade was teaching. In front of the entire class, he shot the instructor to

College campuses may seem like peaceful oases, but they are more similar to tension-filled high schools than we want to admit.

death. When I read about the murder, the thought that it might herald a new era of violence in higher education crossed my mind. Combined with what I've been detecting in my own work with students, the thought still worries me.

More troubling is how unprepared most colleges and universities are to deal with outbreaks of violence. It's common now for U.S. high schools to have a security guard or two. Many have video surveillance systems that monitor areas where students gather. Some schools require students to pass through metal detectors each morning as they arrive.

How do universities compare? Except in areas where sensitive research is conducted or expensive equipment is stored, we seldom use security devices. We settle for parking-lot patrols, or escorts for students going to their cars after night classes. We teach sexual-assault prevention in residence halls and counsel against the pitfalls of substance abuse. Anything more would upset the pleasant climate of the campus and our faith in its sanctity.

I am not necessarily arguing for introducing more-extensive security measures. Like my colleagues, I enjoy the tranquility of academic life and have no desire to turn my campus into a fortress. But students and faculty and staff members should be wary. College campuses may seem like peaceful oases, but they are more similar to tension-filled high schools than we want to admit. We can't afford not to notice what is happening in the schools around us.

Some universities, such as the Massachusetts Institute of Technology, have created "threat teams" to assess and handle potentially dangerous cases. Other institutions, like mine, seem to worry more about trampling on students' privacy rights or fostering an atmosphere of suspicion that hinders trust and collaboration. Those concerns are legitimate, but they shouldn't mean that we do nothing.

To help curb the potential for violence on campus, we should:

• Educate new students early. Beginning with freshman orientation, we need to teach incoming students about our institution's expectations for behavior. Members of the student-affairs and security staffs should lead small groups of new students in discussions about what is and is not acceptable conduct.

• Publicize the student code of conduct, especially the sections dealing with menacing behavior. The code should clearly state that threatening words and actions are prohibited, and should specify the consequences for violations.

• Follow a zero-tolerance policy. Assuming due-process procedures are followed, administrators should apply the appropriate penalties whenever students threaten others or use violence.

• Take every threat seriously. Students and faculty members need to tell college officials when someone threatens another person. Administrators have an obligation to follow up on such reports.

Given what we've witnessed in high schools, we must be careful. The price of ignoring a threat might be someone's life.

Crime on Campus: How Safe are Students?[2]

By Debbie Goldberg
Washington Post, April 6, 1997

In the fall of 1994, just weeks after starting her freshman year at Virginia Polytechnic Institute and State University, Christy Brzonkala claims she was raped by two student-athletes in a dormitory room. After getting no relief from the university's judicial system, which exonerated one of the football players and later rescinded on appeal its suspension of the other, Brzonkala now is pursuing a civil claim in federal court against the university for violating her rights.

At Rice University in Houston, four students were abducted from a campus parking lot at gunpoint two years ago, driven to a nearby bank teller machine, and one was sexually assaulted. At the University of Pennsylvania this fall, a rash of robberies, culminating in the shooting of one student and the stabbing death of a campus researcher, had students and some parents up in arms about the safety of the West Philadelphia campus and its surrounding community.

And it's certainly not only urban campuses such as Rice and Penn that are struggling with violent crime. Howard and Connie Clery were the driving force behind enactment of a federal campus security law after their daughter, Jeanne, in 1986 was brutally raped and murdered by another student who broke into her dormitory room on the seemingly bucolic campus of Lehigh University in Bethlehem, Pa.

Are colleges safe, idyllic havens of higher learning removed from their communities' crime problems, or are they rife with crime fueled in part by student naivete and opportunity?

The answer is that it depends on whom you listen to. According to Alan Lizotte, executive director of the Consortium for Higher Education Campus Crime Research at the State University of New York's Albany campus, crime on

---

campus is "pretty rare, only about one-tenth of the crime rate in the communities" in which the campuses reside.

These findings are echoed by a recent U.S. Education Department report that found, for 1994, a violent crime rate of 65 per 1,000 students on college campuses, compared with a rate of 7.1 per 1,000 people in the general population. (Violent crimes include murders, forcible sex offenses, robbery and aggravated assault.)

On the other hand, Bonnie Fisher, a University of Cincinnati political science professor, found in recent surveys that college students are much more likely to be victims of certain crimes—rape, sexual assault and theft—than 20-to-24-year-olds in the general population.

The discrepancy in these findings stems largely from how the statistics are compiled. Lizotte's data and the Education Department study are based only on those crimes reported to law enforcement agencies. Fisher, on the other hand, went straight to the source, interviewing more than 3,700 students at 12 colleges in 1993 to get her data. When she compared crime data reported to law enforcement officials to what students were telling her, she found that more than 75 percent of crimes against students go unreported, and thus never show up in an official count.

In the case of rape, for instance, the Education Department reported a rate of .09 per 1,000 students in 1993. But Fisher, for approximately the same year, found 31 rapes and sexual assaults per 1,000 students, much higher than the 5.7 cases per 1,000 nationally in the 20-to-24-year-old age group, and far outstripping the Education Department figures. Sexual assaults, in particular, are considered to be vastly underreported by victims.

Thus it's still difficult for students and their parents to gauge how safe a college campus is, despite the 1990 Student Right-To-Know and Campus Security Act that required higher education institutions—from Ivy League universities to cosmetology schools—to annually publish crime statistics and make them available to students, employees and prospective students.

Critics charge that crimes are underreported by some campuses, amid concerns about the public relations aspect of releasing such information. Such underreporting, they say, is fueled by the secret nature of internal judicial proceedings that colleges use to deal with allegations, which often aren't reported as part of the campuses' crime statistics. Colleges "are exploiting loopholes" to keep crime statistics down, charged Daniel Carter, vice president for Security On Campus Inc., a Pennsylvania-based advocacy group started by the Clerys after their daughter's murder.

Specifically, Carter and others say some colleges thwart the intent of the law by using the 1974 Family Educational Rights and Privacy Act to keep school disciplinary records secret, even when they involve issues of crime rather than, say, plagiarism charges. The so-called Bucklay amendment was intended primarily to protect the privacy of educational and financial aid records. For instance, Christy Brzonkala says Virginia Tech failed to include the three rapes she reported in its annual crime statistics for 1994, because her charges were handled through the university's secretive judicial system.

Another controversy has centered on what constitutes a campus's boundary for crime reporting purposes, particularly at urban institutions that may have large stretches of campus that border on or intermingle with city streets. At Penn, for instance, both the student shooting and the researcher's stabbing death last fall happened in the university neighborhood, an area where many students live and frequent stores and restaurants. When the federally mandated crime statistics are compiled for 1996, however, these violent crimes won't show up on the list, because off-campus crimes against students are not part of federal reporting requirements.

Despite the criticisms about how schools handle and report crime, many college security chiefs say that the federal campus security law and increasing publicity about campus crime, have prompted many schools to beef up security and to educate students about crime prevention. After the 1994 student abductions, Rice University took steps to enhance lighting, secured the campus with a locked gate at night, and increased from 16 to 26 the number of campus officers who have full police powers, said Mary Voswinkel, campus police chief. At Penn, additional lighting was added this fall in the off-campus neighborhood bordering the school.

And the Education Department found that most campuses with safety programs improved such services in the last five years: for instance, 71 percent of the 48 percent of institutions that have added a night escort service or improved that service in the last five years.

Still, how can students and parents, not to mention employees, find out how safe their campuses are? Well, it takes a lot of work, as one parent from the Nashville area found out when he started looking into safety at the 13 institutions his college-bound daughter, Jennifer, has applied to for next fall.

The anxious father caved in to his daughter's entreaties not to contact the colleges directly; she was concerned that his inquiries about crime might affect both on her admissions and scholarship applications. (For that reason, he also asked that his name not be published in this article.) So Dad spent much of this school year accumulating whatever data he could find on campus crime, including anecdotes and reported incidents.

He perused college guidebooks to find out if any of the colleges had a reputation as a party school, which he thinks creates a more hospitable environment for crime.

... the caution and common sense that students might otherwise employ in their home towns tend to be "washed away in a flood of alcohol" once they're on campus ...

And since the family visited most of the campuses Jennifer is considering, he was able to check out the surrounding neighborhoods. Right now, he's worried that his daughter may want to attend Illinois Institute of Technology, an excellent academic choice for Jennifer the future engineer, but one in a somewhat seedy part of Chicago. "It's not a very scientific analysis," he conceded.

Statistics aside, there is general agreement that many crimes on campus are crimes of opportunity. Theft is a major problem; consider what the typical residential student now has in his or her dorm room—a computer, compact disc player, television, video cassette recorder, blender, and toaster oven, for starters.

In addition, the caution and common sense that students might otherwise employ in their home towns tend to be "washed away in a flood of alcohol" once they're on campus, noted Sheldon Steinbach, general counsel for the American Council on Education, a Washington, D.C., trade group that represents colleges and universities.

"Eighteen-year-old freshmen are naive and make good victims," agreed Lizotte. "The first line of defense against crime is yourself. You have to be sensible, and young people aren't very sensible."

Indeed, evidence indicates that much of the crime on campus is student-on-student and tends to occur in dormitories, rather than, say, a dark parking lot. The recent Education Department report found that rates for both violent and property crimes increased as the number of residential students on campus increased. "The college years are notorious for drinking, drugs and experimentation, all of which are contributing factors to crime," Fisher explained. And, she added, "we're finding hardly any practice of crime prevention."

The general lack of student responsibility is something nearly everyone agrees on. At many campuses, students routinely leave dormitory doors unlocked, toss their backpacks down on cafeteria tables while they get their food,

---

... evidence indicates that much of the crime on campus is student-on-student and tends to occur in dormitories, rather than, say, a dark parking lot.

---

and leave their wallets on a library desk when they take a bathroom break. It's no wonder that larceny is one of the most common crimes committed on college campuses.

But the stakes may be higher then a stolen portable tape player when drugs and alcohol are involved. Joanna Capozzo, a George Washington University junior, is a sorority sister who hears of "a lot of incidents where girls get really drunk at a frat party, and wake up the next morning in somebody's bed with no recollection of how they got there."

Is it rape? "A lot of them don't think it is rape," acknowledged Capozzo, who is the student association's director of security affairs. In addition to their doubts about whether such acts constitute rape, she said, "Some are afraid to come forward, or don't want to start an ordeal where they might have to transfer." For instance, after she brought charges against the two football players, Christy Brzonkala received threats and, fearful for her safety, transferred to George Mason University.

GWU has reported one rape on campus for the last three years, a figure that Capozzo, given her anecdotal evidence, thinks is low. "But," she pointed out, "that's all that's reported."

Eileen Wagner, Brzonkala's attorney, who herself was raped as a University of Virginia student some three decades ago, calls the widespread misinformation about crimes on campus a "blight on higher education." As for Brzonkala's case—which was the first civil lawsuit brought under the 1994 Violence Against Women Act, and is awaiting oral arguments before the 4th Circuit appeals court—Wagner said, "We don't have much hope of doing anything about the perpetrators, but we do have hopes of putting pressure on institutions to do the right thing."

College Cop-out: Closing the Books on Campus Crime[3]

By Robyn Gearey
The New Republic, November 10, 1997

You're a high-school senior, or maybe the parent of one, and you're weighing an application to the University of Pennsylvania. It's Ivy League all right, but it's an urban campus—right there in the heart of Philadelphia—and, well, it doesn't have the greatest reputation for safety. So you ask the school for a copy of its crime statistics. When the university obliges, you find that there were no murders, just a handful of rapes in the past three years, and a mere eighteen armed robberies in 1995. That doesn't sound quite as bad as you thought.

But it turns out the University of Pennsylvania has neglected to inform you of a few small things. Like the fact that, according to campus police logs, the number of armed robberies in 1995 was closer to two hundred. Like the fact that these statistics do not include the shooting of Patrick Leroy, a senior who was shot on one of the main walkways through campus on September 25, 1996. Why has Penn been so circumspect? Maybe because it's trying to keep up with the competition.

Schools neglect to report as many as 75 percent of the crimes committed on their campuses, according to one recent study. A handful of watchdog groups, led by the Pennsylvania-based Security on Campus (SOC), are trying to change this: in 1990, pressure from the group helped convince Congress to pass the Student Right-to-Know and Campus Security Act (CSA). The law requires schools to compile annual crime statistics from both campus police and other school officials, and then distribute the data to students and staff—as well as any prospective students or staff who request it. But based on interviews with activists, federal officials, and college administrators, it seems clear that only a small percentage of colleges are in full compliance with the law.

College officials complain, with some reason, that they face conflicting legal mandates: while CSA requires schools

---

VIOLENCE IN HIGHER EDUCATION
Recent incidents at U.S. colleges and universities

2000

In February, a young woman at Westchester Community College (Valhalla, NY) was shot by an ex-boyfriend who then killed himself in the middle of the campus.

A 19-year old sophomore was stabbed to death in her Columbia University (New York, NY) dorm room in February. The alleged murderer, an ex-boyfriend who had dropped out of Columbia, killed himself less than a day later.

1999

A young woman was assaulted and raped early one evening at Harvard University's (Cambridge, MA) admissions office in March.

Twenty-one-year-old Babaesu Bay is accused of first-degree murder after firing a stray bullet that killed Temple University (Philadelphia, PA) sophomore Stephen A. Ross Jr. in May.

A female student at the University of Houston (Houston, TX) was the victim of a dorm-room rape in September.

1998

Thirty-one-year-old Oliver Jovanovic, a Columbia University graduate student, was convicted in April of kidnapping, sexually abusing, and assaulting a Barnard College student. In December 1999, after he had served 20 months in prison, the verdict was overturned.

In August a 25-year-old man who had just been fatally shot intruded upon and collapsed in front of a group of students during freshman orientation at Edward Waters College in Jacksonville, Fla.

At the University of Houston, student Dung Van Ha was fatally shot by members of an Asian gang in August.

In November at Chicago's University of Illinois, a 19-year-old student was raped just before 8:00 a.m. as she waited for her classroom door to be unlocked.

In December, Yale University (New Haven, CT) senior Suzanne Jovin, a volunteer who helped the mentally retarded, was fatally stabbed on campus while walking alone one evening.

During a robbery at his apartment on New Year's Eve, a 26-year-old student at Shaw University in Raleigh, N.C., was shot and killed by two masked intruders.

1997

Irma Malloy, dean of education at Texas Southern University in Houston, was shot and killed by 22-year-old Calvin Magee when she screamed during an attempted carjacking perpetrated by Magee and two other men at a Kentucky Fried Chicken drive-through. Magee subsequently received the death penalty.

In November 22-year-old carjacking victim James McCormack of the University of Pennsylvania was shot and wounded for refusing to surrender his keys.

1996

Atlanta's Morehouse College, along with other schools in the city's University Center, became so crime-ridden that police closed a block and a half of the local business district to street traffic.

During a robbery in the fall, a University of Pennsylvania (Philadelphia, PA) senior was shot and wounded.

Biochemist Vladimir Sled was murdered at the University of Pennsylvania during a robbery on Halloween.

1994

In September, while strolling on campus, a student at LeMoyne-Owen College in Tennessee was wounded in the shoulder by a stray bullet fired during a robbery attempt.

to make information about crime public, there is also the 1974 Family Educational Rights and Privacy Act (FERPA), which prevents schools receiving federal funding from releasing a student's educational record without his permission. Many college officials have interpreted that to extend to records of disciplinary proceedings concerning alleged crimes committed on campus. But two state supreme courts have ruled—quite rightly—that FERPA's privacy provisions don't preclude reporting anonymous statistics. And it's hard to believe the colleges have only the students' interests at heart when they fail to meet even the less controversial demands of the law. A 1996 study conducted by University of Cincinnati professor Bonnie Fisher and her colleague Chunmeng Lu found that just 37 percent of the 785 schools surveyed complied with the unambiguous requirement that crime statistics be made available to prospective students.

Recently the Department of Education has investigated a handful of schools accused of not complying with the law. According to the Department, Moorhead University, a Minnesota school with over 6,000 students, underestimated its annual crime rate and underreported illegal incidents at fraternities. After some back-and-forth between the school and the government, federal officials reexamined Moorhead's compliance several months later. Again, the university failed to pass muster: "We believe that the institution has not demonstrated a serious commitment to its obligations under the Campus Security Act and has discounted the seriousness of the issues raised by this office."

Soon the Education Department cited other schools: Virginia Tech had neither "accurately compiled" nor "accurately disclosed" crimes at its Blacksburg, Virginia, campus; in particular, the school had not disclosed an alleged rape in September 1994. Miami University of Ohio was cited for violating six separate CSA provisions: it had "fail[ed] to properly gather the required crime statistics from all pertinent sources," and its office of judicial affairs was not reporting crimes "as a general policy."

The University of Pennsylvania is one of two schools that remain under scrutiny (the other is Clemson University in South Carolina) and it's not hard to see why. According to *The Philadelphia Inquirer,* the school routinely fails to report crimes that occur on the streets and sidewalks connecting campus buildings as well as on property the school leases to businesses. For example, there are the discrepancies, reported by the *Inquirer*, between university police records on robberies and Penn's 1995 crime report. And then there is the fact that Penn excluded the shooting of Patrick Leroy from its report the following year. The university's explanation for the omission: technically speaking, the shooting was on a public walkway that traverses the campus.

Penn is also awaiting another judgment: the *Daily Pennsylvanian* newspaper reports that a former student is suing the school on grounds that university officials neither reported nor acted on a rape charge she filed with a university police officer in November 1994. The plaintiff claims that she was dissuaded from filing criminal charges because the university assured her it would handle the matter. According to the article, the university claims the rape never occurred, despite a statement from the officer at the time that a sexual assault complaint had been made.

One can certainly sympathize with college officials struggling to balance the requirement to release crime figures and the need to protect student privacy. Indeed, representatives from the colleges under investigation counter the Education Department's charges by saying that the reporting requirements are ambiguous. For example, CSA does not explicitly say that crimes committed on public roads or walkways need to be reported—even if those paths are heavily traveled by students and within campus boundaries. And many college officials also realize that violating a student's right to privacy invites lawsuits.

But one reason to question the colleges' explanations is that many institutions actively discourage victims from reporting crimes—even to campus police. A 1992 survey of campus police and security personnel conducted by William Whitman, director of the Campus Safety and Security Institute, found that "students who were victims of reportable violent crimes" were encouraged "not to report the crimes to campus police/security. If the attacker was another student, they encouraged the victim to use the campus judicial system"—where, of course, it's easier to keep things quiet. Sheldon Steinbach, vice president and general counsel for the American Council on Education (ACE), denies that schools would do that, but Whitman reported that "several [college] Directors of Secu-

> *CSA [Campus Security Act] does not explicitly say that crimes committed on public roads or walkways need to be reported—even if those paths are heavily traveled by students and within campus boundaries.*

rity were told they could look for a new job if they ever revealed the institution's true statistics." The Education Department hasn't always helped matters, either. According to a March General Accounting Office report, "the Department has been slow to monitor compliance" with CSA and was over a year late in submitting a required report on campus crime to Congress. More seriously, GAO charged that, although the Department and independent auditors had identified violations at sixty-three colleges since the law's enactment, the Department failed to impose sanctions against any of the violators.

The Education Department blames these failures on a confusion over reporting requirements and difficulties getting complete data from colleges. However, Department officials have also contributed to the general confusion over what colleges are required to do under CSA. In April of 1994, the Department ruled that privacy laws should not prevent schools from releasing statistics of how many crimes occurred, so long as those statistics did not include names or other identifying details. Then, this July, the Ohio supreme court issued a broad ruling that disciplinary records do not qualify as educational records—and, thus, cannot be kept confidential. You'd think the Education Department would applaud such a ruling. Not so. Apparently alarmed that a state court had made too sweeping a rejection of the privacy provisions in FERPA, an Education Department official sent a letter to several colleges in Ohio, criticizing the court's ruling. Whatever the intent of that letter, the effect was to give colleges added credibility in their claim that FERPA laws trump crime reporting laws.

Congress may soon step in to rectify what the universities and the Department of Education have not. The reason has a lot to do with Ben Clery and his parents, Howard and Connie, who, in 1987, founded Security on Campus after Ben's sister Jeanne was beaten, raped, and murdered in her dorm room at Lehigh University. Through its sponsorship of the CSA, the group has almost single-handedly forced the issue of campus crime into the spotlight. Before CSA was passed, most colleges did not compile crime statistics at all: fewer than 5 percent submitted information to the FBI's voluntary crime reporting program.

Because many colleges still seem to be shirking their reporting responsibilities, Security on Campus is now promoting another measure: the Accuracy in Campus Crime

Campus Crimes Reported To The FBI's Uniform Crime Reporting (UCR) Program 1997-1998*

Incidents	1998	1997	1-Year Change
Murder	3	8	+166.7%
Rape	361	402	+11.4%
Robbery	604	535	-11.4%
Aggravated Assault	1,546	1,588	+2.7%
Violent Crime Total	2,514	2,533	+0.8%
Property Crimes**	101,272	96,221	-5.0%
Total	103,789	98,754	-4.8%

*Approximately 500 colleges and universities voluntarily participate in the UCR program, this represents slightly more than 10% of all schools
**Includes burglary, larceny-theft, motor vehicle theft, and arson

Reporting Act (ACCRA), introduced this February in the House by Tennessee Republican John Duncan. In theory, ACCRA would clear up any lingering confusion over just what CSA covers. ACCRA would say explicitly which campus officials must document criminal incidents for inclusion in the CSA-required annual report. It also would require that colleges submit these statistics to the Education Department, which would make them available to the public. The bill's more controversial provisions would require colleges to maintain open crime logs and to make campus judicial hearings open to the public. And, for the first time, violations of the law would provoke mandatory sanctions: at least 1 percent of the school's federal funding per violation.

Congress held preliminary hearings on the proposal in July, in conjunction with the reauthorization of the Higher

Education Act, and more hearings are scheduled for later
this month. But while the bill has fifty-nine co-sponsors in
the House, it has a formidable opponent in ACE, which
represents some 3,600 postsecondary schools. "Some [of the
law's proposals] are highly destructive," says ACE's Steinbach. Especially in hard-to-prosecute sexual assault cases,
he argues, a campus court may be the only recourse available—and many victims even prefer it. "Students often
want the judicial procedure because it's a confidential setting," says Steinbach, who is similarly troubled by the
open-court requirement: "Imagine this," Steinbach says
ominously, "you're alleging a rape and all the guy's frat
brothers show up at the hearing. How willing are people
going to be to testify if they're intimidated?"

On the issue of reporting crime, Steinbach is equally
skeptical. These officials "aren't trained in how to determine what is a crime." Furthermore, he points out, "Some
students may want to talk to someone [about an incident]
but not report it. This could discourage students from seeking counseling" and, in cases where a crime is only
reported to a school counselor, "threaten the doctor-patient
relationship."

ACE has been lobbying hard against the bill, as have
such smaller groups as the National Association of Student
Personnel Administrators. In a four-page letter to
ACCRA's sponsor, several of the measure's opponents
wrote, "We are concerned that [ACCRA] may not provide
the most effective solution" to campus crime problems. The
bill's reporting requirements, the letter said, would have a
"chilling effect on victims" and be "unduly burdensome" for
college authorities. Having the Education Department act
as a central repository for annual crime reports is "a waste
of taxpayer money"; and opening records of criminal activity "will have a devastating impact" on accused students.

Concern over the proposal to open campus disciplinary
proceedings to the public may be plausible, but opposition
to the reporting of anonymous statistics seems pretty inde-
fensible. Students and parents have a right to know how
prevalent crime on campus is. Several courts have said so,
as has Congress. Steinbach scoffs that "Security on Campus is obsessed with reporting as if reporting is a panacea
for campus crime." But the disclosure laws are not about
reducing crime—they're about making educated choices
more effective. You'd think that's a goal universities and
colleges would support.

Crime on Campus: What Colleges Won't Tell You[4]

BY PAUL MCMASTERS
FREEDOM FORUM, AUGUST 23, 1999

In the next few weeks, 10.4 million students will be settling in on the nation's college and university campuses. They look forward to learning, maturing, perhaps partying a little. Some will be more prepared than others for this academic adventure, but very few will be prepared for the amount and nature of crime they will encounter on those campuses.

They won't be prepared because college officials and policies make it difficult, if not impossible, to find out about crime on campus and how it's handled.

For years, colleges have routinely denied students, the public and the press access to information about campus crime and disciplinary actions. In addition, procedures originally developed to handle cases involving academic cheating and related matters has evolved into a full-blown judicial system that also deals with violent crimes such as rape, robbery, assault, weapons possession and drug-dealing.

Campus police operate independently of the regular police and seldom have the resources or expertise to investigate violent crimes fully. The campus courts don't have anything to do with the regular courts, either. They operate in secret, scorn due process, flout accountability, and dispense a peculiar sort of justice where the harshest penalty is expulsion no matter what the crime.

This system seldom serves the victims of crime, those accused of crime, the campus community, prospective students, alumni, or the larger community that pays the bills, directly or indirectly. So the question becomes: Who or what does it serve?

Last week, the Student Press Law Center reported the results of its audit of just how forthcoming college officials are about crime on campus. Staff members at the center recently visited six colleges, public and private, in Maryland, Virginia and the District of Columbia. They went to

---

4. Copyright © 1999 *Freedom Forum.* Reprinted with permission.

campus police departments and judicial affairs offices in search of crime statistics, police logs and the outcomes of student disciplinary proceedings—all clearly releasable information under current law.

The center reported that although some of the colleges visited were more helpful than others, compliance was inconsistent at best. Just finding the proper office and people to ask was difficult. Officials in some cases demanded to know who wanted to know and for what purpose the information was wanted. And when records were provided, they often were less than helpful in determining the full story of criminal incidents and disciplinary actions taken against those who committed them.

Only in recent years have lawsuits and legislation begun to hold colleges and universities to a higher standard of access and accountability when it comes to crime on campus.

Only in recent years have lawsuits and legislation begun to hold colleges and universities to a higher standard of access and accountability when it comes to crime on campus. But those advances more often than not have been two steps forward, then one step back as college administrators lobby against proposed legislation, try to loosen the requirements when the regulations are written, and ignore or misinterpret the law when it's implemented.

An assortment of individuals and organizations have chipped away at college secrecy policies. One of the more significant events was a federal court lawsuit filed by Traci Bauer, editor of the student newspaper at Southwest Missouri State University; in 1991, the court ruled decisively in her case that campus crime reports must be open to the public and press.

Because of the work of individuals like Bauer and groups like the Student Press Law Center, the Society of Professional Journalists, Security on Campus and the Campus Courts Task Force, access to campus crime reports was secured. Then the battle shifted to legislation requiring colleges and universities to report meaningful crime statistics. After favorable legislation was achieved there, efforts were directed toward opening up campus disciplinary records.

The most recent federal legislation is the Higher Education Act of 1998. It requires colleges and universities to maintain for public inspection logs that note crimes within two days of their reporting. It requires them to publish information about crimes in off-campus areas frequented by students. It requires more-extensive reporting of hate crimes, arson and homicide. And it allows colleges and universities to release the final results of disciplinary proceedings against students accused of crimes.

But lobbyists and lawyers for the college administrators managed to get important elements of the law as passed by Congress written out or watered down in the drafting of the implementing regulations.

For example, the regulations as drafted "will almost certainly impede Congress's intent to make key student disciplinary records publicly available," writes Bruce Brown, counsel for the Society of Professional Journalists. In a letter filed as part of the public-comment process, Brown urged Education Department officials to restore to the draft of the rules the term "nonforcible sex offenses" that Congress had expressly written into the law so that information on date rapes would be disclosed.

Further, Brown notes that the draft creates huge loopholes by not meaningfully defining categories to be reported. Without those broad definitions, said Brown, "university officials could believe that they are restricted by the law to releasing no more than a one-sentence record stating that 'John Doe was suspended for one semester for disorderly behavior.'"

And so it goes.

Over the years, college officials have developed elaborate rationales for their reluctance to provide even basic information about crime on campus. They say they want to protect student privacy, but don't explain why privacy should trump safety. They say that it costs too much to maintain and keep reports, but don't mention the millions they spend on fighting disclosure requirements. They say their hands are tied by the law, but don't mention the fact that it was a law they put in place.

Such arguments reflect an attitude among some college administrators that seems to be less about preventing crime than protecting reputations, less about dispensing justice than guarding secrets, less about protecting the safety of innocent students than the privacy of guilty ones.

Until that attitude changes, too many of those millions of college students across the land will have to learn about campus crime the hard way.

Is There Any Justice in Campus Courts?[5]

Critics say secretive university tribunals are not equipped to deal with violent crime

By Dana Hawkins
U.S. News & World Report, November 5, 1999

Up until the moment she got the phone call from the university official, Joanie Giuliani was convinced that the campus court would decide in her favor. A few weeks earlier, the Michigan Technological University junior had filed rape charges against another student through the school's judicial system. University officials had advised her to let them handle the case and had assured her, she says, that her alleged attacker, an athlete, would be punished. But when the phone rang, the official read her a letter stating there was not enough evidence to prosecute. "They give you the impression it's all going to go your way so you'll try it through their system," says Giuliani. "But all they really care about is protecting their reputation, and the athletes who bring in money for the school."

Campus tribunals, which exist in some form at nearly every university in the nation, have stepped beyond adjudicating charges of cheating and plagiarism and are now commonly investigating rapes, assaults, and other serious crimes. Advocates of the judicial boards say they provide students with swift, private resolutions and offer an alternate route to justice for victims of date rape and other assaults whose cases might not meet the "beyond a reasonable doubt" standard of guilt required by criminal courts.

But a growing number of critics say the university judicial system suffers from three basic flaws. First, campus police, often untrained in the techniques of criminal investigations, frequently mishandle evidence and witness interviews. This can compromise a victim's chances for justice in the criminal courts. Second, the harshest sentence the tribunals can impose is expulsion, which is too mild a punishment for violent crimes. Third, the protections granted in a court of law, collectively known as due pro-

---

cess, frequently are absent from university proceedings. As a result, both victims and suspects often come away from a campus trial unsatisfied. "The system is not at all equipped to deal with serious crimes," says S. Daniel Carter, vice president of Security on Campus Inc., based in King of Prussia, Pa.

Beyond Honor Codes

College tribunals primarily enforced academic honor codes until the 1960s and 1970s, when they began accepting cases dealing with underage drinking and other types of youthful misbehavior. It wasn't until the early 1980s—when the college courts began to handle more serious crimes—that they came under scrutiny. Edward Golden, the assistant dean of students at the University of Virginia, conducted a study in 1980 of disciplinary procedures at 58 institutions that showed that many were ignoring due process. He found that 36 percent did not allow cross-examination during proceedings, 55 percent did not guarantee the student an impartial judge or jury, 60 percent did not guarantee students the right to confront their accusers, and 91 percent did not compel witnesses to an alleged crime to testify.

And the courts have not improved in the past decade, say Harvey Silverglate and Alan Charles Kors, authors of the recently published *Shadow University: The Betrayal of Liberty on America's Campuses.* The two spent eight years studying the judicial systems of several hundred American universities. "None of them had a procedure that by any stretch of the imagination could be called fair," says Silverglate. He and Kors found schools where students are even forbidden from discussing their own case publicly. Other campus tribunals bar attorneys, even though a student's testimony can be used later in a criminal trial.

Donald Gehring, the founder and past president of the Association for Student Judicial Affairs, supports college courts. He says they make campuses safer places by swiftly and privately meting out justice in sensitive cases such as date rape, which victims might not otherwise pursue. Gehring contends the courts meet their dual goals of protecting students while educating campus communities. "Even in cases involving violent acts," he says, "suspending someone can be educational."

Law enforcement officials say they increasingly find themselves at odds with university officials over the reach of campus courts. The county prosecutor's criminal division in Dayton, Ohio, is embroiled in a dispute with the University of Dayton about whether campus police and officials should report difficult-to-prove claims of date rape to the prosecutor's office. An Ohio prosecutor familiar with the situation says local law enforcement—not campus police and administrators—should be evaluating whether there is sufficient evidence to prosecute a claim. In some cases, campus officials may be too quick to dismiss a claim as unprovable. The Dayton campus police say they haven't always reported allegations when the victims chose not to file suit. "The philosophy and policy here is the victim drives the car," says John Delamer, the director of public safety at UD.

Under Wraps

University court opponents point out that with prospective students and their parents concerned about crime on campus, schools have an incentive to handle cases internally. Although universities are required by law to make public all crimes reported to campus police, rarely does anyone hear about crimes handled by university tribunals. At most schools, the system operates in absolute secrecy. Universities typically don't disclose the type of crimes adjudicated, the students involved, the number of cases deliberated, or the decisions reached. At the University of Mississippi, a veil of silence covered proceedings against members of the Sigma Chi fraternity after a pledge, Dudley Moore, hanged himself last October. Prior to the suicide, the fraternity was under scrutiny for harassing Moore and other pledges. Judicial inquiry teams, which included some Sigma Chi members, forbade campus police from testifying. Randall Corban, the captain of investigative services with the university police, remains disturbed by the outcome. "I can't tell you the verdict, but I don't think it was as severe as it should have been."

Because the system operates in secrecy, there are frequent charges that the courts favor athletes, fraternity members, and students whose parents are influential or generous contributors. For instance, last year a University of Virginia tribunal expelled Richard Wallace Smith, the son of Federal Express founder Frederick W. Smith, after he pleaded guilty in a criminal court to charges in connection with a 1997 assault on another student. But when later university proceedings resulted in a lesser sentence, students rallied to protest what was viewed as preferential treatment of Smith. His sentence was subsequently stiffened to a two-year suspension. One of Smith's attorneys says the court initially judged her client more harshly because of his father's prominence.

Experts say the case illustrates a crucial weakness of the tribunals. "The key lesson here is that the campus court system collapses under any significant challenge," says Daniel Carter. "Parents would be a lot more disturbed about school crime if they knew how slipshod these proceedings can be." His group, along with student newspapers across the country, has been at the forefront of efforts to open up the courts.

Their efforts may be starting to pay off. Congress repealed a federal privacy law last October that colleges claimed prohibited them from disclosing the outcomes of disciplinary proceedings. The new law doesn't require schools to release the information, but it is causing many institutions, including Michigan Tech and the University of Dayton, to re-examine their secrecy codes. Mark Goodman, executive director of the Student Press Law Center, urges students to learn as much as they can about a prospective school's judicial system, including whether it adjudicates violent crimes and is at least considering releasing trial results. If the school takes a vow of silence on the subject, Goodman advises, that ought to be a deal breaker.

Efforts to End Fraternity Hazing Have Largely Failed, Critics Charge[6]

They say state laws have been ineffective, in part because of a tendency to blame the victims

By Ben Gose
The Chronicle of Higher Education, April 18, 1997

The Presidents of college and university fraternities like to boast that they have hazing under control. Tough policies ban it, they say, and police have state laws at their disposal to deal with houses that violate the prohibitions.

But educators and lawyers familiar with what actually goes on in the pledging process say the reality remains that most pledges don't become members without at least a little abuse, and sometimes quite a bit.

Jonathan Culpepper was apparently determined that John Warren receive his fair share. In October, the two students at Texas A&M University traveled with other members and pledges of Kappa Alpha to a ranch north of Hearne, Tex. There, Mr. Culpepper, a sophomore poured a can of beer on Mr. Warren, held him down while the pledge did pushups, and then yanked up sharply on his underwear, according to a lawsuit filed by Mr. Warren against the fraternity and Mr. Culpepper. Two days later—when Mr. Warren could not walk because of pain—a surgeon removed one of his testicles.

Mr. Warren dropped his classes and sought psychiatric treatment. He is now back at Texas A&M.

"A Slap on the Wrist"

Mr. Culpepper also remains at the university, which imposed some punishment against him but says it cannot reveal the sanction because of privacy laws. He was charged by police with hazing, a misdemeanor punishable by up to a year in jail and a fine of up to $4,000. After

---

6. Copyright © 1997 *The Chronicle of Higher Education.* Reprinted with permission.

pleading no contest, he received a $500 fine and 80 hours of community service. If he completes an 18-month probation period, the "wedgie" incident will be struck from his record.

C. L. Mike Schmidt, Mr. Warren's lawyer, calls that "a slap on the wrist" and says. "Here some kid goes and violates the law, and he doesn't get any real punitive measures."

Twenty years ago, Mr. Culpepper may not have faced any criminal charges. All but 3 of the 40 states with anti-hazing laws, including Texas, have passed them since 1978.

Advocates of greater punishments for hazing say that

Advocates of greater punishments for hazing say that they are still in the early stages of the battle and that hazing—much of it dangerous—remains common.

---

they are still in the early stages of the battle and that hazing—much of it dangerous—remains common. They say that society continues to blame the victims and doesn't strongly punish the perpetrators. Critics cite three recent cases:

• In April, 1995 Gabe Higgins, a pledge of the Texas Cowboys, a "spirit group" at the University of Texas at Austin that is made up mostly of fraternity members, drowned in a river after a night of alleged hazing. Members of the group waited nine hours after discovering he was missing before they notified police, and the only lie detector test given to a member of the group about how Mr. Higgins died indicated deception. No one was indicted.

• This January, William (Trey) Walker III, a freshman at Texas A&M, was doused with water by members of Phi Gamma Delta as part of an initiation ritual on what a university spokeswoman called a "very chilly" day. He died about six hours later of a severe attack of asthma. The university suspended the fraternity for two years for hazing, but a Brazos County grand jury decided that the "hosing down" had not caused Mr. Walker's death. No fraternity members were charged.

• In February, Binaya Oja, a Theta Chi pledge at Clarkson University, choked on his vomit and died after a night of drinking at the fraternity. According to police, 12 men—including seven current and two former Clarkson students—had pressured Mr. Oja and other pledges to drink until they vomited, in order to see who would do so first. Each of the 12 men has been charged with hazing and unlawfully dealing with a child. The police considered filing more-serious charges, such as manslaughter or negligent homicide, but chose, not to.

Mr. Schmidt, the lawyer, says there is an "odd undercurrent among the public" that pins most of the blame for hazing on the victims. "The feeling is, 'Sorry about that. Bud, but you should have thought about the risks before you went out there playing around in the sandbox.'"

> *"People don't seem to take hazing seriously . . . They view these things as college pranks. They don't realize that kids are dying."*
> —**Eileen Stevens, founder of the non-profit Committee to Halt Useless College Killings**

Eileen Stevens, founder of the non-profit Committee to Halt Useless College Killings, has been lobbying for hazing laws since 1978, when her son Chuck died in a hazing incident at Alfred University. "People don't seem to take hazing seriously," she says. "They view these things as college pranks. They don't realize that kids are dying."

Ms. Stevens says 70 college students have died as a result of hazing since 1978. The details of some of these deaths, she says, were related to her by family members and never made public.

In a new twist, police in Austin, Tex., last month charged four female students at Huston-Tillmson College with hazing and assaulting two students who were joining their all-women social club. One pledge alleged that she had been struck on the back and buttocks at least 100 times with a wooden cane. In the past year, criminal hazing charges have also been filed against high-school students in Massachusetts. Ohio, and Texas.

A Vicious Cycle

"Hazing," says David L. Westol, executive director of the national Theta Chi fraternity, "is happening across the board."

But most of the serious hazing incidents still occur in fraternities. Many fraternity members say quietly that hazing is valuable, despite the policies banning it. Some members say most hazing is mild and creates bonds among those who endure it. Other members cite a vicious cycle: Once a student has been hazed, he wants a chance to dole out similar abuse.

Some universities say they are beginning to take hazing more seriously. Texas A&M says it will no longer keep hazing investigations confidential, as it often did until this year. "Now, we're going, to make sure that every time this happens, people know about it," says Mary Jo Powell, a university spokeswoman.

Other universities have tried for years to crack down, to little effect.

An investigation of hazing at the University of Texas at Austin in the early 1990s by the county attorney's office led to fines, probations, and a few short jail sentences. Hazing has not disappeared from the campus, however. Of the 35 fraternities at Texas, 10 have been penalized by the university for hazing in the past four years.

Just last month, police filed criminal charges, ranging from assault to hazing and making terroristic threats, against nine members of Pi Kappa Alpha. The charges stemmed from a complaint filed by a freshman who said he and other pledges had been burned, shocked, and smeared with food. The freshman said one member had choked him and others had threatened to kill him because they thought he had cooperated with a university investigation. Some fraternity member—including the one who allegedly choked the freshman—have called the charges groundless.

Jon Shulkin, a senior at Texas and president of its Interfraternity Council, says his office or the dean of students receives complaints of similar incidents "every couple of weeks."

Ken Oden, the Travis County attorney, has come to realize that arrests won't eradicate hazing. "After three years. you have 100 percent turnover of the people involved in the incident," he says. "No one left in that organization even remembers what happened."

Potential Liabilities

Fraternities have plenty of reasons—besides the obvious goal of preventing deaths—for trying to stamp out hazing.

• Civil suits can be expensive. In February, the parents of Gabe Higgins settled a lawsuit against 18 members of the Cowboys organization, and the owner of the land where Mr. Higgins died, for $1.09 million.

• Reports of hazing may scare off new recruits. Membership in fraternities at the University of Texas is down 29 percent since 1990. Jeremy Gough, president of the Delta Kappa Epsilon chapter there, says that unflattering headlines about hazing discourse freshmen from joining houses. "We've got a bad reputation, and rather than having to deal with that, people are staying away," says Mr. Gough, whose fraternity has shrunk to 12 members from 80 in the past eight years.

• Serious incidents can contribute to a college's decision to do away with fraternities altogether. Bowdoin College's announcement last month that it would force its fraternities to disband by 2000 came just one year after an intoxicated student fell to his death while trying to climb on the roof of a fraternity house. At Clarkson, university officials have formed a committee in the aftermath of Mr. Oja's death to evaluate the role of the fraternity system. One possibility is to do away with fraternities, they have said.

The 63 organizations in the National Interfraternity Conference aren't sitting on their hands. In recent years, many of them have shortened "pledge periods"—the time before a recruit becomes a full-fledged member—from 12 weeks to 6 weeks or less, says the executive director, Jonathan J. Brant.

But he notes that the adults working in the fraternities' national offices can do only so much to control hazing. "Students are still making poor decisions," he says.

Mr. Westol of Theta Chi, says national fraternities now respond more quickly to chapters that engage in hazings. He closed Clarkson's chapter for at least five years within days of Mr. Oja's death. "Our saying is, 'If you're hazing, you're history,'" he says.

In fact, he seems to condemn the actions of Clarkson's former Theta Chi members more strongly than do the police in Potsdam, N.Y., who decided not to file charges of manslaughter or negligent homicide against the students who allegedly pressured Mr. Oja to drink so much that he died.

Police Lieut. John Kaplan says one factor in the decision was, "Is this case winnable?" Another was the fraternity members' remorse.

Lieutenant Kaplan notes his own feelings on making the arrests of the members of Theta Chi. "It's kind of tough to hate them like you think you're going to hate them. These are 19-and 20-year-old kids and they're tremendously affected by this."

Charges at Roanoke College

But Mr. Schmidt and Mr. Stephens, among other critics, argue that the filing of the relatively light charges even in the serious cases has a cascade effect. If incidents of hazing that lead to death draw only misdemeanor charges, what happens, for example, when hazing is interrupted before tragedy occurs?

In February, police charged 10 Roanoke College students with hazing after the students were found standing over four blind-folded men lying in a shallow creek. But the Commonwealth's Attorney for Roanoke County threw out the hazing charges which had been filed against members of an unofficial fraternity called Campus Inter-Action. The attorney said Virginia law implies that a hazing violation must involve physical injury.

Lieut. G. W. Roche, of the Roanoke County police, says that, injured or not, the four students were in mortal danger. The case should have gone forward, he argues.

"It was 30 degrees, and they were soaking wet and they were lying face down in the water," he says. "Who knows what would have happened later? Maybe they would have turned out all right. But maybe they wouldn't have."

Bibliography

Books

Best, Joel. *Random Violence: How We Talk About New Crimes and New Victims.* Los Angeles, California: University of California Press, 1999.

Biskup, Michael D., and Charles P. Cozic (Editors). *Youth Violence (Current Controversies).* San Diego, CA: Greenhaven Press, 1992.

Burke, Helen. *Youth and Justice.* New York, NY: Marion Boyars Publishers, 1982.

Carlsson-Paige, Nancy. *Before Push Comes to Shove.* St. Paul, MN: Redleaf Press, 1998.

Crews, Gordon A. *The Evolution of School Disturbance in America.* Westport, CT: Praeger Pubs., 1997.

Curwin, Richard, and Allen N. Mendler, *As Tough as Necessary: Countering Violence, Agression and Hostility in Our Schools.* Alexandria, VA: Association for Supervision and Curriculum Development, 1997.

Davis, Nanette J. *Youth Crisis.* Westport, CT: Praeger Publisher Text, May 1999.

Devine, John. *Maximum Security: The Culture of Violence in Inner-city Schools.* Chicago, IL: University of Chicago Press, 1996.

Elliott, Delbert S., Beatrix A. Hamburg, and Kirk R. Williams (Editors). *Violence in American Schools: A New Perspective.* New York, NY: Cambridge University Press, 1998.

Empey, Lamar Taylor, Mark C. Stafford, and Carter H. Hay. *American Delinquency: Its Meaning & Construction.* Belmont, CA: Wadsworth Pub. Co., 1999.

Egendorf, Laura K., and Jennifer A. Hurley (Editors). *Teens at Risk: Opposing Viewpoints.* San Diego, CA: Greenhaven Press, 1999.

Flannery, Raymond B. *Violence in America; Coping with Drugs, Distressed Families, Inadequate Schooling and Acts of Hate.* New York, NY: Continuum International, 1997.

Flowers, R. Barri. *The Adolescent Criminal: An Examination of Today's Juvenile Offender.* Jefferson, NC: McFarland & Co., 1990.

Goldstein, Arnold P., and Donald W. Kodluboy. *Gangs in Schools: Signs, Symbols and Solutions.* Champaign, IL: Research Press, 1998.

Guggenbuhl, Allan. *Incredible Fascination of Violence.* New York, NY: Continuum Pub. Corp., 1996.

Hagan, John, Delbert Elliott, and Joan McCord. *Youth Violence: Children at Risk.* Washington, D.C.: American Sociological Association, 1998.

Heide, Kathleen M. *Young Killers: The Challenge of Juvenile Homicide.* Newbury Park, CA: Sage Publications, 1998.

Hoffman, Allan M., John H. Schuh, and Robert H. Fenske. *Violence on Campus: Defining the Problems, Strategies for Action.* Gaithersburg, MD: Aspen Publishers, 1998.

Howard, Matthew O., and Jeffrey M. Jenson (Editors). *Youth Violence: Current Research and Recent Practice Innovations.* Washington, D.C.: National Association of Social Worker, 1999.

Kelleher, Michael D. *When Good Kids Kill.* Westport, CT: Praeger Publisher Trade, 1999.

Kim, Henny H. *Youth Violence (Current Controversies).* San Diego, CA: Greenhaven Press, 1998.

Kindlon, Dan, and Michael Thompson. *Raising Cain: Protecting the Emotional Life of Boys.* New York, NY: Ballantine, 1999.

Kipnis, Aaron R. *Angry Young Men: How Parents, Teachers, and Counselors Can Help Bad Boys Become Good Me.* San Francisco, CA: Jossey-Bass Publishers, 1999.

Kopka, Deborah L. *School Violence.* Santa Barbara, CA: ABC CLIO Incorporated, 1997.

Larson, Bob. *Extreme Evil: Kids Killing Kids.* Nelson Press, August 1999.

Regoli, Robert M., and John D. Hewitt. *Delinquency in Society.* Boston, MA: McGraw-Hill College Division, 1999.

Rojek, Dean G., and Gary F. Jensen (Editors). *Exploring Delinquency: Causes and Control (An Anthology).* Los Angeles, CA: Roxbury Publishers Co., 1996.

Royal, Marcella. *Youth Crime-Violence & the Cause.* Hauppauge, NY: Barron, 1994.

Shoemaker, Donald J. *Theories of Delinquency: An Examination of Explanations of Delinquent Behavior.* New York, NY: Oxford University Press, 2000.

Siegel, Dorothy. *Campuses Respond to Violent Tragedy.* Phoenix, AZ: Oryx Press, 1994.

Smith, Michael Clay, and Richard W. Fossey. *Crime on Campus: Legal Issues & Campus Administration.* Phoenix, AZ: Oryx Press, 1996.

Squyres, Suzanne. *Gun Control-Restricting Rights or Protecting People? (The Information Series on Current Topics).* St. Wylie, TX; Information Plus, 1999.

Steinberg, Laurence. *Beyond the Classroom: Why School Reform has Failed and What Parents Need to Do.* New York, NY: Simon & Schuster, 1997.

Turk, William L. *When Juvenile Crime Comes to School (Criminology Studies, V.7).* Lewiston, NY: Edwin Mellen Press, 1999.

Ungerleider, Dorothy Fink. *Reading, Writing, and Rage: The Terrible Price Paid by Victims of School Failure.* RWR Press, 1996.

Whitaker, Leighton C., and Jeffrey W. Pollard. *Campus Violence: Kinds, Causes, & Cures.* Binghamton, NY: Haworth Press, 1995.

Additional Periodical Articles with Abstracts

For those who wish to read more widely on the subject of School Violence, this section contains abstracts of additional articles that bear on the topic. Readers who require a comprehensive list of materials are advised to consult *Reader's Guide Abstracts* and other Wilson indexes.

A Modest Step Toward Cleaning Up Television. John P. McCarthy. *America* v. 181 pp15-17 July 31/Aug. 7, 1999.

The writer questions Hollywood's resolve to enforce higher standards for television programs and limit the amount of violence portrayed on network television. At the summit on youth violence convened by President Clinton on May 10, 1999, ABC chairman Bob Iger reportedly acknowledged a connection between what people watch and the violence they commit. His fellow television executives, he said, believe that violence portrayed on television has no influence on violent acts committed in the real world, although they tell advertisers the opposite. The writer states that Iger's comments are a considerable step toward better television, one akin to recent admissions by tobacco companies that smoking is addictive and harmful to health. With an industry executive on record as admitting that television has some adverse effects, the writer says it is time to ask what can be done to lessen television's negative influence.

Guns and Politicians. G. Evans Witt. *American Demographics* v. 21 p25 July 1999

The writer asks whether the fact that new gun control legislation has begun to move on Capital Hill in the wake of horrifying school shootings means that public opinion has substantially shifted after the high school tragedies, thus giving impetus to the politicians' actions. According to the writer, a historical look at gun control attitudes, coupled with the recalcitrance of politicians to enact gun control legislation, would appear to suggest that the answer to this question is no. The writer examines the conflicting forces exerted on politicians by public polls and the NRA.

Beyond Total Immersion. Ginger Casey. *American Journalism Review* v. 21 pp30-36 July/Aug. 1999

According to Casey, the media need to rethink the way they cover news events like the Columbine massacre. The writer believes that the rush to immediately find meaning in such chaos results in a skewed form of journalism, one that has become increasingly prevalent. As a result, Casey says, we have turned catastrophic events into news "products," complete with story lines that are, unfortunately, predictable. The search for immediate meaning has also resulted in a rush to facile judgments. Casey questions whether it is time to reevaluate when journalists need to be present at an event and if they have an ethical responsibility that goes beyond providing objective reporting.

The Company They Keep. Deborah Meier. *The American School Board Journal* v. 186 pp25-6 Sept. 1999

In an article that is part of a special section on humanizing high schools, Meier links violence and crime in high schools to the gulf between adolescents and adults. Rather than introducing more laws and rules in the hope of preventing school violence and other problems, Meier says that deeper relationships between adults and young people must be encouraged. She suggests that such a change involves increasing local decision-making powers and limiting the size and bureaucracy of schools.

Looking Closely at Littleton Means Seeing the Corrosive Effects of Humiliation. Matthew Brelis. *Boston Globe* ppE1-2 May 9, 1999

In this article, the effects of public humiliation inflicted on children by their teachers and classmates are examined in relation to the larger problem of school violence. Brelis looks at the case of a student named Nina Campbell, who won a lawsuit against her school district claiming continued psychological scarring after her teacher wrote on her face. Studies done by psychologists suggest the importance of talking about feelings of humiliation to heal inner wounds and prevent the development of violent behavior among young people.

Most Athletes in College Are Hazed, Survey Finds. Eun Lee Koh. *Boston Globe* pA1+ Aug. 31, 1999

Koh cites a survey which claims that 80 percent of all college athletes experience hazing as part of a team initiation process, with as many as one in five being forced to engage in potentially criminal activities. Half of the hazings involved alcohol and about 20 percent of the students admitted committing a criminal act, according to the survey of 10,000 college athletes from 224 NCAA schools. However, Koh points out that only 2,020 students responded to the survey, making the results suggestive rather than conclusive. The research was conducted by Alfred University in New York with the National Collegiate Athletic Association and included athletes from several New England colleges and universities.

From a Daughter's Death, a Life's Work; After Jeanne Clery's Murder at Lehigh University, Her Parents Have Worked to Change Laws and Change Minds About Campus Safety. Bella English. *Boston Globe* Oct. 20, 1999

English examines the failure of many universities to report on-campus crime statistics and its often tragic effect on students. The parents of one student victim—Jeanne Cleary, who was murdered as she slept in her dorm room at Pennsylvania's Lehigh University in 1985—continue to work towards forcing the nation's colleges and universities to publish their crime statistics so that prospective students and their parents can make a more informed decision when choosing which school to attend.

Million-dollar Court Case Sends a Clear Message to Schools: Protect Gay Students Equally or Pay. Deb Price. *Detroit News* Nov. 29, 1996

Price examines the taunting and physical abuse suffered by gay students in elementary and high schools at the hands of their classmates, along with the frequent failure of school administrators to protect these student or punish the offenses committed against them. A 1996 court decision demonstrated the financial penalty which that city's schools and their officials will suffer if they continue to exhibit bias against gay students.

House Demands Enforcement. Debra Gersh Hernandez. *Editor & Publisher* v. 129 pp10-11+ Nov. 2, 1996

Hernandez reports that Congress has put the Department of Education on notice that it has to begin enforcing the law requiring universities to disclose information on campus crime. In order to remedy the problem of college and university officials who either do not release information in a timely manner or do not report statistics accurately, the House of Representatives passed a resolution urging the department to play a more active role in monitoring and enforcing compliance with the Campus Awareness and Security Act of 1990. Meanwhile, the Society of Professional Journalists is urging Congress to proceed even further and is calling for an opening of campus judicial proceedings to the public.

Keep Guns Out of School. Tom Allen. From *Virginia Journal of Education.* Reprinted in *Education Digest* v. 64 pp27-32 Dec. 1998

In an article condensed from the October edition of the *Virginia Journal of Education*, the writer asserts that once a gun appears in a school, teachers, students, and learning all become potential victims. He states that guns are not limited to tough inner-city schools, nor are they carried by any specific type of child. There are measures that schools can take in the face of the growing societal problem of youth and guns, however, to build a nonviolent school climate. The writer outlines some recommendations from experts to increase student and staff safety.

Protecting Gay Students. June Million. *Education Digest* v. 64 pp55-7 March 1999

In an article condensed from the December 1998 *Communicator*, Million says there is a need to train school staff and develop strong policies to prevent antigay bias. Teaching respect for differences and protecting sexual minority students from verbal and physical harm is the direct responsibility of the principal, but most are stymied by a limited knowledge of resources, fear of community or staff backlash or both, and lack of district-wide directives. Million points out that using age and developmentally appropriate materials, including children's literature, and emphasizing respect and safety seem to avoid backlash problems.

School House Hype: Kids' Real Risks. Elizabeth Donohue, Vincent Schiraldi, and Jason Ziedenberg. *Education Digest* v. 64 pp4-10 Feb. 1999

In an article condensed from "School House Hype: School Shootings and the Real Risks Kids Face in America," the writers examine how, following the tremendous news coverage of a number of school shootings during the 1997-1998 academic year, policymakers reacted to a perceived moral panic sweeping the nation. The authors argue that instead of providing context to the events, the media covered the killings as part of a trend in U.S. public schools in a manner that has exacerbated people's fears about school safety. According to the writers, the best data on school-associated violent death suggest that children face a one-in-a-million chance of being murdered at school.

As Students Return, Focus Is on Security. Alan Richard. *Education Week* v. 19 p1 Sept. 8, 1999

Richard considers how school officials in almost every district in the U.S. have been examining their safety and security procedures in the months following the shootings at Columbine High School. Precaution measures, including bans and restrictions on book bags and the installation of video monitoring systems, have been introduced in many districts. However, Richard claims, new research shows a decline in school-related violence, and Secretary of Education Richard W. Riley insists that schools are safe.

The Gunfire Dialogues: Notes on the Reality of Virtuality. Thomas de Zengotita. *Harper's Magazine* v. 299 pp55-8 July 1999

The writer asserts that the shootings at Columbine High School engaged the attention of American society because they strengthened the sense that such shootings reveal something significant about society. Cultural conservatives have focused on the impact of violence in the media, emphasizing the permissive standards applied to content and the extent to which that content has changed over the last 30 years. According to the writer, the violence associated with computer games has made the organized and ritualized fistfight of the 1950s appear quaint. This level of violence may also have a subtle but corrosive impact on those teenagers who do not act out their violent fantasies. The writer then discusses the media's impact on teenagers and on society as a whole.

What Makes Children Kill? Susan C. Vaughan. *Harper's Bazaar* v. 3442 pp546-7+ Sept. 1998

Vaughan considers how the 1990s appears to have been a bloody decade for child-on-child violence. In 1998, four incidents involving suburban and rural boys from middle-class families left 15 dead and 42 injured. As Vaughan reports, a variety of influences have been blamed for these massacres, including the NRA, popular culture, personality disorders, and parental abuse.

It's Not Evil Spirits That Make Teens Kill; Murder: Blaming movies, song lyrics or Satanism lets us ignore the real cause, the breakdown of social safeguards. Helen Smith. *The Los Angeles Times* Dec. 16, 1997

Smith considers American society's many scapegoats for the violent crimes committed by youths, including movies, the gun culture, religious cults, music, video and board games, and the Internet, but she concludes that none of these is responsible. She claims that we blame these forces to give us a greater feeling of control, but in the process, we overlook our own responsibility to instill more positive and enduring values in our children.

Lessons of Littleton. *MacLean's* v. 112 pp18-24+ May 3, 1999
As part of a cover story on the school shootings in Littleton, Colorado, this article examines how the events at Columbine High School caused Littleton to join a growing list of American towns made infamous by murderous teenagers. The April 20, 1999, massacre by Eric Harris and Dylan Klebold was followed by the usual criticisms from media analysts and proponents of gun control. The writer discusses how experts have admitted

that they could not explain why the two middle-class teens had committed the act.

The Guns of Littleton. Bruce Shapiro. *Nation* v. 268 pp4-5 May 17, 1999

Shapiro writes that recent schoolyard shootings have all been marked by greater access to firearms and the corporate-marketed culture of guns. Nonetheless, he says, politicians have depicted Dylan Klebold and Eric Harris, perpetrators of the rampage at Columbine High School, as examples of the dangers of unrestricted Web access, Goth culture, abortion, and atheistic parenting.

Shame You're Not a Girl, Son. Andrew Stephan. *New Statesman* (London, England: 1996) v. 127 p20 May 29, 1998

In all of the recent school shootings, the perpetrators have been teen boys, and according to Stephan, a possible reason is that the U.S. education system no longer knows what to do with boys. When Americans realized that girls were being shortchanged in school and society, they threw themselves into righting and then reversing the injustice. The result of the fact that boys fail to behave like girls, Stephan claims, is the demasculinization of boys and the creation of a "lost generation."

Anatomy of a Massacre. Matt Bai. *Newsweek* pp25-31 May 3, 1999

Bai discusses the shooting at Columbine High School, along with the backgrounds of assailants Eric Harris and Dylan Klebold and the events of that day. The reporter looks at the boys' apparent downward spiral into violence and relates various eye-witness accounts by students of their rampage through the school.

Why the Young Kill. Sharon Begley. *Newsweek* pp32-35 May 3, 1999

Begley looks at evidence presented by neuroscientists and psychologists that certain brains are predisposed to violence. She relates these findings to young killers to explore whether their behavior is influenced by their environments or by innate tendencies.

How Suburban Design Is Failing Teen-agers. William L. Hamilton. *New York Times* pF1+ May 6, 1999

Hamilton examines how the shooting incident at the high school in Littleton has prompted parents and urban planners to question whether the isolation of suburban living is contributing to the alienation of young people. Suburbs, built as safe havens from the sociological ills of cities, now stand accused of creating their own environmental disease. They are said to engender a lack of character and grounding principles of identity, a lack of diversity or tolerances, and a lack of attachment to shared civic ideals. In the article, the designers of the newest American suburbs say they largely ignore the needs of teen-agers in their plans.

Making Kids Safer. Bob Herbert. *New York Times* (Late Edition) pA29 Sept. 9, 1999

According to Herbert, the current concerns over school violence focus attention on murderous incidents that are extremely rare. Rather than attempting quick fixes, criminal justice Professor James Alan Fox and a Washington group called Fight Crime: Invest in Kids say that we should work on the difficult, long-term preventive efforts that can produce major reductions in youth crime and violence. Among the simple approaches recommended by the group are the creation of more early childhood education programs, support for after-school programs for children and teens, and provision of parenting programs and other assistance to young parents whose children are at high risk of getting into trouble.

Violence by Youths: Looking for Answers. Timothy Egan. *New York Times* pA27 April 22, 1999

Egan contends that the shooting at Columbine High School happened in one of those places where Americans tend to move because they are seeking good schools. He maintains that finding common symptoms and patterns to school shootings may be the easy part and asserts that the more troubling question is why normal problems of adolescence seem to be resolved now in extraordinary spasms of violence.

Parents Blaming Parents. Lisa Belkin. *New York Times Magazine* pp60-67+ Oct. 31, 1999

Belkin discusses how, in the wake of school shootings, victims' families are turning to the law for retribution, as grieving parents whose sons have committed murder themselves become the targets of lawsuits. Several such cases are discussed, most notably the lawsuit being brought by Columbine High School victim Isaiah Shoels' parents, Michael and Vonda Shoels, against the parents of Eric Harris and Dylan Klebold.

The Campus Crime Wave. Anne Matthews. *New York Times Magazine* pp38+ March 7, 1993

Matthews discusses the growing problem of crime on the campuses of

American colleges and universities. According to the author, one in three students will be the victim of some kind of campus crime and estimates of the number of women raped during their college years range from 1 in 7 to 1 in 25.

The Clampdown on Teen Rights. Ethan Bronner. *New York Times Upfront* v. 132 pp10-14 Sept. 6, 1999

Bronner explains how authorities' rules dictating acceptable teenage behavior are being rewritten in the wake of the Columbine school killings. Teenagers are being interrogated, suspended, reprimanded, and even arrested for what they say in class, write on tests, post on the Internet, or e-mail, as well as for what they wear and how they do their hair. Concerned parents and school officials say the extra vigilance is justified if it protects children and saves their lives, but civil rights workers, such as Anne Beeson, an attorney with the American Civil Liberties Union, say the crackdown cuts into the rights of teenagers and dangerously erodes the freedoms guaranteed all citizens in the Constitution.

We Are Training Our Kids to Kill. Dave Grossman. *The Saturday Evening Post* v. 271 pp54-5+ Sept./Oct. 1999

Grossman contends that violence in the media must be controlled and violent video games banned. The author asserts that television provides today's children with many of their role models, including the young killers profiled in the news, and although the media is entitled and duty bound to relate events, it must be persuaded not to make heroes of the killers by putting their faces on TV. In addition, Grossman claims that legislation should be introduced to outlaw video games that teach children how to kill with simulations of violence.

The Danger of Suppressing Sadness. Walter Kirn. *Time* v. 153 pp48-9 May 31, 1999

According to Kirn, for better or worse, an institutional drug culture has emerged in American high schools, mimicking that already established among depressed adults. Adolescent rebelliousness, moodiness, and anxiety are increasingly being interpreted as warning signs of chemical imbalances and challenges that teachers used to deal with are being handed over to psychiatrists. In addition, Kirn questions whether there is an unclear distinction between illegal, feel-good drugs such as marijuana and amphetamines, and legal mood-altering substances, such as Luvox, Wellbutrin, and Effexor.

Of Arms and the Boy. John Cloud. *Time* v. 151 pp58-60+ July 6, 1998

In this essay, the writer profiles five boys who are accused of murder in various American communities and tries to identify the factors that sent them over the brink. The boys' common denominators include the fact that they came from areas where guns are available, they felt isolated from family members and girls, and they shared a fascination with forms of alternative popular culture.

Portrait of a Deadly Bond. Eric Pooley. *Time* v. 153 pp26-32 May 10, 1999

In a special section on the high school massacre in Littleton, Colorado, the writer examines the friendship between Eric Harris and Dylan Klebold and their problems leading up to their attack on Columbine High School. Possible motives for their actions, including a feud between their clique and Columbine athletes, are also discussed.

Of a Tender Age: Lawmakers Rush to Stem the Tide of Rising Juvenile Violence. Jean Hellwege. *Trial* v. 32 pp10-12 July 1996

Hellwege describes how, in response to recent studies indicating that juveniles are committing crimes at younger ages and that the crimes they commit are increasingly more violent, lawmakers have been rushing to approve legislation designed to crack down on juvenile lawbreakers with more severe penalties for serious offenses. The writer reviews new statistics that have in part driven the sudden push for juvenile justice and considers some of the popular reform measures.

Making Schools Safe for Kids. Deedee Corradini. *USA Today* v. 127 pp48-9 May 1999

Corradini asserts that the level of youth violence in America's schools has reached a crisis point, and it is therefore time to look at the problem seriously and devise more permanent ways of dealing with it. The writer discusses ways in which youth violence in schools can be overcome.

The Price of Protection. Patrick Welsh. *U.S. News & World Report* v. 126 p28 May 3, 1999

In this essay, the writer discusses efforts to control the potentially volatile student body at the school where he teaches in northern Virginia. The school had the highest reported incidents of violence in that region, and consequently it has been working to increase safety for more than a decade. The school's early warning system incorporates an alternative school on campus with smaller classes, a special crisis center, and at least one police car outside the grounds. Other measures to deter violence include peer mediation and hall monitors equipped with walkie-talkies that are connected to all administrators and the on-duty police officers.

Exorcising the Pain: Littleton Buries its Dead and Tries to Understand. Betsy Streisand and Angie Cannon. *U.S. News & World Report* v. 126 pp18-21 May 10, 1999.

As the writers explain, the community of Littleton, Colorado, which fell victim to the worst school shooting in American history, is struggling to comprehend how so many warning signs were missed. Although Dylan Klebold effectively concealed any indication that he was obsessed with death and violence, signs about Eric Harris were hard to ignore. It appears that he suffered from a specific type of antisocial disorder known as malignant narcissism. He was also taking Luvox, an antidepressant that is often prescribed for depression and obsessive-compulsion disorder, and police had been warned about his chilling Web site, which openly professed his violent tendencies.

Gunning for Hollywood. John Leo. *U.S. News & World Report* v. 126 p16 May 10, 1999

Leo explores the financial connection between Hollywood and Washington, D.C., where, he says, both Republicans and Democrats court the entertainment industry to back their campaigns yet blame these industry executives for youth violence. Some members of both parties have decided to take a middle ground between censorship and liberality by proposing a summit on violence, where the influence of film and television on violent behavior in youths will be discussed. According to Leo, film executives need to assume greater responsibility for the content of their movies and curb the excessive portrayal of pointless and gratuitous violence.

Why? Angie Cannon, Betsy Streisand, Dan McGraw. *U.S. News & World Report* (Online) May 3, 1999

The writers discuss how numerous warning signs that Eric Harris and Dylan Klebold were troubled, angry young men with the potential for violence were ignored by students, teachers, and parents. They point to a "disconnect" that prevented school administrators from listening to the boys and to local law-enforcement, who had warned the school district about escalating violence in the community. The writers question whether teachers, parents, and students did not *want* to notice the boys, whose misfit status resulted in taunting by the school jocks and increased within them an anger they did not know how to manage.

Index